Betty Crocker
GRILLING
MADE EASY

Betty Crocker
GRILLING
MADE EASY

200 SURE-FIRE RECIPES
FROM AMERICA'S MOST TRUSTED KITCHENS

WILEY

Wiley Publishing, Inc.

Library of Congress Cataloging-in-Publication Data:
Betty Crocker grilling made easy : 200 sure-fire recipes from America's most-trusted kitchens.–2nd ed.
    p. cm.
  Rev. ed. of: Betty Crocker's great grilling. 1st ed. New York : Hungry Minds, c2002.
  Includes index.
  ISBN 0-7645-7453-1 (hardcover : alk. paper)
  1. Barbecue cookery. I. Title: Grilling made easy. II. Crocker, Betty. III. Title: Betty Crocker's great grilling.

TX840.B3 B48 2005
641.5'784–dc22

                                          2004011943

GENERAL MILLS

Director, Book and Online Publishing: Kim Walter

Manager, Cookbook Publishing: Lois Tlusty

Editor: Heidi Losleben

Recipe Development and Testing: Betty Crocker Kitchens

Photography and Food Styling: General Mills Photography Studios

WILEY PUBLISHING, INC.

Publisher: Natalie Chapman

Executive Editor: Anne Ficklen

Editor: Kristi Hart

Production Editor: Michael Olivo

Cover Design: Suzanne Sunwoo

Book Design: Melissa Auciello-Brogan, LeAndra Hosier, Kathie Rickard, Erin Zeltner

Manufacturing Manager: Kevin Watt

The Betty Crocker Kitchens seal guarantees success in your kitchen. Every recipe has been tested in America's Most Trusted Kitchens™ to meet our high standards of reliability, easy preparation and great taste.

Find more great ideas and shop for name-brand housewares at

BettyCrocker.com

Manufactured in the United States of America

10 9 8 7 6 5 4 3 2

Second Edition

Cover photo: © Betty Crocker Studios

Dear Friends,

Few aromas signal the start of summer better than grilled food wafting through the air. A single sniff can trigger all sorts of happy memories, from fun family barbecues and spur-of-the-moment neighborhood get-togethers, to an easy, breezy casual meal on a hot summer night.

Whether you're a rookie just learning to make a basic burger or a pro who can sear a sirloin with the best of 'em, *Betty Crocker Grilling Made Easy* provides a recipe for you. Here, you'll find 200 mouthwatering recipes for burgers, steaks, ribs, chicken and fish—not to mention appetizers, sides and desserts—for grillers of all skill levels. And if the weather proves uncooperative, the tasty contact grill recipes in Chapter 6 have got you covered.

In addition to fabulous, no-fuss recipes sure to win rave reviews from family and friends, *Betty Crocker Grilling Made Easy* is packed with grilling terms and techniques, helpful hints, safety tips and simple flavor boosters. To quickly find grilling times for all kinds of foods, turn to the handy charts on pages 20–21.

So what are you waiting for? Let the grilling begin!

Warmly,

Betty Crocker

Contents

Paella on the Grill (page 170)

Let's Get Grilling!

Get in Gear: The Quest for the Best Grill

Make no mistake: there is a grill for everyone. It just takes a little investigative work to find the make and model that suits you best. Begin by asking friends about their grills. What do they like about their grill? What don't they like? Most grill owners welcome the chance to share (and show off) their experience and know-how, so don't be afraid to ask. Who knows? You may even get a personal demo or free meal out of the deal. Then, ask yourself a few simple questions.

- Does building and tending a live fire appeal to you?
- Would you like a perfect flame at the touch of a button?
- How often do you plan to grill?
- Is portability important?
- Do you prefer the taste of food grilled over coals?
- Is precise temperature important?
- How many people do you plan to grill for?
- What's your budget?

A stop at your local hardware store, garden center, discount department store or club store will allow you to see the wide variety of grills available. And, if you come with answers to the questions above, an informed sales person can help you turn your wish list into reality.

Three Ways
to Cook Your Goose

Charcoal and gas are the two fuels typically associated with grilling, but electric grills are also an option. (Keep in mind that grilling purists tend to turn up their noses at the idea of using electricity to grill.) Deciding between the three comes down to personal preference. Once you've chosen a fuel, your next step is to choose a grill type.

1 Charcoal Grill

The simplest charcoal grill consists of a firebox with a grate to hold the charcoal, a grill rack to hold the food and often a cover or lid.

+ Pure charcoal flavor and intense heat
+ Generally less expensive than gas grills
− Starting the fire may be a challenge
− Tend to be messier and require more attention than gas grills

Charcoal square covered grill

Look for These Grill Features

▶ Grills should be made of high-grade U.S. steel.

▶ Stainless-steel cooking grates clean up easily and resist corrosion.

▶ Grills with preassembled and/or welded parts are more stable and rust-resistant.

▶ Charcoal grills should come with a 5-year or more limited warranty; gas grills should come with a 10-year or more limited warranty.

Open Grill or Brazier

This is a charcoal grill in its simplest form: A shallow firebox holds the charcoal and food is placed on a metal grill rack. The grill rack is usually just a few inches from the coals, so these Grills are best for direct-heat grilling of foods such as burgers, chops, steaks and chicken. Braziers can be partially hooded to protect them from wind and retain heat. They may come with electric or battery-powered rotisserie attachments that don't require much attention.

Charcoal open brazier

Kettle Grill

This popular charcoal grill has a deep rounded bottom and a generous lid and comes in many sizes. It can be used for a wide range of cooking methods, from grilling and roasting to steaming or smoking. Without its cover, this grill can be used for direct-heat grilling. Its deep bottom makes it excellent for indirect-heat grilling. When the grill is covered, foods can be grilled and lightly smoked at the same time. Draft vents in the bottom and in the cover help control the temperature. Many optional accessories are available.

Charcoal round covered grill

2 Gas Grill

A gas grill is made up of a metal firebox with tube-shape gas burners at the bottom. Fire from the tubes and heats an element such as ceramic briquettes, lava rock or metal bars. These heating elements are positioned between the grate and the burners. Smoke is created when food drippings hit the hearing element. Gas grills come in all shapes, sizes and price ranges, from tabletop models to elaborate wagons complete with side burners, cutting boards and condiment trays. Some gas grills are fueled by refillable liquid propane (LP) gas tanks; some can be directly hooked up to a natural gas line.

+ Don't require charcoal and are quick to start
+ Feature accurate heat controls and tend to cook food more evenly
- Typically more expensive than charcoal grills
- Foods get their flavor from smoke instead of charcoal

Stand-up LP gas grill   *Permanently installed natural gas grill*

3 Electric Grill

Most electric grills are equipped with a smoking element of some type, such as lava rock. The heating element may be separate under the grill rack or imbedded in the grids of the grill rack. These grills require a separate 110/120-volt grounded outlet, because most require 1,600 to 1,800 watts of power.

+ A great option for apartment and condo dwellers for whom charcoal or gas grills are prohibited
+ A thermostat lets you control the heat
- Because these grills need to be plugged in, they don't have the mobility of other grills
- Foods don't have live-fire flavor

Indoor Electric or Contact Grill

This compact, countertop indoor grill may remind you of a waffle maker at first glance. The exterior is usually made of stainless steel or plastic (sometimes brightly colored). The hinged grill opens up to reveal two nonstick metal grill surfaces that allow you to cook both sides of a food simultaneously. Grooves in the grill surface channel fat away from the food you are cooking into a drip tray, making for healthier cooking. Several sizes are available.

You *Can* Take It with You

Lightweight and portable, tabletop grills can be fueled by charcoal, gas or electricity. They are easy to transport, store and clean. They range from uncovered simple cast-metal hibachis of Japanese origin to miniature versions of kettles and covered cookers. They're great for direct-heat cooking for two, limited storage space, beach cookouts, tailgating and picnics. Because the cooking surface is much smaller than that of standard grills, portable grills are not designed for indirect-heat cooking, large cuts of meat, feeding crowds or long cooking times.

Portable electric tabletop grill

Where There's Smoke . . .
There's Good Food

Smokers

Smokers are cylindrical, covered cookers feature a firebox, a water pan, one or two grill racks and a dome-shaped cover. They can be fueled by charcoal or electricity. The food is placed on a grill rack high above the heat. A pan of water or other liquid (beer, fruit juice, wine, cola) is placed between the heat source and the grill rack holding the food. The food cooks very slowly in a dense cloud of smoke and steam. Aromatic wood chips, which have been soaked in water or other liquids, can be thrown on the heat to create smoke and add another flavor dimension. Smokers are best for slabs of ribs, beef briskets, roasts, whole turkeys and other poultry, and fish.

+ Known for their low, even heat
+ Able to tenderize large cuts of meats
- Because smokers use moist heat, foods do not develop a crisp crust
- Unless you have an electric model, you need to replenish coals or wood hourly

Horizontal Smoker

These barrel-shaped smokers consist of two parts: a firebox set off to the side and a long, cylindrical smoking chamber. Horizontal smokers come in a wide range of sizes and prices. They are typically larger, heavier and more expensive than traditional grills. Dampers on the firebox and chimney control the heat. Horizontal smokers can be fueled by charcoal or small logs.

Vertical Water Smoker

This bullet-shaped smoker has a removable domed top and a firebox. A deep pan of water (or other flavorful liquid) positioned in the middle of the smoker creates a moist, steamy environment. You light a fire at the bottom of the smoker and place a pan of wood chips over it. Vents on the top and bottom of the smoker allow you to control the airflow and temperature. Traditional water smokers burn charcoal, but electric-powered types are available as well.

Charcoal, gas or electric water smoker

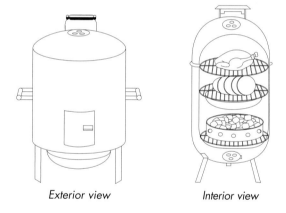

Exterior view   *Interior view*

Clean Up **Your Act**

It's not rocket science: The better care you take of your grill, the longer your grill will last. The following general tips will help you keep your grill looking almost as bright and shiny as the day you bought it. When in doubt, refer to your grill's use-and-care manual for information specific to your model.

Charcoal Grill

▶ Before grilling, take the grill rack off the grill and brush it with vegetable oil (or spray it with cooking spray if the rack doesn't have with a non-stick coating) to help prevent foods from sticking and leaving charred food bits.

▶ Line the bottom of the firebox with heavy-duty foil, shiny side up, to catch the food drippings and ashes. After cooking and when the ashes are cool, bundle up the remains and toss.

▶ Scrub or scrape charred food bits off the grill rack with a brass-bristle brush or a handful of crumpled foil. (Check your grill's use-and-care manual to make sure it's okay to use foil.) Wear hot mitts if the coals are still hot.

▶ Use paper towels and a mild soap and water solution to keep the inside and outside of the lid and the vents clean. A soapy steel wool pad can be used for extremely heavy build up.

▶ Remember to periodically empty the ash catcher (obviously, wait until the ashes are cold).

Gas Grill

▶ Most inside and outside surfaces can be cleaned with warm, soapy water.

▶ A putty knife and a brass-bristle brush are useful in removing grease build up in the bottom tray and the inside cooking box.

▶ Use a brass-bristle brush to clean the metal bars or cooking grates.

▶ Periodically remove the excess grease that may accumulate in the bottom tray and replace the catch pan liner.

▶ Stay away from using cleaning products with chemicals.

Grilling Success Tips

Not all grills are created equal! Read the use-and-care manual that comes with your grill for the best tips and recommendations.

Get to know your grill — whether it has hot spots and where they are, and how long it takes to heat, especially in chilly or windy weather.

To eliminate cleanup when you heat sauces or side dishes on the grill, use an empty coffee can or other can of adequate size.

Keep the heat as even as possible throughout the grilling time. For more even cooking, place thicker foods on the center of the grill rack and smaller pieces on the edges.

Check the food and fire often, for best results. The type of grill, outdoor temperature and wind, position of food on the grill and temperature of the coals all can affect cooking times.

If there isn't a sizzle, the fire may not be hot enough. Increase the heat by raking the coals together, opening the vents, lowering the grill rack and/or adjusting the control on a gas or electric grill.

If the food is browning too quickly on the outside but the middle is not cooked, the fire is too hot. Spread the coals, close the vents halfway, raise the grill rack and/or adjust the control on a gas or electric grill. Covering the grill also will help control the heat.

Grilling Glossary

Before you go shopping and grilling, learning the "lingo" will help you on the way to your quest for success. From tools and utensils to tastes and techniques, you'll soon be speaking the language like a grilling pro.

Barbecue: For some, this word is totally interchangeable with "grilling," while others use it to describe the event of informal entertaining and cooking outdoors. Technically speaking, barbecue describes a method in which whole or pieces of meat, poultry or fish are slowly cooked over low heat in a pit or on a spit. The food is basted with seasoned sauce to keep it moist.

Baste: To brush or spoon liquid over food during grilling.

Brazier: An open or partially covered grill used for charcoal cooking.

Butane Charcoal Lighter: A six- to eight-inch-long tube designed to give you can instant flame and help you light charcoal at a safe distance from the fire.

Ceramic Briquettes: Similar to lava rock, they are used to line the grate of a gas grill. They spread heat evenly and burn off food drippings. Some are wood flavored.

Charcoal: A porous compound made from burned hardwood that's usually compacted and made into the very popular pillow-shaped briquettes or sold in small lumps. Single-use charcoal bags are convenient because you light the entire bag. Damp charcoal can take forever to start, and it burns unevenly. To keep charcoal from becoming damp, store it in a dry place. In humid climates, store charcoal in a tightly closed plastic bag.

Charcoal Chimney Starter: A vented, cylinder-shaped canister with a large, easy-to-grasp handle. You add crumpled newspaper to the bottom and charcoal briquettes to the top; then you light it. Chimney starters are known for their quick, even starting of charcoal. You should remove the chimney and spread the hot coals before grilling food. (You can make a home version by using a two-pound coffee can punched with holes for air circulation.)

Coal Grate or Fire Grate: A rack that holds the charcoal in the firebox.

Composition Charcoal Briquettes: Made from burned wood and scraps, coal dust, borax and petroleum binders, composition briquettes are the most common charcoal briquettes. They are uniform in shape and size. Some brands contain excessive amounts of fillers that can give foods an off-taste. See also "Hardwood Charcoal Briquettes," "Instant Lighting-Briquettes" and "Lump Charcoal."

Direct Heat: Cooking process where food is grilled directly over the heat source.

Drip Pan: A foil pan placed under food to catch drippings during cooking while grilling with indirect heat. It also helps prevent flare-ups.

Electric Starter: A metal loop that heats when 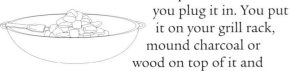 you plug it in. You put it on your grill rack, mound charcoal or wood on top of it and plug it in. The starter is removed when the core of the mound of charcoal turns red.

Firebox, Fire Pan or Fire Bowl: The bottom part of the grill that holds the heat source.

Flare-Up: When fat drippings hit hot coals or lava rock and catch on fire.

Grill: The whole cooking unit, whether fueled by charcoal, gas or electricity.

Grill Rack: The rack on which food is placed for cooking. Also called a grill grid.

Grilling: Cooking foods directly over charcoal, gas or electric heat. Also see "Barbecue."

Grilling Tools: Long handles are a must for sturdy grilling tools, such as turners, tongs, basting brushes and forks to use for turning food. You may want to have a second set of tongs to use just for moving coals around.

Hardwood Charcoal Briquettes: Pieces of pulverized lump charcoal held together by binders such as lime and starch. Because of these binders, hardwood briquettes do not emit off-flavors to foods. See also "Composition Charcoal Briquettes," "Instant-Lighting Briquettes" and "Lump Charcoal."

Hibachi: A small uncovered (usually cast iron) grill of Japanese origin.

Indirect Heat: Cooking process where food is cooked indirectly and over a drip pan, not directly over the heat source.

Instant-Lighting Briquettes: Charcoal briquettes that are saturated with a petroleum product to make them light easily. They typically ash over in about 20 minutes. See also "Composition Charcoal Briquettes," "Hardwood Charcoal Briquettes" and "Lump Charcoal."

Lava Rock: Used in place of charcoal, volcanic lava bits are heated in gas and electric grills to cook food.

Liquid Lighter Fluid: A liquid specially formulated to light charcoal quickly.

Lump Charcoal: When whole logs or aged low-resin hardwoods are burned in a kiln and become carbonized, lump charcoal is the result. Lump charcoal contains no binders or fillers. It lights easily and burns cleanly. It occasionally sparks and can be expensive. See also "Composition Charcoal Briquettes," "Hardwood Charcoal Briquettes" and "Instant-Lighting Briquettes."

Marinade: Mixture of herbs, spices and liquid in which food is soaked to add flavor. If an acid such as lemon juice, vinegar or a tomato-based food is added, it can also tenderize.

Marinate: Soak a food such as meat or vegetables in a seasoned liquid mixture, called a marinade, to add flavor or tenderize.

Meat Thermometer: Using a thermometer is the best way to determine the correct doneness of meat, from burgers to roasts. An instant-read thermometer will give an accurate reading about five seconds after being inserted into the food. Keep the thermometer clean and in working order. Insert the thermometer tip into the center of the food or into the largest meat muscle. Keep the tip away from bone, fat or rotisserie rod.

Mop: A thin sauce frequently brushed on foods during grilling to help keep foods moist and tender. Clean cloth strips tied together, a clean "dish mop," a cluster of fresh herb sprigs or a barbecue brush can be used as the "mop" to add the sauce.

Paraffin Starters: Nontoxic, compact ice-cube shapes made from paraffin wax. These starters light even when wet and help get charcoal lit in a minimum amount of time.

Rub: A dry or wet mixture of seasonings rubbed into foods before cooking to add flavor.

Skewers: Long, thin pointed rods (the best are  flat or square) made from metal or wood. *Kabob* is the name given to foods threaded on skewers.

Smoker Cooking: Barrel-shaped grilling equipment, fueled by charcoal or electricity, that allows slow cooking over low heat with hot smoke that flavors as it cooks.

Spray Bottle: Plastic container that can spray, but preferably squirt, water in a small stream to extinguish flare-ups.

Wire Grill Brush: Long-handled brush with brass or steel bristles used for scraping cooked bits of food off the grill rack and the grill. Follow the grill manufacturer's directions for the type of grill brush to purchase; grill racks vary in material and finish, and some may not withstand brushes that have extremely stiff wire.

Wood Bits, Chips and Chunks: Various-sized pieces of aromatic woods soaked in water and then added to the coals to impart their distinctive flavors to the food being grilled.

Be Safe—Not Sorry

Grilling creates such a laid-back, relaxing atmosphere, it's easy to forget you're playing with fire. Keep the following safety tips in mind and you won't get burned.

Food Safety

▶ Use long-handled barbecue tools to keep a safe distance between you and the intense heat of the grill.

▶ Use long, heatproof mitts to protect hands and arms when working with the grill, heat source and food.

▶ Keep a spray bottle filled with water on hand to quickly douse flare-ups.

▶ Trim visible fat from meat to avoid flare-ups.

▶ Don't use the same platter to carry raw meat to the grill as you do to serve the cooked meat.

▶ Marinate foods in the refrigerator, not on the kitchen counter (unless for 30 minutes or less). Use a nonmetal container.

▶ The same brush used for brushing marinades on raw meat should not be used on cooked meat. Either have two on hand or wash the brush in hot, soapy water, and dry thoroughly before using again.

▶ If a marinade in which raw meat was placed is to be used as a sauce after the meat is cooked, be sure to bring the marinade to boiling and then boil one minute before serving.

▶ Open foil food packets carefully and facing away from you to let out the steam. Steam burns can be painful.

▶ Perishable food should be consumed within two hours; one hour if the outside temperature is over 90°F.

Going Public

If you live in an apartment, townhouse or condo, always check with your building supervisor or association before grilling.

Always keep a bucket of water on hand to quickly douse any flare-ups.

Follow local rules, regulations and fire laws when camping or hosting a cookout on the beach or in the park.

When using public facilities, respect others and clean up when you leave.

Fuel and Flame Safety

▶ Place the grill in a well-ventilated area, away from buildings, dry leaves or brush.

▶ Grilling on a wooden deck requires extra precautions; place a metal sheet or several sheets of heavy-duty foil under the grill to catch any hot ashes that might fall through an open vent.

▶ Never add more liquid fire starter after a charcoal fire is started. The fluid can catch fire as you pour it and the flame could travel upstream to the container. If needed, start three or four more pieces of charcoal separately in a can or on a piece of heavy-duty foil and then add them using tongs. Keep cans and bottles of fire starter away from open flames.

▶ Extinguish coals completely after food is removed. Close the vents on a covered grill to cut off the supply of oxygen. If there is no cover, spread the coals or let them burn completely and then cool.

▶ Dispose of ashes properly. On the chance there is a live coal left, use a covered metal pail.

▶ Never store spare gas tanks under the grill or in the house.

▶ Refillable gas tanks of fuel for gas grills have the potential to cause explosions and fires. Fill a portable gas tank to only 80-percent capacity for maximum efficiency and safety. Secure the tank when transporting it so that it can't tip over. Be careful not to tip the tank when it's connected to the regulator. When attaching a refill tank, check the connection by rubbing it with a liquid detergent. If bubbles appear, there is a leak.

Start It Up: Simple Ways to Light Your Fire

Charcoal Grilling

Charcoal produces lots of heat, and a little goes a long way. Use enough briquettes to form a solid bed of coals under the grilling area that is a little larger than the area the food will cover. It takes about 30 briquettes to grill one pound of meat. (One pound of charcoal equals about 15 to 20 briquettes.)

Any food that grills longer than one hour will require about 10 additional briquettes per hour. When adding extra briquettes, place them around the edges so that they touch the already burning coals, or give them a head start by lighting them separately (in a can or charcoal chimney starter) before adding.

1 Light the Coals

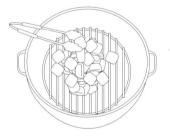

Pyramid shape starter

Arrange the desired number of charcoal briquettes in a slight pyramid shape on the coal grate in the firebox. This shape allows air to circulate, heating the briquettes faster.

▶ **Charcoal Chimney Starters:** Place crumpled newspaper in the bottom of the chimney, add charcoal briquettes and light. Remove the chimney and spread the hot coals before grilling food.

▶ **Electric Coil Starters:** Arrange the charcoal pyramid over the coil and plug in the starter. After about 10 minutes, unplug and remove the starter to a fireproof spot out of the way. The coals will take about 20 minutes before they are ready for grilling.

▶ **Liquid Fire Starters:** Look for those specially intended for charcoal and carefully follow the manufacturer's directions. Never use gasoline or kerosene because it could cause an explosion. Drizzle the charcoal lighter generously (about 1/2 cup) over the charcoal pyramid and wait about one minute to let the liquid soak into the charcoal. Stand back (in case of a possible flare-up) and light the outer edges of the briquettes. The coals will be ready for grilling in about 30 minutes. You want to allow enough time to let the charcoal to evenly burn as well as vaporize the fire starter so that any odor is not absorbed by the food. You're ready to grill when the coals look ashy gray.

2 Get Ready to Cook

Coals are ready

When the coals are 80 percent ashy gray in daylight, they are ready for grilling. (After dark, coals are ready when they have an even red glow.) Bright red coals are too hot, black coals are too cool and a mix of red and black coals gives off uneven heat. Coals that are too cool can cause the food to have an off-flavor from charcoal lighter that has not vaporized.

▶ **Spread a single layer of coals** in an even pattern on the coal grate in an area just slightly larger than the area on the cooking grill rack that will be covered by the food.

▶ **Check the temperature of the coals** by placing your hand, palm side down, near but not touching the cooking grill rack. If you can keep your hand there for two seconds (one-thousand one, one-thousand two), the temperature is high; three seconds is medium-high; four seconds is medium; five seconds is low.

3 Control the Heat

Keep the heat as even as possible throughout the grilling time. If the food does not sizzle, the fire may be too cool.

▶ **Raise the heat** by raking the coals closer together and knocking off a bit of the ash, lowering the cooking grill rack or opening the vents.

▶ **Lower the heat** by doing the opposite: spread and separate the coals, raise the cooking grill rack or close the vents halfway.

▶ **Occasional flare-ups** are a normal part of grilling. Control flare-ups by spacing out the coals or covering the grill. Or keep a spray bottle filled with water handy for spraying; take care not to soak the coals.

Gas Grilling

Generally, heating a gas grill evenly will take about 10 minutes.

▶ **Follow the manufacturer's directions** for heating the grill for direct- or indirect-heat grilling. (Also see "Grilling with Direct and Indirect Heat," page 20.)

▶ **Adjust the heat control,** reposition the grill rack or cover the grill.

▶ **Most gas grills have faster and slower cooking areas,** which can be used effectively when grilling foods with different donenesses. Take the time to learn where these areas are on your grill.

▶ **Lava rock in a gas grill can be used over and over.** When lava rock becomes extremely greasy, however, it contributes to flare-ups. Avoid flare-ups and lengthen the life of lava rock by turning the rock over every once in a while (between grilling times) to burn off the grease that accumulates from cooking meat with fat. If flare-ups occur, do not use water on a gas grill. Just close the hood and reduce the heat until it subsides.

Grilling with
Direct & Indirect Heat

Direct-Heat Grilling

Food is cooked on the grill rack directly over the heat source.

▶ On a charcoal grill, food is cooked over the evenly distributed hot coals.

▶ On a gas grill, food is cooked directly over the heated burner.

Indirect-Heat Grilling

Food is cooked away from the heat. This is the preferred method for longer-cooking foods, such as whole poultry, whole turkey breasts and roasts.

▶ For a charcoal grill, place a drip pan directly under the grilling area and arrange the coals around edge of the firebox.

▶ For a dual-burner gas grill, heat only one side and place the food over the burner that is not lit. For a single-burner grill, place food in a foil tray or on several layers of foil and use low heat.

Gas grill
(side view)

Charcoal grill
(top view)

Indirect grilling
(side view)

Indirect grilling
(aerial view)

Timetable for Grilling Poultry with Direct Heat

First heat the coals or your gas grill for direct heat (above). Then cover and grill poultry over medium heat for the time listed until your thermometer reaches the doneness temperature or until juice is no longer pink when centers of thickest pieces are cut, turning once halfway through grilling (turn cut-up broiler-fryer pieces 2 or 3 times).

Type of Poultry		Weight (pounds)	Approximate Total Grilling Time (minutes)	Doneness
Chicken	Cut-Up Broiler-Fryer	3 to 3 1/2	35 to 40	170°F
	Bone-In Split Breasts (Breast Halves)	2 1/2 to 3	20 to 25	170°F
	Boneless Skinless Breast Halves	1 1/4	15 to 20	170°F
Turkey	Tenderloins	1 to 1 1/2	8 to 12	170°F
	Breast Slices	1 to 1 1/2	6 to 7	No longer pink in center

Timetable for Grilling Meat with Direct Heat

First, heat the coals or your gas grill for direct heat (page 20).* Then cover and grill meat over medium heat for the time listed until your thermometer reaches the doneness temperature, turning once halfway through grilling (turn beef and pork tenderloins 2 or 3 times).

Meat Type	Meat Cut	Thickness (inches)	Approximate Total Grilling Time (minutes)	Doneness
Beef	Rib Eye Steak	3/4 1 1 1/2	6 to 8 11 to 14 17 to 22	145°F medium-rare to 160°F medium
	Porterhouse/T-Bone Steaks	3/4 1 1 1/2	10 to 121 14 to 16 20 to 24	145°F medium-rare to 160°F medium
	Top Loin Strip Steak	3/4 1	10 to 12 15 to 18	145°F medium-rare to 160°F medium
	Tenderloin	1 1 1/2	13 to 15 14 to 16	145°F medium-rare to 160°F medium
	Top Sirloin	3/4 1 1 1/2	13 to 16 17 to 21 22 to 26	145°F medium-rare to 160°F medium
	Top Round Steak (best when marinated before cooking)	3/4 1 1 1/2	8 to 9 16 to 18 25 to 28	145°F medium-rare to 160°F medium
	Flank Steak (best when marinated before cooking)	1 to 1 1/2 pounds	17 to 21	145°F medium-rare to 160°F medium
	Ground Patties (4 per pound)	1/2 inch thick (4-inch diameter)	10 to 12	160°F medium
	(4 per 1 1/2 pounds)	3/4 inch thick (4-inch diameter)	12 to 15	160°F medium
Veal	Chop, Loin or Rib	3/4 to 1	14 to 16	160°F medium
Pork	Chop (boneless or bone-in)	3/4 to 1 1 1/2	9 to 12 12 to 16	160°F medium 160°F medium
	Tenderloin	1 to 1 1/2	15 to 25	160°F medium
	Loin Back Ribs or Spareribs *Use indirect heat*	— — —	1 1/2 to 2 hours	Tender
	Ground Patties	1/2	8 to 10	160°F medium
Lamb	Chop, Loin or Rib	1	10 to 15	160°F medium
	Chop, Sirloin	1	12 to 15	160°F medium

*Use indirect heat for pork loin back or spareribs.

Grilling Gadgets

What would grilling be without gadgets? We've certainly come a long way from the primitive fire pits and iron grates our predecessors used. When shopping for grilling accessories, keep your budget, your grilling style and the storage space you have available in mind. Like any tool, some are more useful than others. Only you know which ones will work for you.

Basting Topper:  Simply screw the basting topper on any bottle of marinade, basting sauce or barbecue sauce and brush over chicken, ribs or roasts to coat the food without a mess. When you're done, remove the brush top, clean and replace the original lid.

Branding Iron:  Miniature branding irons (some with real cowboy brands) can be purchased as a fun way to personalize steaks, chops and burgers. A three-way brand offers "rare," "medium" and "well" brands to take the guesswork out of meat doneness.

Charcoal Baskets:  These metal baskets allow coals to be started on top of the grill grate and then moved to the sides to provide a larger cooking area. Charcoal baskets are good when you're using indirect heat to grill large cuts of meat or other foods that require a long, slow cooking time.

Grill Basket: Grill baskets, also called grill "woks," are great for grilling vegetables or small pieces of meat. A hinged grill basket can be easily flipped to turn everything over at once and ensure even cooking.

Grill basket   Fish grill basket

Grilling Screen or Grid: This flat, metal screen (or metal sheet with holes) can be used with delicate foods, such as fish or shellfish, or small pieces of food such as cut-up vegetables. The screen or grid keeps food from falling through the grill rack.

Grill or Smoker Thermometer: This metal thermometer measures the temperature of the coals. Some thermometers magnetically attach to the outside of steel grills; others can be placed directly on the grill rack or cooking surface.

Hood Holder: This props the hood open to three different heights to allow better temperature control and easy access for turning and basting foods.

Injectors: These syringes with a needlelike end allow you to inject a marinade into meat, seasoning it from the inside out.

Instant-Read Thermometer: An instant-read thermometer quickly checks the internal temperature of foods. They come in a variety of styles; some show doneness levels (very rare to well), while others show an actual digital temperature. Some are shaped like a fork, others are just a probe.

Kabob or Skewer Rack: This rack lets you space kabobs evenly and holds kabobs off the grill rack so they don't stick and are easy to turn.

Rib Rack: Not just for ribs, this self-contained rack increases the cooking capacity of your grill while allowing smoke and heat to evenly penetrate food. Some racks also come with spikes for holding corn, potatoes and other vegetables.

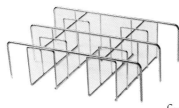

Rotisserie: Food is threaded and then suspended over the heat source with this large skewer-type rod (spit). Holders automatically turn it during grilling.

Skewer: Great for kabobs, these small diameter, long thin rods are usually made from stainless steel. Lengths vary from about 8 to 16 inches.

Unlike round skewers, flat skewers keep food from "spinning" when turned, making it easier to cook both sides evenly. Bamboo or wooden skewers are also available but must be soaked in water at least 30 minutes before using so they don't burn while on the grill.

Smoker Bags: These bags are a mess-free way to lend food a mellow, smoky flavor. Food is placed directly in the bag and then grilled, giving the food a wonderful smoky flavor without soaking wood chips and having clouds of smoke.

Smoker Box: Used to flavor food without a lot of mess, these vented aluminum or cast-iron boxes can be filled with wood chips or pellets (no need to soak), garlic or fresh herbs. Because the boxes contain the ash from these items, they won't burn up your gas grill. They also extend the smoke in charcoal grills.

Tumble Basket: This drum-shaped wire basket attaches to the spit rod of a rotisserie and allows grilling without frequent attention. Great for chicken pieces, large vegetable chunks and shellfish (whole lobster, crab legs, clams, mussels).

Vertical Poultry Rack: Grilling (or roasting) poultry vertically allows the fat to drip down (to keep the bird moist) and away from the bird (to reduce fat) as it cooks. The result is a deliciously moist bird. There are a variety of poultry racks, including stainless steel, nonstick and terra cotta. Less-expensive racks don't have a juice-catching tray at the bottom so more flare-ups will result.

Flavor Boosters: From Marinades & Mops to Sauces & Seasonings

If you're looking for big, bold flavors, marinades, mops, rubs and sauces are a good bet. These flavorizers are about complementing and enhancing grilled foods, not masking their flavor. For definitions, see the Grilling Glossary on page 14.

Marinades

Marinades can play double duty: They add bold flavor, but when an acid such as tomato juice or vinegar is added, they also can tenderize. For marinades with oil, mixing in a blender or food processor will keep the mixture from separating.

Marinades can add flavor in as little as 15 minutes to 2 hours. Although meats can stand at room temperature up to 30 minutes, marinating meats in the refrigerator is safest. Marinating longer than 24 hours is not recommended. The flavor will not change much, and if an acid is included, the meat fibers can break down, resulting in a mushy texture.

Always marinate food in a nonmetal dish, such as glass or plastic, just a bit larger than the food itself, or use a heavy-duty plastic bag that can be tightly sealed. Acid-based marinades can react with some metals, such as aluminum. As a general guideline, marinate delicate fish fillets and vegetables about 30 minutes; fish steaks, meat chops and chicken pieces at least 1 hour; and larger meat cuts up to 24 hours. Turn the food once or twice during the marinating time so the marinade can reach all surfaces. Marinades are not reusable; discard any leftover marinade that is not boiled at least one minute and used as a sauce.

Mops

Mops were originally used in large southern wood-burning barbecue pits and applied with a new, clean floor mop. Barbecue mops are available at stores specializing in outdoor cooking equipment or restaurant supplies. Fresh herb sprigs, such as rosemary or thyme, tied together can also be used as a mop and will add extra flavor. Most often, mops are used when cooking slowly and smoking larger cuts of meat.

Mops can be as simple as broth or beer or as complex as you can imagine. If meats are fatty, use a mop made without oil or butter. In general, you can mop meats whenever you remove the lid from a grill to turn the food. Water smokers, on the other hand, keep meats very moist, so mopping isn't needed.

Rubs

Rubs traditionally were used for barbecued meats cooked in dug-out earth pits, where the "pitmasters" had their own "secret rub." You can add a rub and immediately grill the food or, for more flavor, cover and refrigerate about 1 hour.

Rubs may contain sugar or salt or even ground nuts. The "wet" seasonings get their name from added liquid, such as oil, mustard and reduced liquids such as wine, mixed with the dry seasonings and creating a paste. When grilled, the flavored surface provides a greater flavor contrast with the interior of the meat than do marinades, which tend to meld with the flavor of the meat.

You can easily mix together seasonings from your spice cabinet, or purchase ready-to-use rubs at the supermarket. Rubs also can be used to flavor a wide range of dishes such as condiments, soups and stews.

Sauces

The king of sauces for grilling is barbecue sauce. For years, cooks prided themselves on using their own barbecue sauce recipes, which were brushed or rubbed on foods during grilling or served on top or alongside meats afterward. Most recipes are based on ketchup, chili sauce or canned tomato products, with extra flavors added to make them special. If sauces are thick or contain sugar or other ingredients that will burn, brush them on during the last 15 to 20 minutes of grilling.

Bottled barbecue sauces are popular and readily available in national and regional brands. About 75 percent of all barbecue sauces sold are tomato-based sauces in one of two varieties, either regular/ original or hickory/smoke flavor. The other 25 percent are made up of specialty flavors such as Honey-Dijon, Cajun or Jamaican.

Special Note for Safe Marinades, Mops and Sauces

Leftover marinades, mops and sauces that have been in contact with raw meat should be discarded. Or, to use as a sauce with the grilled meat, heat a leftover marinade, mop or sauce to boiling, then boil for one minute. Boiling will destroy any bacteria that may have been transferred back and forth by brushing it on the uncooked meat, and keep sauces safe.

Other Sensational Seasonings

You can enhance the traditional grilled flavor of foods by adding aromatic woods, herbs or other seasonings to the fire or heat source. These flavorizers should smolder and smoke, not immediately burn to a crisp. Like marinades, mops, rubs and sauces, they should enhance and add a new dimension to food, not mask its true flavor.

It is important to soak all wood pieces, herbs (dried or fresh) and spices, and all other flavorings in water for at least 30 minutes before draining and scattering on the hot coals or lava rock.

▶ **For most gas grills,** place in a drip pan or open-ended foil packet and place directly on the grill rack, or sprinkle directly on the lava rock.

▶ **For electric grills,** place flavorings on the bottom of the grill, under the heating element.

A handful of wood chips usually will be enough for direct grilling. Two handfuls, one added at the beginning of grilling and the second added halfway through, will work well for indirect grilling. Replenish as necessary, and adjust amounts according to the package directions and your personal preference.

Wood Chips and Chunks

Wood is the most popular added flavor when grilling. Use only hardwoods. Do not use softwoods, such as cedar, pine or spruce, because they contain resin or sap that gives off fumes that impart an "off" flavor to foods. Hardwoods are available in bits, chips and chunks. Bits or sawdust are used for a subtle flavor. Chips give true wood-smoke flavor. Chips can be soaked in liquid (water, coffee, beer) for at least 30 minutes, then drained and sprinkled over hot coals or lava rock for rich flavor. Chunks are ideal for longer-cooking foods, such as ribs, roasts and whole poultry. Soak chunks at least 3 hours in liquid before using on hot coals.

Wood Chips and Chunks

Type	Flavor	Use With
Alder	Light, delicate, mildly sweet smoky flavor; associated with Pacific Northwest. If not available, substitute fruitwoods.	Salmon and other fish, scallops, chicken, pork
Fruit (apple, apricot, pork, cherry, peach)	Light, slightly sweet, fragrant smoke.	Poultry and game, veal, ham, vegetables, fish and shellfish
Grapevine cuttings (or grapevine wreaths)	Sweet and subtle, winelike flavor. Popular in wine-producing regions.	Poultry, veal, lamb, fish, vegetables
Hickory	Most popular wood flavor; pungent, smoky, robust, sweet and baconlike. Associated with southern cooking.	Ham, ribs, pork, beef
Mesquite	Smoky but sweeter, tangy and more delicate than hickory. Rich and woody. Burns very hot and can become bitter with long cooking times.	Steak, beef, lamb, poultry
Nut (walnut, pecan)	Sweet, delicate.	Poultry and game, fish
Oak	Smoky but pleasant, robust and tangy.	Beef, pork, ham, poultry
Sugar Maple	Mildly smoky and sweet.	Ham, poultry, vegetables

Other Flavor Enhancers

Type	Flavor	Use With
Flavored charcoals	Varied flavors such as hardwood, bourbon.	See suggestions on package
Cinnamon sticks, whole nutmeg, whole cloves	Spicy, slightly sweet.	Poultry, pork
Citrus peel	Tangy, sharp.	Beef, poultry, pork, ribs, duck
Coffee grounds	Rich, musty; too much can become bitter.	Beef, pork
Corn cobs, dried	Mellow, slightly sweet.	Beef, pork
Garlic cloves	Mellow, nutty.	Beef, poultry
Herbs (fresh or dried)	Basil, bay leaves, cilantro, dill weed, fennel leaves, rosemary, tarragon, thyme. Flavor varies with the herb.	Poultry, fish, shellfish, beef
Herb packets	Special herb blends available in tea-bag form.	Poultry, fish, shellfish, beef, vegetables
Nut shells	From hardwood trees, such as almonds, hazelnuts, pecans, pistachios, walnuts. Flavor varies with the nut.	Poultry, pork, fish
Seaweed (washed and dried)	Somewhat tangy.	Shellfish, mild-flavored fish

Microwave-to-Grill Cooking

To cut your grilling time in half, simply combine the benefits of your microwave and grill. When you go the microwave-to-grill route, you get moist, fast-cooking food with unmistakable grill flavor and appeal. This method is great when grilling dense vegetables, bone-in chicken pieces, meaty spareribs or fresh raw sausage like bratwurst, which are known to overbrown on the outside before the center is cooked. This technique is nice when your coals are burning too hot. Also, much of the fat cooks away from foods during microwaving, which results in fewer flare-ups and healthier cooking.

To Partially Microwave

▶ While the coals are heating to the desired temperature, start the food in the microwave.

▶ Use microwavable casseroles and dishes with covers to partially cook foods most quickly. If you do not have a cover, use plastic wrap and turn back a corner to allow steam to escape. Plastic dishes are nice, because they're lighter in weight and can be safer outdoors than glass dishes.

▶ For added flavor, brush 2 to 4 tablespoons of your favorite barbecue sauce or marinade on the meat before microwaving.

▶ Add 1/4 cup of water or broth to vegetables before microwaving.

▶ Arrange food with thickest parts to the outside edge of the dish.

▶ Cover tightly and microwave on High following the Microwave-to-Grill Guide.

▶ Turn over, rotate or stir food after half the microwave time.

▶ Drain well and immediately place food on the grill to complete cooking.

To Finish on the Grill

As a guide, grill food for about half the time recommended in the recipe. Additional time may be needed because microwave wattages vary as do grills and grilling conditions, so use the doneness test in the recipe as the final guide.

Food Safety Tips

▶ Plan prep time so food can go right from the microwave to the grill.

▶ For food-safety reasons, don't refrigerate partially cooked meat or let it stand at room temperature before grilling. Plan to have the coals ready by the time foods are removed from the microwave.

Microwave-to-Grill Guide

Food	Time on High (per pound)	What to Look For
Chicken pieces (bone-in)	4 to 6 minutes	Edges of pieces will be cooked; parts will be pink but hot
Ribs	6 to 8 minutes	No longer pink; may not be cooked through
Sausage links, raw	4 to 6 minutes	No longer pink; may not be cooked through
Vegetable pieces (3/4 to 1 inch) such as potatoes, carrots or winter squash	4 to 6 minutes	Softened

Note: If grilling more than 4 pounds of food, microwave in two batches.

Grilling Top Ten

Juicy Hamburgers

Juicy Hamburgers

Photo on page 28

Prep: 10 min
Grill: 15 min
4 sandwiches

1 pound lean (at least 80%) ground beef
3 tablespoons water
1/2 teaspoon salt
1/4 teaspoon pepper
4 hamburger buns

1. Heat coals or gas grill for direct heat. Heat to medium heat, which will take about 40 minutes for charcoal or about 10 minutes for a gas grill.

2. In medium bowl, mix beef, water, salt and pepper. Shape mixture into 4 uniform, flat patties, each about 3/4 inch thick. Shaping the patties to have smooth edges will keep them together during cooking and result in uniform doneness. Gently pinch to close any cracks in the patty. Handle the patties as little as possible. The more the beef is handled, the less juicy the burgers will be.

3. Place patties on grill. Cover and grill 13 to 15 minutes, turning once, until beef is no longer pink in center and meat thermometer inserted in center of patties reads 160°F. Loosen patties gently with a turner to prevent crumbling. Serve on buns.

Cheeseburgers: About 1 minute before hamburgers are done, top each burger with 1 slice (1 ounce) American, Cheddar, Swiss or Monterey Jack cheese. Grill until cheese is melted.

Shaping the patties to have smooth edges will keep them together during cooking and result in uniform doneness. Gently pinch to close any cracks in the patty.

Storage **Tip**

If you choose not to grill all the patties at once, it's important to immediately store the uncooked meat in the coldest part of your refrigerator, or freeze it ASAP. Ground meat deteriorates more quickly than other cuts, so it should be used—or stored—quickly.

1 Sandwich: Cal. 390 (Cal. from Fat 170); Fat 19g (Sat. fat 7g); Chol. 65mg; Sodium 670mg; Carbs. 29g (Fiber 2g); Pro. 26g • **% Daily Value:** Vit. A 2%; Vit. C 0%; Calc. 8%; Iron 20% • **Exchanges:** 2 Starch, 3 Medium-Fat Meat • **Carb. Choices:** 2

Basic Brats

Prep: 5 min
Grill: 25 min
6 sandwiches

6 fresh bratwurst (1 pound)
1/3 cup Dijon mustard
2 teaspoons chopped fresh or 1/2 teaspoon dried oregano leaves
6 bratwurst buns, split

1. Heat coals or gas grill for direct heat. Heat to medium heat, which will take about 40 minutes for charcoal or about 10 minutes for a gas grill.

2. Place bratwurst on grill. Cover and grill about 25 minutes, turning occasionally, until no longer pink in center.

3. In small bowl, mix mustard and oregano; spread on cut sides of buns. Serve bratwurst on buns.

Healthful Hint

If you're looking to lower the fat in your diet, use turkey Polish sausage instead of bratwursts.

1 Sandwich: Cal. 390 (Cal. from Fat 215); Fat 24g (Sat. fat 8g); Chol. 45mg; Sodium 1300mg; Carbs. 30g (Fiber 1g); Pro. 14g •
% Daily Value: Vit. A 0%; Vit. C 0%; Calc. 6%; Iron 12% •
Exchanges: 2 Starch, 1 High-Fat Meat, 3 Fat • **Carb. Choices:** 2

Foot-Long Hot Dogs

Prep: 5 min
Grill: 20 min
6 sandwiches

6 long hot dogs (12 inches)
1 tablespoon butter or margarine, melted
6 long hot dog buns, split

1. Brush grill rack with vegetable oil. Heat coals or gas grill for direct heat. Heat to medium heat, which will take about 40 minutes for charcoal or about 10 minutes for a gas grill.

2. In each hot dog, cut crosswise diagonal slashes 1/2 inch apart and 1/4 inch deep.

3. Place hot dogs on grill. Cover and grill 15 to 20 minutes, turning frequently and brushing occasionally with butter, until hot and slashes begin to open. Serve on buns.

Try This

Divide a can of chili with beans, 3/4 cup shredded Cheddar cheese and a cup of chopped onion among these six foot-long hot dogs and presto! You've got Foot-Long Coney Island Dogs.

1 Sandwich: Cal. 535 (Cal. from Fat 280); Fat 31g (Sat. fat 12g); Chol. 55mg; Sodium 1530mg; Carbs. 46g (Fiber 2g); Pro. 17g • **% Daily Value:** Vit. A 2%; Vit. C 0%; Calc. 14%; Iron 18% • **Exchanges:** 3 Starch, 1 High-Fat Meat, 4 1/2 Fat • **Carb. Choices:** 3

Great Steak

porterhouse   rib eye   sirloin   T-bone   tenderloin

1 steak (about 8 ounces)

1. Select a 3/4- to 1-inch-thick steak from those shown in the photos above.

2. Heat coals or gas grill for direct heat. Heat to medium heat, which will take about 40 minutes for charcoal or about 10 minutes for a gas grill.

3. To prevent steak from curling during broiling, cut outer edge of fat on steak diagonally at 1-inch intervals with sharp knife. Do not cut into the meat or it will dry out during grilling.

4. Place steak on grill. Cover and grill for about half the time listed in the chart or until the steak is brown on one side.

5. Turn the steak and continue grilling until desired doneness. To check doneness, cut a small slit in the center of boneless cuts or in the center near the bone of bone-in cuts. Medium-rare is very pink in the center and slightly brown toward the edges. Medium is light pink in center and brown toward the edges. Or insert a meat thermometer in the center of the steak to check for desired doneness. Sprinkle salt and pepper over both sides of steak after cooking if desired. Serve immediately.

Timetable for Grilling Steaks

| | Approximate Total Grilling Time in Minutes | |
Type of Steak	145°F (medium-rare)	160°F (medium)
Porterhouse and T-Bone	10 to 12	14 to 16
Rib Eye	6 to 8	11 to 14
Sirloin (boneless)	13 to 16	17 to 21
Tenderloin	13 to 14	14 to 15

1 Serving: Cal. 350 (Cal. from Fat 140); Fat 16g (Sat. fat 6g); Chol. 130mg; Sodium 120mg; Carbs. 0g (Fiber 0g); Pro. 49g • **% Daily Value:** Vit. A 2%; Vit. C 0%; Calc. 0%; Iron 20% • **Exchanges:** 8 Lean Meat • **Carb. Choices:** 0

Classic Chicken Breasts

Prep: 5 min
Grill: 15 to 25 min
1 serving

1 skinless, boneless chicken breast half (about 1/4 pound)

1. Select boneless, skinless chicken breast halves (about 1/4 pound each) or skinless bone-in chicken breast halves (about 1/2 pound each). If chicken is frozen, place in refrigerator the night before you plan to use it or for at least 12 hours to thaw. Cut and discard fat from chicken with kitchen scissors or knife. Rinse chicken under cold water, and pat dry with paper towels.

2. Brush grill rack with vegetable oil. Heat coals or gas grill for direct heat. Heat to medium heat, which will take about 40 minutes for charcoal or about 10 minutes for a gas grill.

3. Place chicken breasts on grill. Cover and grill for the time listed in the chart, turning once with tongs. If desired, brush chicken with sauce during the last 10 minutes of grilling. Grill until juice of chicken is no longer pink when centers of thickest pieces are cut.

Timetable for Grilling Chicken Breasts

Cut of Chicken	Approximate Grilling Time
Breast halves (bone-in)	20 to 25 minutes
Breast halves (boneless)	15 to 20 minutes

1 Serving: Cal. 140 (Cal. from Fat 30); Fat 3.5g (Sat. fat 1g); Chol. 70mg; Sodium 60mg; Carbs. 0g (Fiber 0g); Pro. 25g • **% Daily Value:** Vit. A 0%; Vit. C 0%; Calc. 0%; Iron 4% • **Exchanges:** 3.5 Very Lean Meat • **Carb. Choices:** 0

Terrific Turkey Breast

Prep: 5 min
Grill: 1 hr 5 min
Stand: 10 min
6 servings

2-pound boneless turkey breast half
Olive or vegetable oil
1/2 teaspoon lemon pepper

1. If using charcoal grill, place drip pan directly under grilling area, and arrange coals around edge of firebox. Heat coals or gas grill for indirect heat. Heat to medium heat, which will take about 40 minutes for charcoal or about 10 minutes for a gas grill.

2. Rub turkey skin with oil; sprinkle with lemon pepper. Insert barbecue meat thermometer so tip is in thickest part of turkey.

3. Place turkey, skin side down, on grill over drip pan or over unheated side of gas grill. Cover and grill 20 minutes; turn. Cover and grill 35 to 45 minutes longer or until thermometer reads 170°F and juice of turkey is no longer pink when center is cut.

4. Remove turkey from grill; cover with foil tent and let stand 10 minutes. Slice turkey.

Success Tip

The turkey will lose a lot of its juices if you slice it right after you take it off the grill. To keep the juices in, cover the turkey with foil and let it rest for a few minutes before you slice it.

1 Serving: Cal. 225 (Cal. from Fat 110); Fat 12g (Sat. fat 3g); Chol. 80mg; Sodium 95mg; Carbs. 0g (Fiber 0g); Pro. 29g • **% Daily Value:** Vit. A 0%; Vit. C 0%; Calc. 0%; Iron 6% • **Exchanges:** 4 Lean Meat • **Carb. Choices:** 0

Fish Steak

Fish steak, about 3/4 inch thick (1/4 to 1/3 pound)
Salt and pepper to taste
1 tablespoon butter or margarine, melted
1 teaspoon lemon juice

1. Heat coals or gas grill for direct heat. Heat to medium heat, which will take about 40 minutes for charcoal or about 10 minutes for a gas grill.

2. Sprinkle both sides of the fish steak with salt and pepper. In small bowl, mix butter and lemon juice.

3. Place fish steak on grill. Cover and grill 7 to 10 minutes, brushing 2 or 3 times with butter mixture. Carefully turn fish with a turner. If fish sticks to the grill, loosen it gently with a turner. Brush other side with butter mixture.

4. Cover and grill 7 to 10 minutes longer or until fish flakes easily with a fork. Brush with butter mixture.

Shop Talk

When you select fresh fish, the scales should be bright with a sheen, the flesh should be firm and elastic and there should be no smell. Frozen fish should be tightly wrapped and frozen solid; there should be no discoloration and no smell.

1 Serving: Cal. 220 (Cal. from Fat 115); Fat 13g (Sat. fat 8g); Chol. 100mg; Sodium 1370mg; Carbs. 1g (Fiber 0g); Pro. 25g • **% Daily Value:** Vit. A 8%; Vit. C 0%; Calc. 2%; Iron 2% • **Exchanges:** 3 1/2 Lean Meat, 1/2 Fat • **Carb. Choices:** 0

Succulent Pork Chop

| loin or rib chop | loin chop | blade chop |

1 pork chop, with bone (3/4-inch thick)

1. Select pork chop from those shown in the photos above.

2. Heat coals or gas grill for direct heat. Heat to medium heat, which will take about 40 minutes for charcoal or about 10 minutes for a gas grill.

3. Place pork chop on grill. Cover and grill for about half the time listed in the chart or until pork chop is brown on one side.

4. Turn the pork chop and continue grilling until the doneness listed in the chart. To check doneness, cut a small slit in the center of boneless cuts or in the center near the bone of bone-in cuts; pork is done when it is no longer pink in center. Or insert a meat thermometer in the center of the pork chop to check for medium doneness (160°F). Sprinkle salt and pepper over both sides of pork chop after cooking if desired. Serve immediately.

Timetable for Grilling Pork Chops

Pork Cut	Approximate Thickness	Approximate Doneness	Grilling Time in Minutes
Loin or Rib Chop (bone-in)	3/4 inch	160°F (medium)	9 to 12
	1 1/2 inches	160°F (medium)	12 to 16
Loin Chop (boneless)	1 inch	160°F (medium)	9 to 12
Blade Chop (bone-in)	3/4 inch	160°F (medium)	9 to 12
	1 1/2 inches	160°F (medium)	12 to 16

1 Serving: Cal. 170 (Cal. from Fat 70); Fat 8g (Sat. fat 3g); Chol. 65mg; Sodium 40mg; Carbs. 0g (Fiber 0g); Pro. 23g • **% Daily Value:** Vit. A 0%; Vit. C 0%; Calc. 0%; Iron 4% • **Exchanges:** 3 Lean Meat • **Carb. Choices**: 0

Pork Tenderloins

Prep: 10 min
Marinate: 8 hr
Grill: 30 min
6 servings

Peppery Teriyaki Marinade (page 294)
2 pork tenderloins (about 3/4 pound each)

1. In small bowl, make Peppery Teriyaki Marinade.

2. Fold thin end of each pork tenderloin under so that pork is an even thickness; secure with toothpicks. Place pork in shallow glass or plastic dish or resealable plastic food-storage bag. Pour marinade over pork; turn pork to coat. Cover dish or seal bag and refrigerate, turning pork occasionally, at least 8 hours but no longer than 24 hours.

3. If using charcoal grill, place drip pan directly under grilling area, and arrange coals around edge of firebox. Brush grill rack with vegetable oil. Heat coals or gas grill for indirect heat. Heat to medium heat, which will take about 40 minutes for charcoal or about 10 minutes for a gas grill.

4. Remove pork from marinade; reserve marinade. Place pork on grill over drip pan or over unheated side of gas grill. Cover and grill 25 to 30 minutes, brushing occasionally with marinade and turning once, until pork has slight blush of pink in center and meat thermometer inserted in center reads 160°F. Discard any remaining marinade.

5. Remove toothpicks. To serve, cut pork across grain into thin slices.

Success Tip

When marinating meats of any kind, it's important to use a resealable plastic food-storage bag, or a glass or plastic dish. Acidic ingredients, such as lemon juice and tomatoes, can react with a metal pan and give foods an off flavor.

1 Serving: Cal. 190 (Cal. from Fat 65); Fat 7g (Sat. fat 2g); Chol. 70mg; Sodium 860mg; Carbs. 5g (Fiber 0g); Pro. 26g • **% Daily Value:** Vit. A 0%; Vit. C 0%; Calc. 0%; Iron 8% • **Exchanges:** 4 Very Lean Meat, 1 Fat • **Carb. Choices:** 0

Barbecue Pork Ribs

Prep: 10 min
Grill: 1 hr 10 min
Cook: 20 min
4 servings

4 pounds pork loin back ribs (not cut into serving pieces)
1 tablespoon vegetable oil
4 teaspoons chopped fresh or 1 1/2 teaspoons dried thyme leaves
Smoky Barbecue Sauce (below)

1. If using charcoal grill, place drip pan directly under grilling area, and arrange coals around edge of firebox. Brush grill rack with vegetable oil. Heat coals or gas grill for indirect heat. Heat to medium heat, which will take about 40 minutes for charcoal or about 10 minutes for a gas grill.

2. Brush meaty sides of pork with oil. Sprinkle with thyme.

3. Place pork, meaty sides up, on grill over drip pan or over unheated side of gas grill. Cover and grill 1 hour to 1 hour 10 minutes or until no longer pink when cut near bone. Meanwhile, make Smoky Barbecue Sauce. Brush sauce over pork 2 or 3 times during the last 15 minutes of grilling.

4. Heat any remaining sauce to boiling; boil and stir 1 minute. To serve, cut pork into serving pieces. Serve with sauce.

Smoky Barbecue Sauce

1/2 cup ketchup
1/4 cup water
3 tablespoons packed brown sugar
2 tablespoons white vinegar
2 teaspoons celery seed
1/4 teaspoon liquid smoke
1/4 teaspoon red pepper sauce

In 1-quart saucepan, heat all ingredients to boiling; reduce heat. Simmer uncovered 15 minutes, stirring occasionally. About 1 cup.

Try This

Don't feel limited to using the Smoky Barbecue Sauce included with this recipe. Experiment with one of the other barbecue sauces found in the Sauces, Marinades & Rubs chapter. Or skip making your own sauce and use your favorite purchased barbecue sauce instead.

1 Serving: Cal. 960 (Cal. from Fat 650); Fat 70g (Sat. fat 25g); Chol. 265mg; Sodium 570mg; Carbs. 19g (Fiber 1g); Pro. 64g • **% Daily Value:** Vit. A 8%; Vit. C 4%; Calc. 14%; Iron 28% • **Exchanges:** 1 Starch, 8 1/2 Medium-Fat Meat, 5 1/2 Fat • **Carb. Choices:** 1

Beef, Pork & Lamb

Sour Cream and Onion Burgers

Backyard Beer Burgers

Prep: 10 min
Grill: 15 min
6 sandwiches

1 1/2 pounds lean (at least 80%) ground beef
1 small onion, finely chopped (1/4 cup)
1/4 cup regular or nonalcoholic beer
1 tablespoon Worcestershire sauce
1 teaspoon salt
1/4 teaspoon pepper
2 cloves garlic, finely chopped
6 rye or whole wheat hamburger buns, split
Ketchup, if desired
Pickle planks, if desired

1. Heat coals or gas grill for direct heat.

2. In medium bowl, mix all ingredients except buns, ketchup and pickles. Shape mixture into 6 patties, about 3/4 inch thick.

3. Cover and grill patties over medium heat 13 to 15 minutes, turning once, until meat thermometer inserted in center reads 160°F and patties are no longer pink in center. Add buns, cut sides down, for last 4 minutes of grilling or until toasted. Serve burgers in buns with ketchup and pickles.

Success Tip

Though you may have seen it done time and time again, resist the urge to press a metal spatula down on a hamburger patty while it's cooking. You'll wind up squeezing out much of the flavorful juices.

1 Sandwich: Cal. 325 (Cal. from Fat 125); Fat 14g (Sat. fat 5g); Chol. 70mg; Sodium 620mg; Carbs. 23g (Fiber 2g); Pro. 27g • **% Daily Value:** Vit. A 2%; Vit. C 0%; Calc. 4%; Iron 22% • **Exchanges:** 1 1/2 Starch, 3 Medium-Fat Meat • **Carb. Choices:** 1 1/2

Sour Cream and Onion Burgers

Prep: 10 min
Grill: 13 min
8 sandwiches

Photo on page 44

2 pounds lean (at least 80%) ground beef
2 envelopes (1 ounce each) onion recipe and soup mix
1 cup sour cream
1/2 cup dry bread crumbs
1/8 teaspoon pepper
8 hamburger buns, split, or 1 round focaccia bread (10 inch), cut
    horizontally in half, then cut into 8 wedges
Leaf lettuce, if desired

1. Heat coals or gas grill for direct heat.

2. In large bowl, mix all ingredients except buns and lettuce. Shape mixture into 8 patties, about 1/2 inch thick.

3. Cover and grill patties over medium heat 11 to 13 minutes, turning once, until meat thermometer inserted in center reads 160°F and patties are no longer pink in center. Serve in buns with lettuce.

Try This

Tired of shaping patties into the ordinary rounds? Shape them into wedges and serve on slices of focaccia instead of the usual sandwich buns.

1 Sandwich: Cal. 425 (Cal. from Fat 190); Fat 21g (Sat. fat 9g); Chol. 85mg; Sodium 820mg; Carbs. 31g (Fiber 2g); Pro. 28g • **% Daily Value:** Vit. A 4%; Vit. C 2%; Calc. 12%; Iron 24% • **Exchanges:** 2 Starch, 3 Medium-Fat Meat, 1 Fat • **Carb. Choices:** 2

Jalapeño Burgers

Prep: 10 min
Grill: 13 min
6 sandwiches

1 1/2 pounds lean (at least 80%) ground beef
1 medium onion, finely chopped (1/2 cup)
2 to 3 jalapeño chilies, seeded and finely chopped
1 clove garlic, finely chopped

1. Brush grill rack with vegetable oil. Heat coals or gas grill for direct heat.

2. In medium bowl, mix all ingredients. Shape mixture into 6 patties, about 1/2 inch thick.

3. Cover and grill patties over medium heat 11 to 13 minutes, turning once, until meat thermometer inserted in center reads 160°F and patties are no longer pink in center.

Try This

For a Mexican twist, serve these zesty burgers in flour tortillas accompanied by Fresh Tomato Salsa (page 295), taco sauce or chili sauce.

1 Sandwich: Cal. 220 (Cal. from Fat 115); Fat 13g (Sat. fat 5g); Chol. 70mg; Sodium 55mg; Carbs. 2g (Fiber 0g); Pro. 23g • **% Daily Value:** Vit. A 2%; Vit. C 2%; Calc. 0%; Iron 14% • **Exchanges:** 3 Medium-Fat Meat • **Carb. Choices:** 0

Gingery Pepper Steak

Prep: 15 min
Marinate: 1 hr
Grill: 16 min
4 servings

1-pound beef boneless top sirloin steak, 3/4 inch thick
1/4 cup red wine vinegar
1 1/2 tablespoons chopped fresh or 1 1/2 teaspoons dried
    oregano leaves
1 tablespoon grated gingerroot
2 tablespoons olive or vegetable oil
2 tablespoons water
2 teaspoons cracked black pepper
4 large cloves garlic, crushed

1. Cut beef into 4 serving pieces. In shallow glass or plastic dish or resealable plastic food-storage bag, mix remaining ingredients. Add beef; turning to coat. Cover dish or seal bag and refrigerate, turning once, at least 1 hour but no longer than 24 hours.

2. Brush grill rack with vegetable oil. Heat coals or gas grill for direct heat. Remove beef from marinade; discard marinade.

3. Cover and grill beef over medium heat 13 to 16 minutes for medium beef doneness, turning once.

Shop Talk

Look for the freshest gingerroot you can find; it shouldn't be shriveled or cracked, and the cut surfaces shouldn't be dried out. Take a whiff— gingerroot should smell fresh, not musty.

1 Serving: Cal. 165 (Cal. from Fat 65); Fat 7g (Sat. fat 2g); Chol. 60mg; Sodium 45mg; Carbs. 2g (Fiber 0g); Pro. 22g • **% Daily Value:** Vit. A 0%; Vit. C 0%; Calc. 0%; Iron 12% • **Exchanges:** 3 Lean Meat • **Carb. Choices:** 0

Taco Burgers

Prep: 10 min
Grill: 18 min
4 sandwiches

1 pound lean (at least 80%) ground beef
1 envelope (1.25 ounces) taco seasoning mix
4 slices (1 ounce each) Monterey Jack cheese
4 hamburger buns, split
1 avocado, pitted, peeled and sliced
1/4 cup thick-and-chunky salsa

1. Heat coals or gas grill for direct heat.

2. In medium bowl, mix beef and taco seasoning mix. Shape mixture into 4 patties, each about 3/4 inch thick.

3. Cover and grill patties over medium heat 13 to 15 minutes, turning once, until meat thermometer inserted in center reads 160°F and patties are no longer pink in center. Top each patty with cheese slice. Grill 1 to 2 minutes or until cheese begins to melt. Serve in buns with avocado and salsa.

Substitute

This recipe calls for ground beef, but feel free to use ground turkey instead.

1 Sandwich: Cal. 540 (Cal. from Fat 270); Fat 30g (Sat. fat 12g); Chol. 95mg; Sodium 880mg; Carbs. 32g (Fiber 4g); Pro. 35g • **% Daily Value:** Vit. A 26%; Vit. C 6%; Calc. 30%; Iron 28% • **Exchanges:** 2 Starch, 4 Medium-Fat Meat, 2 Fat • **Carb. Choices:** 2

Lemon Pepper Steaks

Prep: 5 min
Grill: 16 min
4 servings

4 beef sirloin or rib eye steaks, 1 inch thick (about 2 pounds)
1/2 teaspoon garlic salt
1/4 cup butter or margarine, melted
2 tablespoons chopped fresh or 1 tablespoon dried basil leaves
2 teaspoons lemon pepper
2 medium bell peppers (any color), cut lengthwise in half
    and seeded

1. Brush grill rack with vegetable oil. Heat coals or gas grill for direct heat.

2. Trim fat on beef steaks to 1/2-inch thickness if necessary. Sprinkle garlic salt over beef. In small bowl, mix butter, basil and lemon pepper; brush over beef and bell pepper halves.

3. Cover and grill beef and bell peppers over medium heat 12 to 16 minutes for medium beef doneness, turning once. Brush tops of steaks with butter mixture. Cut bell peppers into strips; serve over beef.

Success Tip

One of the best ways to keep steaks moist and juicy is to make sure the grill is hot before adding the steaks. A hot grill quickly sears the outside of the meat and seals in the juices.

1 Serving: Cal. 525 (Cal. from Fat 325); Fat 36g (Sat. fat 17g); Chol. 165mg; Sodium 470mg; Carbs. 5g (Fiber 1g); Pro. 45g • **% Daily Value:** Vit. A 18%; Vit. C 48%; Calc. 2%; Iron 28% • **Exchanges:** 1 Vegetable, 6 Medium-Fat Meat, 1 Fat • **Carb. Choices:** 0

Steak with Feta

Prep: 10 min
Marinate: 8 hr
Grill: 20 min
8 servings

Greek Marinade (below)
2-pound beef boneless sirloin steak, about 1 inch thick
2 medium red onions, cut into 1/2-inch slices
1 package (4 ounces) crumbled feta cheese
Chopped fresh parsley, if desired

1. In shallow glass or plastic dish or resealable plastic food-storage bag, make Greek Marinade. Pierce beef with fork several times on both sides. Add beef and onions to marinade; turn to coat. Cover dish or seal bag and refrigerate, turning beef occasionally, at least 8 hours but no longer than 24 hours.

2. Heat coals or gas grill for direct heat. Remove beef from marinade; reserve marinade.

3. Cover and grill beef and onions over medium heat 15 to 20 minutes for medium beef doneness, brushing occasionally with marinade and turning once. Discard any remaining marinade.

4. Cut beef across grain into thin slices. Sprinkle beef with feta and parsley; serve with onion slices.

Greek Marinade

1/2 cup dry red wine or beef broth
1 tablespoon packed brown sugar
3 tablespoons olive or vegetable oil
1 1/2 teaspoons dried oregano leaves
1/2 teaspoon salt
1/4 teaspoon ground cinnamon
2 cloves garlic, finely chopped

In small bowl, mix all ingredients. About 3/4 cup.

1 Serving: Cal. 225 (Cal. from Fat 110); Fat 12g (Sat. fat 4g); Chol. 70mg; Sodium 380mg; Carbs. 5g (Fiber 1g); Pro. 25g • **% Daily Value:** Vit. A 2%; Vit. C 0%; Calc. 8%; Iron 12% • **Exchanges:** 1 Vegetable, 3 Lean Meat, 1 Fat • **Carb. Choices:** 0

Steak and Potato Salad

Prep: 15 min
Grill: 14 min
4 servings

3/4 pound small red potatoes, cut in half
2/3 cup honey Dijon dressing and marinade
3/4-pound beef boneless top sirloin steak, 3/4 inch thick
1/4 teaspoon salt
1/4 teaspoon coarsely ground pepper
4 cups bite-size pieces romaine lettuce
2 medium tomatoes, cut into thin wedges
1/2 cup thinly sliced red onion

1. Heat coals or gas grill for direct heat.

2. In 2- or 2 1/2-quart saucepan, place potatoes; add enough water to cover potatoes. Heat to boiling; reduce heat to medium. Cook uncovered 5 to 8 minutes or just until potatoes are tender.

3. Drain potatoes; place in medium bowl. Add 2 tablespoons of the dressing; toss to coat. Place potatoes in grill basket (grill "wok") if desired. Brush beef steak with 1 tablespoon of the dressing; sprinkle with salt and pepper.

4. Cover and grill beef and potatoes over medium heat 10 to 14 minutes, turning once, until beef is desired doneness and potatoes are golden brown. Cut beef into thin slices.

5. On 4 plates, arrange lettuce, tomatoes and onion. Top with beef and potatoes; drizzle with remaining dressing. Sprinkle with additional pepper if desired.

Healthful Hint

Looking to cut down on fat? Substitute fat-free salad dressing for the regular dressing and marinade.

1 Serving: Cal. 310 (Cal. from Fat 145); Fat 16g (Sat. fat 3g); Chol. 45mg; Sodium 450mg; Carbs. 21g (Fiber 3g); Pro. 20g • **% Daily Value:** Vit. A 34%; Vit. C 52%; Calc. 2%; Iron 16% • **Exchanges:** 1 Starch, 1 Vegetable, 2 Medium-Fat Meat, 1 Fat • **Carb. Choices:** 1 1/2

Garlic Steak Salad

Spicy Garlic Dressing (below)
1-pound beef boneless sirloin steak, 1 to 1 1/2 inches thick
1 large red or yellow bell pepper, cut into strips
1 cup sliced fresh mushrooms (3 ounces)
1/4 teaspoon salt
1/8 teaspoon pepper
6 cups bite-size pieces salad greens

1. Heat coals or gas grill for direct heat. Make Spicy Garlic Dressing; reserve 1/4 cup.

2. Cover and grill beef steak over medium heat 15 to 20 minutes, turning once, until desired doneness. Meanwhile, in medium bowl, toss bell pepper and mushrooms with 2 tablespoons of the dressing; place in grill basket (grill "wok"). Cover and grill vegetables 5 minutes, shaking basket or stirring vegetables occasionally, until bell pepper is crisp-tender.

3. Sprinkle beef with salt and pepper; cut into 1/4-inch slices. In medium bowl, toss beef and reserved 1/4 cup dressing. In large bowl, place salad greens, vegetables and beef. Add remaining dressing; toss.

Spicy Garlic Dressing

1/3 cup olive or vegetable oil
2 tablespoons chopped fresh parsley
3 tablespoons red wine vinegar
1 tablespoon lemon juice
1 teaspoon chopped fresh or 1/2 teaspoon dried oregano leaves
1/2 teaspoon crushed red pepper
2 cloves garlic, finely chopped

In tightly covered container, shake all ingredients. About 1/2 cup.

1 Serving: Cal. 225 (Cal. from Fat 135); Fat 15g (Sat. fat 2g); Chol. 40mg; Sodium 140mg; Carbs. 5g (Fiber 2g); Pro. 17g • **% Daily Value:** Vit. A 68%; Vit. C 100%; Calc. 4%; Iron 14% • **Exchanges:** 1 Vegetable, 2 Medium-Fat Meat, 1 Fat • **Carb. Choices:** 0

Sizzling Fajitas

Prep: 30 min
Marinate: 8 hr
Grill: 24 min
12 servings

Fajita Marinade (page 291)
2 beef boneless top sirloin steaks, 1 1/2 inches thick
    (1 1/2 pounds each)
4 large onions, sliced
4 medium green or red bell peppers, cut into 1/4-inch strips
1/4 cup vegetable oil
24 flour tortillas (8 to 10 inches in diameter)

Serve with One or More of These Toppings:
1 jar (16 ounces) picante sauce (2 cups)
2 cups shredded Cheddar or Monterey Jack cheese (8 ounces)
3 cups purchased guacamole
1 1/2 cups sour cream

1. In shallow glass or plastic dish or resealable plastic food-storage bag, make Fajita Marinade. Trim excess fat from beef steaks. Pierce beef with fork several times on both sides. Add beef to marinade; turn to coat. Cover dish or seal bag and refrigerate, turning beef occasionally, at least 8 hours but no longer than 24 hours.

2. Heat coals or gas grill for direct heat. Remove beef from marinade; reserve marinade.

3. Cover and grill beef over medium heat 18 to 24 minutes for medium doneness, brushing occasionally with marinade and turning once. Discard any remaining marinade. Meanwhile, in large bowl, toss onions and bell peppers with oil; place in grill basket (grill "wok"). Cover and grill vegetables 6 to 8 minutes, shaking basket or stirring vegetables once or twice, until crisp-tender.

4. While beef and vegetables are grilling, heat oven to 325°F. Wrap tortillas in foil. Heat in oven about 15 minutes or until warm. Remove tortillas from oven; keep wrapped.

5. Cut beef across grain into very thin slices. For each fajita, layer beef, vegetables and desired Toppings on tortilla. Roll or fold tortilla around filling. Serve with desired Toppings.

1 Serving (without Toppings): Cal. 610 (Cal. from Fat 250); Fat 28g (Sat. fat 8g); Chol. 75mg; Sodium 830mg; Carbs. 60g (Fiber 6g); Pro. 36g • **% Daily Value:** Vit. A 12%; Vit. C 40%; Calc. 18%; Iron 32% • **Exchanges:** 3 Starch, 3 Vegetable, 3 Medium-Fat Meat, 1 1/2 Fat • **Carb. Choices:** 4

Barbecued London Broil

Prep: 15 min
Marinate: 8 hr
Grill: 17 min
4 servings

1/3 cup white vinegar
1/3 cup olive or vegetable oil
3 tablespoons packed brown sugar
3 tablespoons soy sauce
1/2 teaspoon coarsely ground pepper
2 medium onions, sliced
1 clove garlic, finely chopped
1 1/2-pound beef flank steak

1. In shallow glass or plastic dish or resealable plastic food-storage bag, mix all ingredients except beef. Add beef; turn to coat. Cover dish or seal bag and refrigerate, turning beef occasionally, at least 8 hours but no longer than 24 hours.

2. Brush grill rack with vegetable oil. Heat coals or gas grill for direct heat. Remove beef and onions from marinade; discard marinade. In 9-inch round foil pan, place onions.

3. Cover and grill beef over medium heat 12 to 17 minutes for medium-rare doneness, turning once. At same time, grill onions in pan, stirring occasionally, until tender.

4. Cut beef diagonally across grain into very thin slices. Top beef with onions.

Success Tip

You can make this less-tender cut of beef taste great by grilling it to medium-rare and cutting it across the grain into thin diagonal slices.

1 Serving: Cal. 370 (Cal. from Fat 190); Fat 21g (Sat. fat 6g); Chol. 95mg; Sodium 430mg; Carbs. 8g (Fiber 1g); Pro. 37g • **% Daily Value:** Vit. A 2%; Vit. C 0%'; Calc. 2%; Iron 20% • **Exchanges:** 1/2 Other Carbs., 5 Lean Meat, 1 1/2 Fat • **Carb. Choices:** 1/2

Steak with Parsley Pesto

Prep: 5 min
Grill: 15 min
4 servings

1/4 cup chopped fresh parsley
1/4 cup olive or vegetable oil
4 cloves garlic, cut into pieces
4 beef T-bone steaks, about 1 inch thick (about 8 ounces each)
1 teaspoon salt
1/2 teaspoon freshly ground pepper

1. Heat coals or gas grill for direct heat.

2. In food processor or blender, cover and process parsley, oil and garlic until smooth.

3. Cut outer edge of fat on beef steaks diagonally at 1-inch intervals to prevent curling (do not cut into beef).

4. Cover and grill beef over medium heat 5 minutes for medium-rare or 7 minutes for medium, brushing frequently with parsley mixture. Turn; brush generously with parsley mixture. Grill 5 to 8 minutes longer until desired doneness. Sprinkle with salt and pepper. Discard any remaining parsley mixture.

Try This

Here's a quick and easy way to cut up fresh parsley: Snip it with kitchen scissors into little pieces over a measuring cup or small bowl.

1 Serving: Cal. 325 (Cal. from Fat 205); Fat 23g (Sat. fat 5g); Chol. 80mg; Sodium 660mg; Carbs. 1g (Fiber 0g); Pro. 30g • **% Daily Value:** Vit. A 8%; Vit. C 4%; Calc. 2%; Iron 16% • **Exchanges:** 4 Medium-Fat Meat, 1/2 Fat • **Carb. Choices:** 0

Beer-Marinated Rump Roast

Prep: 20 min
Marinate: 8 hr
Grill: 2 hr
Stand: 15 min
8 servings

2 tablespoons vegetable oil
1 medium onion, chopped (1/2 cup)
1 clove garlic, finely chopped
1/2 cup chili sauce
1/2 teaspoon salt
1/4 teaspoon pepper
1 can or bottle (12 ounces) regular or nonalcoholic beer
3 1/2- to 4-pound beef rolled rump roast
2 cups hickory wood chips

1. In 1-quart saucepan, heat oil over medium-high heat. Cook onion and garlic in oil, stirring frequently, until onion is tender; remove from heat. Stir in chili sauce, salt, pepper and beer.

2. In shallow glass or plastic dish or resealable plastic food-storage bag, place beef roast. Pour beer mixture over beef; turn beef to coat. Cover dish or seal bag and refrigerate, turning beef occasionally, at least 8 hours but no longer than 24 hours.

3. In medium bowl, cover wood chips with water; soak 30 minutes.

4. Brush grill rack with vegetable oil. Heat coals or gas grill for indirect heat. Remove beef from marinade; reserve marinade.

5. Insert spit rod lengthwise through center of beef; hold firmly in place with adjustable holding forks. Insert barbecue meat thermometer so tip is near center of beef but not touching spit rod. Drain wood chips. Add about 1/2 cup wood chips to hot coals. For gas grill, place wood chips on piece of foil; seal tightly. Poke 6 to 8 slits in top of foil packet with sharp knife. Place on grill rack; cover grill and let packet get hot enough to start smoking, about 10 minutes. Leave packet on grill while grilling food.

6. Cover and grill beef on rotisserie over drip pan over medium-low heat about 2 hours for medium doneness (160°F on meat thermometer), brushing occasionally with marinade and adding 1/2 cup wood chips every 30 minutes.

7. Remove spit rod, holding forks and thermometer. Discard any remaining marinade. Cover beef with foil and let stand 15 minutes before slicing.

1 Serving: Cal. 260 (Cal. from Fat 80); Fat 9g (Sat. fat 2g); Chol. 105mg; Sodium 310mg; Carbs. 4g (Fiber 0g); Pro. 40g • **% Daily Value:** Vit. A 4%; Vit. C 2%; Calc. 0%; Iron 20% • **Exchanges:** 5 Lean Meat • **Carb. Choices:** 0

Glazed Beef Tenderloin with Herbed Potatoes

Prep: 15 min
Marinate: 1 hr
Grill: 15 min
4 servings

1/3 cup steak sauce
1 1/2 tablespoons packed brown sugar
4 beef tenderloin steaks, about 1 inch thick (about 1 pound)
8 small new potatoes (1 pound), cut lengthwise in half
2 tablespoons water
Cooking spray
1 teaspoon chopped fresh or 1/4 teaspoon dried
     rosemary leaves, crumbled
1 teaspoon chopped fresh or 1/4 teaspoon dried thyme leaves
1/4 teaspoon paprika
1/2 teaspoon salt
1/4 teaspoon pepper

1. In shallow glass or plastic dish, mix steak sauce and brown sugar; reserve 2 tablespoons sauce. Add beef to remaining sauce (about 1/4 cup); turn to coat. Cover and refrigerate, turning beef 2 or 3 times, at least 1 hour but no longer than 24 hours.

2. Heat coals or gas grill for direct heat.

3. In 2-quart microwavable casserole, place potatoes and water. Cover and microwave on High 3 to 5 minutes or until potatoes are just tender. Place potatoes on sheet of heavy-duty foil. Spray potatoes with cooking spray; sprinkle with rosemary, thyme and paprika. Wrap securely in foil.

4. Cover and grill beef and packet of potatoes over medium heat 7 minutes. Turn beef and potatoes; brush reserved sauce over beef. Cover and grill about 6 to 8 minutes longer for medium beef doneness; remove from heat. Sprinkle salt and pepper over potatoes.

1 Serving: Cal. 260 (Cal. from Fat 65); Fat 7g (Sat. fat 3g); Chol. 55mg; Sodium 660mg; Carbs. 28g (Fiber 2g); Pro. 23g • **% Daily Value:** Vit. A 2%; Vit. C 10%; Calc. 2%; Iron 18% • **Exchanges:** 2 Starch, 2 Lean Meat • **Carb. Choices:** 2

Peppercorn T-Bones

Prep: 10 min
Grill: 16 min
6 servings

6 beef T-bone steaks, 1 inch thick (about 1 1/2 pounds)
3 cloves garlic, cut in half
1 1/2 tablespoons black peppercorns, crushed
1/3 cup butter or margarine, softened
1 1/2 tablespoons Dijon mustard
3/4 teaspoon Worcestershire sauce
1/4 teaspoon lime juice
Salt and pepper, if desired

1. Heat coals or gas grill for direct heat.

2. Trim fat on beef steaks to 1/4-inch thickness. Rub garlic on beef. Press crushed peppercorns into beef. In small bowl, mix remaining ingredients except salt and pepper; set aside.

3. Cover and grill beef over medium heat 12 to 16 minutes for medium doneness, turning once. Sprinkle with salt and pepper. Serve with butter mixture.

Try This

To crush peppercorns, place them in a heavy-duty resealable plastic food-storage bag and use a rolling pin to crush them into smaller pieces.

1 Serving: Cal. 200 (Cal. from Fat 135); Fat 15g (Sat. fat 8g); Chol. 65mg; Sodium 200mg; Carbs. 1g (Fiber 0g); Pro. 15g • **% Daily Value:** Vit. A 8%; Vit. C 0%; Calc. 0%; Iron 8% • **Exchanges:** 2 High-Fat Meat • **Carb. Choices:** 0

Easy Steak Kabobs

Prep: 15 min
Grill: 18 min
4 servings

1 pound beef boneless top sirloin steak
1 medium bell pepper (any color)
16 medium mushrooms
1 tablespoon chopped fresh or 1 teaspoon dried dill weed
1 tablespoon lemon juice
1 tablespoon olive or vegetable oil
1 tablespoon honey mustard
1/4 teaspoon salt
1/4 teaspoon pepper

1. Heat coals or gas grill for direct heat.

2. Cut beef into 24 one-inch pieces. Cut bell pepper into 16 one-inch wedges. On each of eight 10- to 12-inch metal skewers, alternately thread beef, bell pepper and mushrooms, leaving 1/4-inch space between each piece. In small bowl, mix remaining ingredients.

3. Cover and grill kabobs over medium heat 15 to 18 minutes, turning and brushing kabobs 3 or 4 times with oil mixture, until beef is desired doneness and vegetables are tender.

Substitute

If you'd like, you can substitute chicken for the sirloin steak in this recipe. Use boneless skinless chicken breasts or thighs, cut into 1-inch pieces. Grill until the chicken is no longer pink in center.

1 Serving: Cal. 185 (Cal. from Fat 65); Fat 7g (Sat. fat 2g); Chol. 60mg; Sodium 240mg; Carbs. 5g (Fiber 2g); Pro. 25g • **% Daily Value:** Vit. A 4%; Vit. C 24%; Calc. 0%; Iron 16% • **Exchanges:** 1 Vegetable, 3 Very Lean Meat, 1 Fat • **Carb. Choices:** 0

Honey-Mustard Pork Chops

Prep: 10 min
Grill: 16 min
4 servings

Honey-Mustard Glaze (below)
4 pork butterfly loin chops, 1 inch thick (about 1 pound)

1. Brush grill rack with vegetable oil. Heat coals or gas grill for direct heat.

2. Make Honey-Mustard Glaze.

3. Cover and grill pork chops over medium heat 12 to 16 minutes, brushing occasionally with glaze and turning once, until no longer pink in center. Discard any remaining glaze.

Honey-Mustard Glaze

1/4 cup honey
2 tablespoons Dijon mustard
1 tablespoon orange juice
1 teaspoon chopped fresh or 1/4 teaspoon dried tarragon leaves
1 teaspoon balsamic or cider vinegar
1/2 teaspoon white Worcestershire sauce
Dash of onion powder

In small bowl, mix all ingredients. About 1/2 cup.

Shop Talk

If you're having a hard time finding white Worcestershire sauce, feel free to substitute regular Worcestershire sauce instead. Your glaze will be darker in color, but it will still taste delicious.

1 Serving: Cal. 250 (Cal. from Fat 90); Fat 10g (Sat. fat 3g); Chol. 75mg; Sodium 190mg; Carbs. 14g (Fiber 0g); Pro. 26g • **% Daily Value:** Vit. A 0%; Vit. C 0%; Calc. 0%; Iron 6% • **Exchanges:** 1 Other Carbs., 4 Very Lean Meat, 1 Fat • **Carb. Choices:** 1

Basil-Lemon Pork Chops with Melon

Prep: 20 min
Marinate: 1 hr
Grill: 16 min
4 servings

Basil-Lemon Marinade (below)
4 pork loin or rib chops, 1 inch thick (about 2 pound)
1/4 honeydew melon, peeled and cut into 4 wedges
1/4 cantaloupe, peeled and cut into 4 wedges
Salt and white pepper, to taste

1. In small bowl, make Basil-Lemon Marinade; reserve 3/4 cup for brushing on pork and melon during grilling. In shallow glass or plastic dish or resealable plastic food-storage bag, place pork chops. Pour remaining marinade over pork; turn pork to coat. Cover dish or seal bag and refrigerate, turning once, at least 1 hour but no longer than 2 hours.

2. Brush grill rack with vegetable oil. Heat coals or gas grill for direct heat. Drain pork; discard marinade.

3. Cover and grill pork over medium heat 12 to 16 minutes, turning once and brushing with reserved marinade, until no longer pink when cut near bone. Add honeydew and cantaloupe wedges for last 3 to 4 minutes of grilling, turning and brushing 2 to 3 times with reserved marinade, until hot. Discard any remaining marinade.

4. Sprinkle pork with salt and white pepper. Serve pork with melon.

Basil-Lemon Marinade

1 can (12 ounces) frozen lemonade concentrate, thawed
1/2 cup slivered fresh basil leaves or 2 1/2 tablespoons dried basil
    leaves
1/4 cup olive or vegetable oil

In small bowl, mix all ingredients. About 1 1/4 cups.

1 Serving: Cal. 370 (Cal. from Fat 145); Fat 16g (Sat. fat 5g); Chol. 100mg; Sodium 375mg; Carbs. 20g (Fiber 1g); Pro. 36g • **% Daily Value:** Vit. A 20%; Vit. C 32%; Calc. 2%; Iron 8% • **Exchanges:** 1 Fruit, 5 Lean Meat, 1 Fat • **Carb. Choices:** 1

Wild Rice- and Almond-Stuffed Pork Chops

Prep: 20 min
Grill: 45 min
4 servings

Wild Rice and Almond Stuffing (below)
1/3 cup apricot preserves
1 tablespoon dry white wine or apple juice
1/8 teaspoon ground cinnamon
4 pork loin chops, 1 inch thick (about 2 1/2 pounds)

1. Brush grill rack with vegetable oil. Heat coals or gas grill for direct heat.

2. Make Wild Rice and Almond Stuffing. In small bowl, mix apricot preserves, wine and cinnamon.

3. Make a horizontal cut in side of each pork chop on the meatiest side of the bone, forming a pocket (do not cut through to opposite side). Press about 1/3 cup stuffing mixture into each pocket. Secure openings with toothpicks.

4. Cover and grill pork over medium-low heat 40 to 45 minutes, brushing occasionally with apricot mixture and turning 2 or 3 times, until pork is no longer pink when cut near bone on the unstuffed sides of chops. Remove toothpicks; discard any remaining apricot mixture.

Wild Rice and Almond Stuffing

1 teaspoon butter or margarine
1/3 cup finely chopped celery
1 medium green onion, finely chopped (1 tablespoon)
1 cup cooked wild rice
1 tablespoon sliced almonds
1/4 teaspoon salt
1/8 teaspoon pepper

In 8-inch skillet, melt butter over medium heat. Cook celery and onion in butter, stirring frequently, until celery is crisp-tender. Stir in remaining ingredients. About 1 1/3 cups.

1 Serving: Cal. 450 (Cal. from Fat 170); Fat 19g (Sat. fat 74g); Chol. 135mg; Sodium 260mg; Carbs. 24g (Fiber 1g); Pro. 46g • **% Daily Value:** Vit. A 2%; Vit. C 2%; Calc. 2%; Iron 10% • **Exchanges:** 1 1/2 Starch, 6 Lean Meat • **Carb. Choices:** 1 1/2

Jamaican Jerk Pork Chops with Mango Salsa

Prep: 20 min
Marinate: 30 min
Grill: 12 min
4 servings

Jamaican Jerk Seasoning (below)
4 pork loin or rib chops, about 3/4 inch thick (about 2 pounds)
Mango Salsa (below)

1. Make Jamaican Jerk Seasoning. Rub seasoning into pork chops. Cover and refrigerate at least 30 minutes but no longer than 1 hour.

2. Meanwhile, make Mango Salsa.

3. Heat coals or gas grill for direct heat.

4. Cover and grill pork chops over medium heat 9 to 12 minutes, turning once, until no longer pink when cut near bone. Serve with salsa.

Jamaican Jerk Seasoning

2 teaspoons dried thyme leaves
1 teaspoon ground allspice
1 teaspoon packed brown sugar
1/2 teaspoon salt
1/2 teaspoon cracked black pepper
1/4 to 1/2 teaspoon ground red pepper (cayenne)
1/4 teaspoon crushed dried sage leaves
4 cloves garlic, finely chopped

In small bowl, mix all ingredients. About 2 tablespoons.

Mango Salsa

1 medium mango, cut lengthwise in half, seed removed and chopped (1 cup)
1/4 cup finely chopped red onion
1 tablespoon finely chopped fresh or 1 teaspoon dried mint leaves
1 small jalapeño chili, finely chopped (2 to 3 teaspoons)
2 tablespoons lime juice
1/8 teaspoon salt

In small glass or plastic bowl, mix all ingredients. Cover and refrigerate until serving. About 1 1/4 cups.

1 Serving: Cal. 215 (Cal. from Fat 70); Fat 8g (Sat. fat 3g); Chol. 65mg; Sodium 410mg; Carbs. 14g (Fiber 2g); Pro. 24g • **% Daily Value:** Vit. A 30%; Vit. C 32%; Calc. 2%; Iron 10% • **Exchanges:** 1 Starch, 3 Very Lean Meat, 1 Fat • **Carb. Choices:** 1

Balsamic Pork with Mixed-Herb Brush

Prep: 15 min
Marinate: 1 hr
Grill: 15 min
6 servings

2 pork tenderloin (about 1 1/2 pounds)
8 large sprigs rosemary
8 large sprigs thyme
1/2 cup balsamic vinegar
1/4 cup olive or vegetable oil

1. Cut each pork tenderloin crosswise into 6 pieces. Press each piece, cut side down, to form a round, about 1 1/2 inches thick. If end pieces are thin, coil into round fillets; secure with toothpicks.

2. In shallow glass or plastic dish or resealable plastic food-storage bag, place rosemary and thyme sprigs. Stir in vinegar and oil. Add pork; turn to coat. Cover dish or seal bag and refrigerate, turning pork 2 to 3 times, at least 1 hour but no longer than 24 hours.

3. Brush grill rack with vegetable oil. Heat coals or gas grill for direct heat. Remove pork and herbs from marinade; reserve marinade. Place herbs directly on hot coals, lava rock or ceramic briquettes.

4. Immediately cover and grill pork over medium heat 7 minutes, turning and brushing frequently with marinade. Discard any remaining marinade. Cover and grill pork 6 to 8 minutes longer, turning frequently, until no longer pink in center. Remove toothpicks.

Success Tip

Prevent the tenderloin from overcooking by securing the thin ends with toothpicks.

1 Serving: Cal. 200 (Cal. from Fat 90); Fat 9g (Sat. fat 2g); Chol. 70mg; Sodium 50mg; Carbs. 1g (Fiber 0g); Pro. 26g • **% Daily Value:** Vit. A 0%; Vit. C 0%; Calc. 0%; Iron 8% • **Exchanges:** 3 1/2 Lean Meat • **Carb. Choices:** 0

Pork Tenderloin Sandwiches

Prep: 5 min
Grill: 20 min
6 sandwiches

1/2 cup orange marmalade
1/4 cup Dijon mustard
1 tablespoon olive or vegetable oil
1 pork tenderloin (3/4 to 1 pound)
1 loaf (1 pound) French bread, cut into thin slices
Lettuce leaves

1. Heat coals or gas grill for direct heat.

2. In small bowl, mix marmalade and 1 tablespoon of the mustard. Brush oil over pork.

3. Cover and grill pork over medium heat 15 to 20 minutes, turning occasionally and lightly brushing 1 tablespoon marmalade mixture over pork for last few minutes of grilling, until pork has slight blush of pink in center and meat thermometer inserted in center reads 160°F.

4. Spread remaining 3 tablespoons mustard on one side of bread slices. Cut pork into thin slices. Place lettuce and pork on half of bread slices. In 1-quart saucepan, heat remaining marmalade mixture to boiling; boil and stir 1 minute. Drizzle over pork. Top with remaining bread.

Try This

Instead of Dijon mustard, try yellow, spicy or country-style mustard. They're all great tasting.

1 Sandwich: Cal. 360 (Cal. from Fat 70); Fat 8g (Sat. fat 2g); Chol. 35mg; Sodium 730mg; Carbs. 56g (Fiber 3g); Pro. 20g • **% Daily Value:** Vit. A 6%; Vit. C 4%; Calc. 8%; Iron 18% • **Exchanges:** 4 Starch, 1 Lean Meat • **Carb. Choices:** 4

Sweet Lemon Spareribs

Prep: 15 min
Cook: 1 hr 30 min
Marinate: 4 hr
Grill: 30 min
6 servings

6 pounds pork spareribs, cut into serving pieces
1/2 can (12-ounce size) frozen lemonade concentrate, thawed
3/4 cup barbecue sauce

1. In 4-quart Dutch oven, place pork. Add enough water to cover pork. Heat to boiling; reduce heat to low. Cover and simmer about 1 hour 30 minutes or until tender.

2. Remove pork to 13 × 9-inch glass baking dish. In small bowl, mix lemonade concentrate and barbecue sauce. Pour sauce mixture over pork; turn pork to coat. Cover and refrigerate, turning pork occasionally, at least 4 hours but no longer than 24 hours.

3. Brush grill rack with vegetable oil. Heat coals or gas grill for direct heat. Remove pork from marinade; reserve marinade.

4. Cover and grill pork, meaty sides up, over medium-hot heat about 30 minutes, turning and brushing frequently with marinade, until glazed and heated through. Discard any remaining marinade.

Try This

Use a sharp knife or kitchen scissors to cut pork ribs into serving-size pieces.

1 Serving: Cal. 775 (Cal. from Fat 485); Fat 54g (Sat. fat 20g); Chol. 215mg; Sodium 440mg; Carbs. 21g (Fiber 0g); Pro. 52g • **% Daily Value:** Vit. A 2%; Vit. C 4%; Calc. 8%; Iron 20% • **Exchanges:** 1 1/2 Other Carbs., 7 High-Fat Meat • **Carb. Choices:** 1 1/2

Sesame Pork
with Garlic Cream Sauce

Prep: 15 min
Grill: 15 min
6 servings

1 1/2 pounds pork tenderloin
2 tablespoons vegetable oil
1/4 cup sesame seed
Garlic Cream Sauce (below)

1. Brush grill rack with vegetable oil. Heat coals or gas grill for direct heat.

2. Cut pork crosswise into 12 slices. Between sheets of plastic wrap or waxed paper, flatten slices with a meat mallet or rolling pin to 1/2-inch thickness. Brush pork with oil; coat with sesame seed.

3. Cover and grill pork over medium heat 12 to 15 minutes, turning once, until no longer pink in center.

4. Meanwhile, make Garlic Cream Sauce. Serve sauce with pork.

Garlic Cream Sauce

1 tablespoon butter or margarine
2 cloves garlic, finely chopped
1 package (3 ounces) cream cheese, cut into cubes
1/3 cup milk
1 tablespoon chopped fresh or 1 teaspoon freeze-dried chives

In 10-inch skillet, melt butter over medium heat. Cook garlic in butter about 2 minutes, stirring occasionally; until golden; reduce heat to low. Add cream cheese and milk. Cook, stirring constantly, until smooth and hot. Stir in chives. Serve warm. About 2/3 cup.

1 Serving: Cal. 290 (Cal. from Fat 170); Fat 19g (Sat. fat 7g); Chol. 95mg; Sodium 110mg; Carbs. 2g (Fiber 0g); Pro. 28g • **% Daily Value:** Vit. A 6%; Vit. C 0%; Calc. 4%; Iron 10% • **Exchanges:** 4 Lean Meat, 1 1/2 Fat • **Carb. Choices:** 0

Cajun Pork Loin Ribs

**Prep: 15 min
Grill: 1 hr
6 servings**

2 teaspoons chili powder
2 teaspoons ground mustard
1 teaspoon ground red pepper (cayenne)
1/4 teaspoon salt
4 pounds pork loin back ribs (not cut into serving pieces)
Sweet and Spicy Glaze (below)

1. Brush grill rack with vegetable oil. Heat coals or gas grill for indirect heat.

2. In small bowl, mix chili powder, mustard, red pepper and salt. Sprinkle evenly over meaty sides of pork.

3. Cover and grill pork, meaty sides up, over drip pan and over medium heat 50 to 60 minutes or until pork is no longer pink when cut near bone. Meanwhile, make Sweet and Spicy Glaze. Brush pork with glaze 2 or 3 times during last 15 minutes of grilling. Discard any remaining glaze.

4. To serve, cut pork into serving pieces.

Sweet and Spicy Glaze

1 tablespoon vegetable oil
2 cloves garlic, finely chopped
1/2 cup chili sauce
3 tablespoons packed brown sugar
1/4 teaspoon ground red pepper (cayenne)

In 1-quart saucepan, heat oil over medium heat. Cook garlic in oil, stirring frequently, until golden. Stir in remaining ingredients; heat just to boiling. About 3/4 cup.

1 Serving: Cal. 650 (Cal. from Fat 425); Fat 47g (Sat. fat 17g); Chol. 175mg; Sodium 520mg; Carbs. 13g (Fiber 1g); Pro. 43g • **% Daily Value:** Vit. A 12%; Vit. C 2%; Calc. 8%; Iron 18% • **Exchanges:** 1 Other Carbs., 6 High-Fat Meat • **Carb. Choices:** 1

Glazed Country Ribs

Prep: 15 min
Microwave: 18 min
Grill: 12 min
4 servings

3 pounds pork country-style ribs, cut into serving pieces
1/2 cup orange juice
3/4 cup cocktail sauce
1/2 cup orange marmalade

1. Brush grill rack with vegetable oil. Heat coals or gas grill for direct heat.

2. While grill is heating, in 3-quart microwavable casserole, arrange pork with meatiest pieces to outside edge. Add orange juice. Cover and microwave on High 5 minutes. Rearrange and turn over pork, so less-cooked pieces are to outside edge of casserole. Cover and microwave on High 3 minutes; rearrange pork. Cover and microwave on Medium (50%) 8 to 10 minutes or until very little pink remains.

3. While pork is microwaving, in small bowl, mix cocktail sauce and marmalade; reserve 1/2 cup to serve with pork.

4. Drain pork; discard cooking liquid. Cover and grill pork over medium heat 10 to 12 minutes, turning and brushing generously with sauce mixture 2 or 3 times, until pork is glazed, browned and no longer pink when cut near bone. Serve pork with reserved sauce mixture.

Success Tip

Precooking these ribs in the microwave means faster grilling. Because the ribs are precooked, the sweet sauce can be added when you start grilling.

1 Serving: Cal. 540 (Cal. from Fat 200); Fat 22g (Sat. fat 8g); Chol. 115mg; Sodium 690mg; Carbs. 45g (Fiber 1g); Pro. 40g • **% Daily Value:** Vit. A 12%; Vit. C 18%; Calc. 2%; Iron 10% • **Exchanges:** 1 Fruit, 2 Other Carbs., 6 Lean Meat, 1 Fat • **Carb. Choices:** 3

Sausage and Potato Kabobs

Prep: 15 min
Cook: 15 min
Grill: 25 min
4 servings

8 new potatoes (3/4 pound)
1 pound fully cooked smoked Polish sausage, cut into 12 pieces
12 baby dill pickles
1/4 cup butter or margarine, melted
2 teaspoons chopped fresh or 1/2 teaspoon dried dill weed

1. In 2-quart saucepan, heat 1 inch water to boiling. Add potatoes. Boil about 15 minutes or until almost tender; drain. Cool slightly.

2. Brush grill rack with vegetable oil. Heat coals or gas grill for direct heat.

3. Cut potatoes in half. On each of four 15-inch metal skewers, alternately thread sausage pieces, potatoes and pickles, leaving 1/4-inch space between each piece.

4. Cover and grill kabobs over medium heat 20 to 25 minutes, turning frequently, until sausage is hot. Meanwhile, in small bowl, mix butter and dill weed; brush over potatoes for last 5 minutes of grilling.

Success Tip

Try to keep the new potatoes, sausage pieces and pickles all about the same size. It helps ensure even cooking.

1 Serving: Cal. 545 (Cal. from Fat 385); Fat 43g (Sat. fat 19g); Chol. 100mg; Sodium 2560mg; Carbs. 25g (Fiber 4g); Pro. 15g • **% Daily Value:** Vit. A 16%; Vit. C 12%; Calc. 6%; Iron 18% • **Exchanges:** 1 1/2 Starch, 1 1/2 High-Fat Meat, 6 Fat • **Carb. Choices:** 1 1/2

Italian Panini

1 round loaf (1 pound) unsliced French or Italian bread
4 ounces thinly sliced salami
1 jar (7 or 7.25 ounces) roasted red bell peppers, well drained
1/2 cup olive tapenade
4 ounces sliced provolone cheese
Olive oil, if desired

1. Heat coals or gas grill for direct heat.

2. In top of bread loaf, cut a circle 1/2 inch from edge of bread, cutting 2 inches down into loaf but not all the way through. Remove center of bread loaf and set aside. Arrange salami inside bread loaf; top with peppers, tapenade and cheese. Place center of bread loaf over filling to fit tightly. Wrap tightly in aluminum foil.

3. Cover and grill loaf over low heat 15 to 20 minutes, turning once, until cheese is melted.

4. Brush olive oil over top of loaf. Cut loaf into 4 wedges.

Tapenade is a paste usually made of ground-up capers, anchovies, olives, olive oil and seasonings. You'll find it shelved with the olives at your grocery store. If you prefer, you can use 1/2 cup basil pesto instead.

1 Sandwich: Cal. 485 (Cal. from Fat 170); Fat 19g (Sat. fat 8g); Chol. 45mg; Sodium 1390mg; Carbs. 62g (Fiber 4g); Pro. 21g • **% Daily Value:** Vit. A 62%; Vit. C 70%; Calc. 32%; Iron 24% • **Exchanges:** 4 Starch, 1 1/2 High-Fat Meat, 1/2 Fat • **Carb. Choices:** 4

Sizzling Sausage Hoagies

Prep: 10 min
Grill: 12 min
6 sandwiches

6 fully cooked sausages or hot dogs
1 large bell pepper (any color), cut into 6 strips
About 3/4 cup Italian dressing
1 loaf (1 pound) unsliced French bread, cut horizontally in half
Spicy brown mustard, if desired

1. Brush grill rack with vegetable oil. Heat coals or gas grill for direct heat.

2. On 14-inch flat metal skewer, alternately thread whole sausages and bell pepper strips crosswise. Brush some of the dressing on cut sides of bread.

3. Cover and grill sausages and pepper strips over medium heat 8 to 12 minutes, turning and brushing frequently with dressing, until sausages are brown. Add bread, cut sides down, for last 3 to 4 minutes of grilling until golden brown.

4. To serve, place skewer of sausages and pepper strips on bottom half of bread. Top with top of bread; pull out skewer. Cut bread crosswise into 6 servings. Serve with mustard.

Success Tip

To keep the sausage and bell pepper from spinning around on the skewer, use a flat-bladed skewer. If you don't have one, thread sausages and peppers on two round-bladed skewers placed side by side.

1 Sandwich: Cal. 555 (Cal. from Fat 315); Fat 35g (Sat. fat 10g); Chol. 40mg; Sodium 1480mg; Carbs. 45g (Fiber 3g); Pro. 15g • **% Daily Value:** Vit. A 2%; Vit. C 20%; Calc. 10%; Iron 18% • **Exchanges:** 3 Starch, 1 High-Fat Meat, 3 Fat • **Carb. Choices:** 3

Mint-Smoked Lamb Chops

Prep: 10 min
Grill: 12 min
4 servings

2 tablespoons dry white wine or chicken broth
2 tablespoons honey
1 tablespoon butter or margarine, melted
1 teaspoon chopped fresh mint leaves
1/4 teaspoon salt
1/8 teaspoon pepper
1 cup whole fresh mint leaves
8 lamb rib or loin chops, about 1 inch thick (about 2 pounds)

1. Brush grill rack with vegetable oil. Heat coals or gas grill for direct heat.

2. In small bowl, mix all ingredients except 1 cup mint and the lamb.

3. Sprinkle 1 cup mint over hot coals, lava rock or ceramic briquettes. Immediately cover and grill lamb over hot heat 6 minutes. Brush with wine mixture. Turn lamb; brush with wine mixture. Cover and grill about 6 minutes longer for medium doneness (160°F). Discard any remaining wine mixture.

Success **Tip**

To capture the wonderful fresh mint smoke, quickly cover the grill after adding the mint and the lamb chops.

1 Serving: Cal. 230 (Cal. from Fat 115); Fat 13g (Sat. fat 5g); Chol. 75mg; Sodium 230mg; Carbs. 9g (Fiber 0g); Pro. 20g • **% Daily Value:** Vit. A 18%; Vit. C 0%; Calc. 2%; Iron 10% • **Exchanges:** 1/2 Other Carbs., 3 Lean Meat, 1 Fat • **Carb. Choices:** 1/2

Marinated Lamb and Veggie Kabobs

Prep: 20 min
Marinate: 6 hr
Grill: 20 min
4 servings

1/4 cup lemon juice
2 tablespoons olive or vegetable oil
1 1/2 teaspoons chopped fresh or 1/2 teaspoon dried
    oregano leaves
1 teaspoon salt
1/4 teaspoon pepper
1 pound lamb boneless shoulder, cut into 1-inch cubes
1 medium green bell pepper, cut into 1-inch pieces
1 medium onion, cut into eighths
1 cup 1-inch cubes eggplant

1. In shallow glass or plastic dish or resealable plastic food-storage bag, mix lemon juice, oil, oregano, salt and pepper. Add lamb; turn to coat. Cover dish or seal bag and refrigerate 6 to 8 hours, stirring occasionally.

2. Heat coals or gas grill for direct heat.

3. Remove lamb from marinade; reserve marinade. On each of four 11-inch metal skewers, thread lamb, leaving 1/4-inch space between each piece.

4. Cover and grill lamb kabobs over medium heat 10 minutes, brushing frequently with marinade. Meanwhile, on each of four 11-inch metal skewers, alternately thread bell pepper, onion and eggplant, leaving 1/4-inch space between each piece.

5. Add vegetable kabobs to grill. Cover and grill vegetable and lamb kabobs 6 to 10 minutes, brushing frequently with marinade, until lamb is slightly pink in center and vegetables are crisp-tender. Discard any remaining marinade.

1 Serving: Cal. 245 (Cal. from Fat 115); Fat 13g (Sat. fat 4g); Chol. 80mg; Sodium 510mg; Carbs. 6g (Fiber 2g); Pro. 26g • **% Daily Value:** Vit. A 2%; Vit. C 26%; Calc. 2%; Iron 12% • **Exchanges:** 1 Vegetable, 3 1/2 Lean Meat, 1/2 Fat • **Carb. Choices:** 1/2

Herbed Butterflied Leg of Lamb

Prep: 10 min
Marinate: 8 hr
Grill: 35 min
9 servings

2 tablespoons chopped fresh or 2 teaspoons dried
     rosemary leaves, crumbed
3 large cloves garlic, finely chopped
2 tablespoons olive or vegetable oil
1 cup dry sherry or nonalcoholic white wine
1 teaspoon salt
1/2 teaspoon pepper
3 1/2-pound butterflied leg of lamb

1. In 10-inch skillet, cook rosemary and garlic in oil over medium heat, stirring frequently, until garlic is golden; remove from heat. Stir in sherry, salt and pepper.

2. In shallow glass or plastic dish, place lamb. Pour sherry mixture over lamb; turn lamb to coat. Cover and refrigerate 8 to 10 hours, turning lamb occasionally.

3. Heat coals or gas grill for direct heat. Remove lamb from marinade; reserve marinade.

4. Cover and grill lamb over medium heat 30 to 35 minutes for medium doneness (160°F), turning lamb and brushing with marinade every 10 minutes. Discard any remaining marinade.

Did You Know?

To "butterfly" a piece of meat means to split it in half down the center without completely cutting it in two pieces. When you spread open the piece of meat, it looks like a butterfly.

1 Serving: Cal. 285 (Cal. from Fat 135); Fat 15g (Sat. fat 5g); Chol. 120mg; Sodium 270mg; Carbs. 0g (Fiber 0g); Pro. 37g • **% Daily Value:** Vit. A 0%; Vit. C 0%; Calc. 0%; Iron 16% • **Exchanges:** 5 Lean Meat • **Carb. Choices:** 0

Chicken & Turkey

Pesto-Chicken Sandwiches

Tequila-Lime Chicken

Prep: 10 min
Marinate: 30 min
Grill: 20 min
4 servings

Tequila-Lime Marinade (below)
4 boneless, skinless chicken breast halves (about 1 1/4 pounds)

1. In shallow glass or plastic dish or resealable plastic food-storage bag, make Tequila-Lime Marinade. Between sheets of plastic wrap or waxed paper, flatten each chicken breast half to 1/4-inch thickness. Add chicken to marinade; turn to coat. Cover dish or seal bag and refrigerate at least 30 minutes but no longer than 24 hours.

2. Heat coals or gas grill for direct heat. Remove chicken from marinade; discard marinade.

3. Cover and grill chicken over medium heat 15 to 20 minutes, turning once, until juice of chicken is no longer pink when centers of thickest pieces are cut.

Tequila-Lime Marinade

2 teaspoons grated lime peel
1/4 cup lime juice
1/4 cup olive or vegetable oil
2 tablespoons chopped fresh cilantro
1/2 teaspoon sugar
1/2 teaspoon salt
1 small jalapeño chili, seeded and finely chopped
1 clove garlic, finely chopped

In small bowl, mix all ingredients. About 2/3 cup.

Substitute

If you don't care for the taste of cilantro in the marinade, try using chopped fresh parsley instead.

1 Serving: Cal. 175 (Cal. from Fat 65); Fat 7g (Sat. fat 2g); Chol. 75mg; Sodium 160mg; Carbs. 1g (Fiber 0g); Pro. 27g • **% Daily Value:** Vit. A 0%; Vit. C 0%; Calc. 0%; Iron 4% • **Exchanges:** 4 Very Lean Meat, 1 Fat • **Carb. Choices:** 0

Orange-Tarragon Chicken

Prep: 15 min
Marinate: 8 hr
Grill: 20 min
Cook: 2 min
4 servings

Orange-Tarragon Marinade (below)
4 boneless, skinless chicken breast halves (about 1 1/4 pounds)
Chopped tomato, if desired
Chopped fresh tarragon leaves, if desired

1. In shallow glass or plastic dish or resealable plastic food-storage bag, make Orange-Tarragon Marinade. Add chicken; turn to coat. Cover dish or seal bag and refrigerate at least 8 hours but no longer than 24 hours.

2. Brush grill rack with vegetable oil. Heat coals or gas grill for direct heat. Remove chicken from marinade; reserve marinade.

3. Cover and grill chicken, skin sides up, over medium heat 15 to 20 minutes, turning once and brushing with marinade, until juice of chicken is no longer pink when centers of thickest pieces are cut.

4. In 1-quart saucepan, heat remaining marinade to boiling; boil and stir 1 minute. Serve with chicken. Garnish with tomato and tarragon.

Orange-Tarragon Marinade

2 teaspoons grated orange peel
1/2 cup orange juice
1/4 cup vegetable oil
1/4 cup white wine vinegar
2 tablespoons chopped shallots
1 teaspoon dried tarragon leaves
1/2 teaspoon salt

In small bowl, mix all ingredients. About 1 1/4 cups.

1 Serving: Cal. 315 (Cal. from Fat 190); Fat 21g (Sat. fat 4g); Chol. 75mg; Sodium 360mg; Carbs. 4g (Fiber 0g); Pro. 27g • **% Daily Value:** Vit. A 0%; Vit. C 8%; Calc. 2%; Iron 6% • **Exchanges:** 4 Medium-Fat Meat • **Carb. Choices:** 0

Teriyaki Chicken

Prep: 10 min
Marinate: 1 hr
Grill: 25 min
8 servings

Teriyaki Marinade (below)
8 bone-in chicken breast halves (about 3 pounds)

1. In shallow glass or plastic dish or heavy-duty resealable plastic food-storage bag, make Teriyaki Marinade. Add chicken; turn to coat. Cover dish or seal bag and refrigerate, turning chicken occasionally, at least 1 hour but no longer than 24 hours.

2. Heat coals or gas grill for direct heat. Remove chicken from marinade; reserve marinade.

3. Cover and grill chicken, skin sides up, over medium heat 10 minutes; turn chicken. Cover and grill 10 to 15 minutes longer, turning and brushing 2 or 3 times with marinade, until juice of chicken is no longer pink when centers of thickest pieces are cut. Discard any remaining marinade.

Teriyaki Marinade

1/2 cup soy sauce
1/2 cup dry sherry or orange juice
2 tablespoons sugar
2 tablespoons vegetable oil
2 teaspoons grated gingerroot or 1/2 teaspoon ground ginger
2 cloves garlic, crushed

In small bowl, mix all ingredients. About 2/3 cup.

Try This

For a handheld style of this favorite dish, cut the grilled chicken into thin strips, then wrap 'em up in flour tortillas. Add some chopped fresh cilantro or shredded lettuce if you like.

1 Serving: Cal. 220 (Cal. from Fat 90); Fat 10g (Sat. fat 2g); Chol. 75mg; Sodium 790mg; Carbs. 4g (Fiber 0g); Pro. 28g • **% Daily Value:** Vit. A 2%; Vit. C 0%; Calc. 2%; Iron 6% • **Exchanges:** 4 Lean Meat • **Carb. Choices:** 0

Spicy Caribbean Chicken

Prep: 15 min
Marinate: 2 hr
Grill: 20 min
6 servings

Spicy Marinade (below)
6 boneless, skinless chicken breast halves (about 1 3/4 pounds)

1. Make Spicy Marinade.

2. In shallow glass or plastic dish or resealable plastic food-storage bag, place chicken. Pour marinade over chicken; turn chicken to coat. Cover and refrigerate at least 2 hours but no longer than 6 hours.

3. Brush grill rack with vegetable oil. Heat coals or gas grill for direct heat. Remove chicken from marinade; reserve marinade.

4. Cover and grill chicken over medium heat 15 to 20 minutes, turning and brushing frequently with marinade, until juice of chicken is no longer pink when centers of thickest pieces are cut. Discard any remaining marinade.

Spicy Marinade

4 medium green onions, sliced (1/4 cup)
2 jalapeño chilies, seeded and chopped
1/3 cup lemon juice
1/4 cup honey
2 tablespoons chopped fresh or 2 teaspoons dried thyme leaves
2 tablespoons vegetable oil
1/2 teaspoon salt
1/4 teaspoon ground allspice
1/4 teaspoon ground nutmeg

In food processor or blender, cover and process all ingredients about 20 seconds or until smooth. About 1 cup.

1 Serving: Cal. 210 (Cal. from Fat 65); Fat 7g (Sat. fat 2g); Chol. 75mg; Sodium 200mg; Carbs. 10g (Fiber 0g); Pro. 27g • **% Daily Value:** Vit. A 0%; Vit. C 2%; Calc. 2%; Iron 6% • **Exchanges:** 1/2 Starch, 4 Very Lean Meat, 1/2 Fat • **Carb. Choices:** 1/2

Citrus Chicken

Prep: 10 min
Marinate: 2 hr
Grill: 20 min
Cook: 2 min
6 servings

Citrus Marinade (below)
6 boneless, skinless chicken breast halves (about 1 3/4 pounds)

1. In shallow glass or plastic dish or resealable plastic food-storage bag, make Citrus Marinade. Add chicken; turn to coat. Cover dish or seal bag and refrigerate, turning chicken occasionally, at least 2 hours but no longer than 24 hours.

2. Heat coals or gas grill for direct heat. Remove chicken from marinade; reserve marinade.

3. Cover and grill chicken over medium heat 15 to 20 minutes, turning and brushing with marinade occasionally, until juice of chicken is no longer pink when centers of thickest pieces are cut.

4. In 1-quart saucepan, heat remaining marinade to boiling; boil and stir 1 minute. Serve with chicken.

Citrus Marinade

1/2 cup frozen (thawed) orange juice concentrate
1/4 cup vegetable oil
1/4 cup lemon juice
2 tablespoons grated orange peel
1/2 teaspoon salt
1 clove garlic, finely chopped

In small bowl, mix all ingredients. About 1 cup.

1 Serving: Cal. 265 (Cal. from Fat 115); Fat 13g (Sat. fat 2g); Chol. 75mg; Sodium 270mg; Carbs. 10g (Fiber 0g); Pro. 27g • **% Daily Value:** Vit. A 2%; Vit. C 30%; Calc. 2%; Iron 6% • **Exchanges:** 1/2 Fruit, 4 Lean Meat • **Carb. Choices:** 1/2

Cheddar-Stuffed Chicken Breasts

Prep: 15 min
Grill: 20 min
4 servings

4 boneless, skinless chicken breast halves (about 1 1/4 pounds)
1/4 teaspoon salt
1/4 teaspoon pepper
3 ounces Cheddar cheese or Monterey Jack cheese
    with jalapeño peppers
1 tablespoon butter or margarine, melted
1/3 cup sour cream
1/4 cup salsa
Chopped fresh cilantro, if desired

1. Brush grill rack with vegetable oil. Heat coals or gas grill for direct heat.

2. Between sheets of plastic wrap or waxed paper, flatten each chicken breast half to 1/4-inch thickness. Sprinkle with salt and pepper. Cut cheese into 4 slices, about 3 × 1 × 1/4 inch. Place 1 slice cheese in center of each chicken breast half. Roll chicken around cheese, folding in sides. Brush rolls with butter.

3. Cover and grill chicken rolls, seam sides down, over medium heat 15 to 20 minutes, turning after 10 minutes, until juice of chicken is no longer pink when centers of thickest pieces are cut.

4. Serve chicken with sour cream and salsa. Sprinkle with cilantro.

Try This

This chicken dish has a Mexican twist with the addition of sour cream and salsa. For a super-easy sauce, mix the two together just before serving.

1 Serving: Cal. 300 (Cal. from Fat 160); Fat 18g (Sat. fat 10g); Chol. 115mg; Sodium 440mg; Carbs. 2g (Fiber 0g); Pro. 33g • **% Daily Value:** Vit. A 12%; Vit. C 2%; Calc. 14%; Iron 6% • **Exchanges:** 4 1/2 Lean Meat, 1 Fat • **Carb. Choices:** 0

Chicken with Tomato Pesto Sauce

Prep: 20 min
Grill: 20 min
8 servings

Tomato Pesto Sauce (below)
8 boneless, skinless chicken breast halves (about 2 1/2 pounds)
2 tablespoons olive or vegetable oil
1 1/2 teaspoons garlic pepper
Fresh small basil leaves, if desired

1. Make Tomato Pesto Sauce; cover and refrigerate until serving.

2. Heat coals or gas grill for direct heat.

3. Brush chicken with oil; sprinkle with garlic pepper.

4. Cover and grill chicken over medium heat 15 to 20 minutes, turning once, until juice of chicken is no longer pink when centers of thickest pieces are cut. Serve with sauce. Garnish with basil.

Tomato Pesto Sauce

1 can (6 ounces) tomato paste
1/3 cup olive or vegetable oil
3 tablespoons water
1/2 teaspoon salt
1/2 cup shredded Parmesan cheese
1 clove garlic, finely chopped
1/2 cup chopped fresh basil leaves

In small bowl, mix tomato paste, oil, water and salt until smooth. Stir in cheese, garlic and basil. About 1 1/4 cups.

1 Serving: Cal. 285 (Cal. from Fat 145); Fat 16g (Sat. fat 4g); Chol. 80mg; Sodium 550mg; Carbs. 6g (Fiber 1g); Pro. 30g • % Daily Value: Vit. A 16%; Vit. C 10%; Calc. 10%; Iron 8% • Exchanges: 1 Vegetable, 4 Lean Meat, 1 Fat • Carb. Choices: 1/2

Lemon Chicken with Fennel and Onions

6 bone-in chicken breast halves (about 3 pounds)
1/3 cup olive or vegetable oil
1 teaspoon grated lemon peel
1/4 cup lemon juice
2 tablespoons chopped fresh or 2 teaspoons dried oregano leaves
1/2 teaspoon salt
2 medium fennel bulbs, cut into wedges
1 medium red onion, cut into wedges

1. In shallow glass or plastic dish, place chicken. In small bowl, mix oil, lemon peel, lemon juice, oregano and salt; pour over chicken. Cover and let stand 15 minutes.

2. Heat coals or gas grill for direct heat. Remove chicken from marinade; reserve marinade. Brush fennel and onion with marinade.

3. Cover and grill chicken, skin sides down, over medium heat 10 minutes. Turn chicken; add fennel and onion to grill. Cover and grill 10 to 15 minutes longer, brushing frequently with marinade, until juice of chicken is no longer pink when centers of thickest pieces are cut. Discard any remaining marinade.

Substitute

Use whatever fresh herbs you have on hand—chopped fresh thyme and rosemary are both equally delicious.

1 Serving: Cal. 265 (Cal. from Fat 135); Fat 15g (Sat. fat 3g); Chol. 75mg; Sodium 210mg; Carbs. 8g (Fiber 3g); Pro. 28g • **% Daily Value:** Vit. A 4%; Vit. C 10%; Calc. 6%; Iron 8% • **Exchanges:** 4 Lean Meat, 1 Vegetable, 1 Fat • **Carb. Choices:** 1/2

Chicken BLT Sandwiches

Prep: 10 min
Grill: 20 min
4 sandwiches

4 boneless, skinless chicken breast halves (about 1 1/4 pounds)
1/4 cup Thousand Island dressing
4 whole wheat sandwich buns, split
4 lettuce leaves
8 slices tomato
4 slices bacon, cooked, drained and broken in half

1. Heat coals or gas grill for direct heat.

2. Cover and grill chicken over medium heat 15 to 20 minutes, turning once, until juice of chicken is no longer pink when centers of thickest pieces are cut.

3. Spread dressing on cut sides of buns. Layer chicken, lettuce, tomato and bacon in buns.

Substitute

If you like, you can substitute ranch dressing for the Thousand Island. Or try marinating the chicken in ranch dressing for extra flavor.

1 Sandwich: Cal. 320 (Cal. from Fat 125); Fat 14g (Sat. fat 3g); Chol. 80mg; Sodium 450mg; Carbs. 20g (Fiber 3g); Pro. 33g • **% Daily Value:** Vit. A 12%; Vit. C 18%; Calc. 6%; Iron 14% • **Exchanges:** 1 Starch, 1 Vegetable, 4 Lean Meat • **Carb. Choices:** 1

Honey Mustard Chicken Sandwiches

1/4 cup Dijon mustard
2 tablespoons honey
1 tablespoon chopped fresh or 1 teaspoon dried oregano leaves
1/8 to 1/4 teaspoon ground red pepper (cayenne)
4 boneless, skinless chicken breast halves (about 1 1/4 pounds)
4 whole-grain sandwich buns, split
4 slices tomato
Leaf lettuce

1. Heat coals or gas grill for direct heat.

2. In small bowl, mix mustard, honey, oregano and red pepper. Brush on chicken.

3. Cover and grill chicken over medium heat 15 to 20 minutes, brushing frequently with mustard mixture and turning once, until juice of chicken is no longer pink when centers of thickest pieces are cut. Discard any remaining mustard mixture.

4. Serve chicken on buns with tomato and lettuce.

Try This

Broil these sandwiches on rainy days or when you don't feel like firing up the grill. Place the chicken on the rack of the broiler pan, and brush with the mustard mixture. Broil 4 to 6 inches from heat for 15 to 20 minutes, turning once and brushing with additional mustard mixture.

1 Sandwich: Cal. 270 (Cal. from Fat 55); Fat 6g (Sat. fat 1g); Chol. 75mg; Sodium 560mg; Carbs. 26g (Fiber 3g); Pro. 31g • **% Daily Value:** Vit. A 8%; Vit. C 12%; Calc. 4%; Iron 14% • **Exchanges:** 2 Starch, 3 1/2 Very Lean Meat • **Carb. Choices:** 2

Pesto-Chicken Sandwiches

Prep: 15 min
Marinate: 1 hr
Grill: 20 min
4 sandwiches

Photo on page 88

4 boneless, skinless chicken breast halves
    (about 1 1/4 pounds)
3/4 cup basil pesto
1/2 teaspoon salt
1 bell pepper (any color), cut into fourths
8 slices French bread, 3/4 inch thick
8 to 12 large fresh basil leaves

1. In shallow glass or plastic dish, place chicken. Brush 2 tablespoons of the pesto over tops of chicken; turn chicken. Brush with 2 tablespoons of the pesto; sprinkle with salt. Cover and refrigerate at least 1 hour but no longer than 24 hours.

2. Heat coals or gas grill for direct heat.

3. Cover and grill chicken over medium heat 15 to 20 minutes, turning once, until juice is no longer pink when centers of thickest pieces are cut. Add bell pepper for last 10 minutes of grilling until bell pepper is crisp-tender. Add bread for last 3 minutes of grilling, turning once, until toasted.

4. Cut bell pepper into strips. Spread remaining 1/2 cup pesto on one side of bread slices. Place chicken on 4 bread slices; top with bell pepper, basil and remaining bread.

Serving Idea

Enjoy these sandwiches with purchased potato salad and your favorite fresh fruit.

1 Sandwich: Cal. 530 (Cal. from Fat 280); Fat 31g (Sat. fat 6g); Chol. 80mg; Sodium 1050mg; Carbs. 30g (Fiber 2g); Pro. 36g • **% Daily Value:** Vit. A 12%; Vit. C 12%; Calc. 24%; Iron 20% • **Exchanges:** 2 Starch, 4 Medium-Fat Meat, 2 1/2 Fat • **Carb. Choices:** 2

Chicken Satay Salad

Prep: 20 min
Marinate: 1 hr
Grill: 20 min
6 servings

1 flour tortilla (8 inches in diameter), cut in half, then cut crosswise
  into 1/8- to 1/4-inch strips
Peanut Satay Dressing (below)
4 boneless, skinless chicken breast halves (about 1 1/4 pounds)
6 cups bite-size pieces mixed salad greens
1 cup finely shredded red cabbage
1/3 cup shredded carrot
1/4 cup chopped fresh cilantro or parsley

1. Heat oven to 350°F. On ungreased cookie sheet, arrange tortilla strips in single layer. Bake 7 to 11 minutes or until lightly browned.

2. Meanwhile, make Peanut Satay Dressing. In resealable plastic food-storage bag, place chicken; add 3 tablespoons of the dressing. Seal bag; turn to coat chicken. Refrigerate 1 to 2 hours. Refrigerate remaining dressing. In large bowl, toss remaining ingredients; cover and refrigerate.

3. Brush grill rack with vegetable oil. Heat coals or gas grill for direct heat.

4. Cover and grill chicken over medium heat 15 to 20 minutes, turning once, until juice of chicken is no longer pink when centers of thickest pieces are cut.

5. Cut chicken into strips. Add chicken and remaining dressing to salad; toss. On 6 plates, arrange salad. Sprinkle with tortilla strips.

Peanut Satay Dressing

1/3 cup rice vinegar or cider vinegar
1/4 cup creamy peanut butter
3 tablespoons finely chopped peanuts
2 tablespoons sugar
2 tablespoons vegetable oil
2 tablespoons sesame oil
1 tablespoon soy sauce
1/2 teaspoon finely chopped gingerroot
1 clove garlic, finely chopped

In small bowl, beat all ingredients with wire whisk until smooth and creamy. About 1 cup.

1 Serving: Cal. 335 (Cal. from Fat 180); Fat 20g (Sat. fat 4g); Chol. 50mg; Sodium 320mg; Carbs. 15g (Fiber 3g); Pro. 24g • **% Daily Value:** Vit. A 58%; Vit. C 24%; Calc. 6%; Iron 10% • **Exchanges:** 1/2 Starch, 1 Vegetable, 3 Lean Meat, 2 Fat • **Carb. Choices:** 1

Italian Chicken Salad

Prep: 10 min
Marinate: 15 min
Grill: 20 min
4 servings

1/3 cup raspberry vinegar
2 tablespoons balsamic vinegar
1/4 cup water
1 envelope (0.7 ounces) Italian dressing mix
1 tablespoon olive or vegetable oil
4 boneless, skinless chicken breast halves (about 1 1/4 pounds)
6 cups bite-size pieces mixed salad greens
2 roma (plum) tomatoes, chopped (2/3 cup)

1. In medium bowl, mix vinegars and water. Stir in dressing mix. Stir in oil. Divide dressing mixture in half.

2. In shallow glass or plastic dish or resealable plastic food-storage bag, place chicken. Pour half of the dressing mixture over chicken; turn chicken to coat. Cover dish or seal bag and refrigerate 15 minutes. Cover and refrigerate remaining dressing mixture.

3. Heat coals or gas grill for direct heat. Remove chicken from marinade; reserve marinade.

4. Cover and grill chicken over medium heat 15 to 20 minutes, turning and brushing with marinade occasionally, until juice of chicken is no longer pink when centers of thickest piece are cut. Discard any remaining marinade.

5. Cut chicken into slices. Serve chicken on salad greens with remaining dressing mixture. Top with tomatoes.

Substitute

Balsamic vinegar adds a wonderful distinctive flavor to this pretty salad, but red wine vinegar will work, too.

1 Serving: Cal. 205 (Cal. from Fat 80); Fat 9g (Sat. fat 2g); Chol. 75mg; Sodium 720mg; Carbs. 7g (Fiber 2g); Pro. 28g • **% Daily Value:** Vit. A 56%; Vit. C 32%; Calc. 6%; Iron 12% • **Exchanges:** 4 Very Lean Meat, 1 Vegetable, 1 Fat • **Carb. Choices:** 1/2

Buffalo Chicken Kabobs

Prep: 20 min
Grill: 20 min
4 servings

1 pound boneless, skinless chicken breasts, cut into 24 cubes
24 (about 1 1/2 cups) refrigerated new potato wedges (from
    1-pound 4-ounce bag)
24 pieces (about 1 inch) celery
2 tablespoons olive or vegetable oil
1 teaspoon red pepper sauce
1/2 teaspoon black and red pepper blend
1/2 teaspoon seasoned salt
6 cups bite-size pieces romaine lettuce
1/2 cup shredded carrot
1/2 cup blue cheese dressing

1. Heat coals or gas grill for direct heat.

2. On each of eight 8- to 10-inch metal skewers, alternately thread chicken, potatoes and celery, leaving 1/4-inch space between each piece. In small bowl, mix oil and pepper sauce; brush over chicken and vegetables. Sprinkle with pepper blend and seasoned salt.

3. Cover and grill kabobs over medium heat 15 to 20 minutes, turning occasionally, until chicken is no longer pink in center and potatoes are tender.

4. On 4 plates, arrange romaine and carrot. Top each with 2 kabobs. Serve with dressing.

Substitute

If you don't have the refrigerated potatoes, use fresh new red potatoes. Because the refrigerated potatoes are partially cooked, you'll need to slightly cook the fresh ones. Place 2 cups of new potato wedges in a glass casserole. Cover and microwave on High for 3 to 5 minutes, stirring once, until slightly cooked.

1 Serving: Cal. 445 (Cal. from Fat 215); Fat 24g (Sat. fat 3g); Chol. 75mg; Sodium 590mg; Carbs. 28g (Fiber 4g); Pro. 29g • **% Daily Value:** Vit. A 88%; Vit. C 28%; Calc. 10%; Iron 16% • **Exchanges:** 1 1/2 Starch, 1 Vegetable, 3 Lean Meat, 3 Fat • **Carb. Choices:** 2

Beer Can Chicken

Prep: 10 min
Grill: 1 hr 30 min
Stand: 15 min
6 servings

Basic Barbecue Rub (below)
4- to 4 1/2-pound whole broiler-fryer chicken
1 can (12 ounces) beer or lemon-lime soda pop

1. If using charcoal grill, place drip pan directly under grilling area, and arrange coals around edge of firebox. Heat coals or gas grill for indirect heat.

2. Make Basic Barbecue Rub. Fold wings of chicken across back with tips touching. Sprinkle rub inside cavity and all over outside of chicken; rub in with fingers.

3. Pour 1/2 cup of beer from can. Hold chicken upright, with opening of body cavity down; insert beer can into cavity. Insert barbecue meat thermometer so tip is in thickest part of inside thigh muscle and does not touch bone.

4. Cover and grill chicken upright over drip pan or over unheated side of gas grill over medium heat 1 hour 15 minutes to 1 hour 30 minutes or until thermometer reads 180°F and juice is no longer pink when center of thigh is cut.

5. Using tongs, carefully lift chicken to 13 × 9-inch pan, holding large metal spatula under beer can for support. Let stand 15 minutes before carving. Remove beer can; discard.

Basic Barbecue Rub
1 tablespoon paprika
2 teaspoons salt
1/2 teaspoon garlic powder
1/2 teaspoon onion powder
1/2 teaspoon pepper

In small bowl, mix all ingredients. About 2 tablespoons.

1 Serving: Cal. 315 (Cal. from Fat 160); Fat 18g (Sat. fat 5g); Chol. 115mg; Sodium 890mg; Carbs. 3g (Fiber 0g); Pro. 35g • **% Daily Value:** Vit. A 2%; Vit. C 0%; Calc. 2%; Iron 8% • **Exchanges:** 5 Lean Meat, 1 Fat • **Carb. Choices:** 0

1. Insert the beer can into the cavity of the chicken.

2. Cover and grill the chicken over indirect heat until the thermometer reads 180°.

3. After grilling, use tongs to carefully lift the bird to the pan, holding a metal spatula under the beer can for support.

Peanutty Chicken Kabobs

Prep: 15 min
Grill: 20 min
4 servings

Spicy Peanut Sauce (below)
1 pound boneless, skinless chicken breast halves or thighs, cut
     into 1 1/2-inch pieces
Chopped peanuts, if desired

1. Brush grill rack with vegetable oil. Heat coals or gas grill for direct heat.

2. Make Spicy Peanut Sauce; reserve 1/2 cup sauce to serve with cooked kabobs.

3. On four 10- to 12-inch metal skewers, thread chicken pieces, leaving 1/4-inch space between each piece. Brush chicken with half of the remaining sauce.

4. Cover and grill kabobs over medium heat 15 to 20 minutes, turning and brushing occasionally with remaining sauce, until chicken is no longer pink in center.

5. Serve kabobs with reserved sauce and the peanuts.

Spicy Peanut Sauce

1/3 cup crunchy peanut butter
1/3 cup boiling water
1 tablespoon grated gingerroot or 1 teaspoon ground ginger
1 tablespoon lemon juice
1/8 teaspoon crushed red pepper

In small bowl, mix all ingredients. About 3/4 cup.

1 Serving: Cal. 260 (Cal. from Fat 125); Fat 14g (Sat. fat 3g); Chol. 70mg; Sodium 160mg; Carbs. 5g (Fiber 1g); Pro. 30g • **% Daily Value:** Vit. A 0%; Vit. C 0%; Calc. 2%; Iron 8% • **Exchanges:** 4 Lean Meat, 1 Fat • **Carb. Choices:** 0

Peppery Horseradish Chicken

Prep: 5 min
Grill: 55 min
6 servings

1/4 cup prepared horseradish
1/4 cup sour cream
1/4 teaspoon pepper
3- to 3 1/2-pound cut-up broiler-fryer chicken

1. Brush grill rack with vegetable oil. Heat coals or gas grill for direct heat.

2. In small bowl, mix horseradish, sour cream and pepper.

3. Place chicken, skin sides up, on grill over medium heat; brush with horseradish mixture. Cover and grill 15 minutes. Turn chicken; brush with horseradish mixture. Cover and grill 20 to 40 minutes longer, turning and brushing with horseradish mixture occasionally, until juice of chicken is no longer pink when centers of thickest pieces are cut. Discard any remaining horseradish mixture.

Serving Idea

A perfect choice for picnics, this zesty chicken is great paired with cool, creamy potato salad from the deli and crisp carrot sticks.

1 Serving: Cal. 325 (Cal. from Fat 155); Fat 17g (Sat. fat 5g); Chol. 120mg; Sodium 125mg; Carbs. 1g (Fiber 0g); Pro. 41g • **% Daily Value:** Vit. A 2%; Vit. C 0%; Calc. 0%; Iron 8% • **Exchanges:** 6 Lean Meat • **Carb. Choices:** 0

Best Barbecued Chicken

Prep: 10 min
Cook: 12 min
Grill: 55 min
6 servings

1 1/4 cups Best Barbecue Sauce (below)
3- to 3 1/2-pound cut-up broiler-fryer chicken

1. Heat coals or gas grill for direct heat.

2. Make Best Barbecue Sauce.

3. Cover and grill chicken, skin sides up, over medium heat 15 minutes. Turn chicken; brush with sauce. Cover and grill 20 to 40 minutes longer, turning occasionally and brushing 2 or 3 times with sauce, until juice of chicken is no longer pink when centers of thickest pieces are cut.

4. Heat remaining sauce to boiling; boil and stir 1 minute. Serve with chicken.

Best Barbecue Sauce

1 cup ketchup
1/2 cup chili sauce
1/2 cup packed brown sugar
2 tablespoons cider vinegar
1 tablespoon lemon juice
1 tablespoon liquid smoke

In 2-quart saucepan, heat all ingredients to boiling; reduce heat. Simmer uncovered 10 minutes, stirring occasionally. About 2 cups.

Serving Idea

Add corn on the cob, a crisp mixed-greens salad and baked beans for a perfect summer meal.

1 Serving: Cal. 365 (Cal. from Fat 115); Fat 13g (Sat. fat 4g); Chol. 85mg; Sodium 830mg; Carbs. 35g (Fiber 1g); Pro. 28g • **% Daily Value:** Vit. A 16%; Vit. C 8%; Calc. 4%; Iron 10% • **Exchanges:** 2 Other Carbs., 4 Lean Meat, 1/2 Fat • **Carb. Choices:** 2

Chicken with Caramelized Onions

Prep: 15 min
Grill: 55 min
Cook: 15 min
6 servings

3- to 3 1/2-pound cut-up broiler-fryer chicken
1/8 teaspoon pepper
1 tablespoon butter or margarine, melted
1 tablespoon vegetable oil
1 tablespoon honey
Honey-Caramelized Onions (below)

1. Brush grill rack with vegetable oil. Heat coals or gas grill for direct heat.

2. Sprinkle chicken with pepper. In small bowl, mix butter and oil.

3. Place chicken, skin sides up, on grill over medium heat; brush with butter mixture. Cover and grill 15 minutes. Turn chicken; brush with butter mixture. Cover and grill 20 to 40 minutes longer, turning occasionally, until juice of chicken is no longer pink when centers of thickest pieces are cut. Brush with honey.

4. Meanwhile, make Honey-Caramelized Onions. Serve with chicken.

Honey-Caramelized Onions

2 tablespoons butter or margarine
3 large onions, thinly sliced
2 tablespoons honey
1 teaspoon ground mustard
1/4 cup sweet white wine or nonalcoholic white wine

In 10-inch skillet, melt butter over medium-high heat. Cook onions in butter about 8 minutes, stirring frequently, until transparent. Stir in honey. Cook about 3 minutes, stirring frequently, until onions are caramel colored. In small bowl, mix mustard and wine; pour over onions. Cook over medium heat about 2 minutes, stirring frequently, until liquid is absorbed. About 1 1/2 cups.

1 Serving: Cal. 360 (Cal. from Fat 190); Fat 21g (Sat. fat 8g); Chol. 100mg; Sodium 120mg; Carbs. 16g (Fiber 1g); Pro. 28g • **% Daily Value:** Vit. A 8%; Vit. C 4%; Calc. 2%; Iron 8% • **Exchanges:** 1/2 Other Carbs., 1 Vegetable, 4 Medium-Fat Meat • **Carb. Choices:** 1

Greek Chicken with Red Wine and Garlic

Prep: 10 min
Marinate: 1 hr
Grill: 55 min
4 servings

Red Wine Garlic Marinade (below)
1 1/2 to 2 pounds broiler-fryer chicken pieces
3/4 cup pitted Kalamata or ripe olives, drained

1. In shallow glass or plastic dish or resealable plastic food-storage bag, make Red Wine Garlic Marinade. Add chicken; turn to coat. Cover and refrigerate 1 hour.

2. Heat coals or gas grill for direct heat. Remove chicken from marinade; reserve marinade.

3. Cover and grill chicken, skin sides down, over medium heat 15 minutes. Turn chicken; brush with marinade. Cover and grill 20 to 40 minutes longer, brushing occasionally with marinade, until juice of chicken is no longer pink when centers of thickest pieces are cut. Discard any remaining marinade. Serve chicken with olives.

Red Wine Garlic Marinade

1/2 cup dry red wine or chicken broth
2 tablespoons chopped fresh or 1 tablespoon dried basil leaves
1 tablespoon chopped fresh or 1 teaspoon dried mint leaves
3 tablespoons olive or vegetable oil
2 cloves garlic, finely chopped

In small bowl, mix all ingredients. About 2/3 cup.

Success Idea

Cook chicken pieces evenly by placing the meatier pieces in the center of the grill rack and smaller pieces around the edges.

1 Serving: Cal. 270 (Cal. from Fat 180); Fat 20g (Sat. fat 4g); Chol. 65mg; Sodium 360mg; Carbs. 3g (Fiber 1g); Pro. 20g • **% Daily Value:** Vit. A 6%; Vit. C 0%; Calc. 4%; Iron 12% • **Exchanges:** 3 Lean Meat, 1 Fat • **Carb. Choices:** 0

Three-Herb Chicken

Prep: 10 min
Marinate: 30 min
Grill: 55 min
4 servings

Herb Marinade (below)
4 chicken thighs (about 1 pound)
4 chicken drumsticks (about 1 pound)

1. In shallow glass or plastic dish or heavy-duty resealable plastic food-storage bag, make Herb Marinade. Add chicken thighs and drumsticks; turn to coat. Cover dish or seal bag and refrigerate, turning chicken occasionally, at least 30 minutes but no longer than 24 hours.

2. Heat coals or gas grill for direct heat. Remove chicken from marinade; reserve marinade.

3. Cover and grill chicken, skin sides down, over medium heat 15 minutes. Turn chicken; brush with marinade. Cover and grill 20 to 40 minutes longer, brushing occasionally with marinade, until juice of chicken is no longer pink when centers of thickest pieces are cut. Discard any remaining marinade.

Herb Marinade

1/2 cup vegetable oil
1/2 cup lime juice
2 tablespoons chopped fresh or 2 teaspoons dried basil leaves
2 tablespoons chopped fresh or 2 teaspoons dried oregano leaves
2 tablespoons chopped fresh or 2 teaspoons dried thyme leaves
1 teaspoon onion powder
1/4 teaspoon lemon pepper

In small bowl, mix all ingredients. About 1 1/4 cups.

1 Serving: Cal. 435 (Cal. from fat 305); Fat 34g (Sat. fat 7g); Chol. 105mg; Sodium 115mg; Carbs. 2g (Fiber 0g); Pro. 30g • **% Daily Value:** Vit. A 4%; Vit. C 4%; Calc. 2%; Iron 10% • **Exchanges:** 4 High-Fat Meat • **Carb. Choices:** 0

Asian Chicken Drumsticks

Prep: 10 min
Grill: 1 hr
4 servings

2 tablespoons soy sauce
1 tablespoon olive or vegetable oil
1 teaspoon Dijon mustard
1/4 teaspoon salt
1/8 teaspoon ground red pepper (cayenne)
2 cloves garlic, finely chopped
8 chicken drumsticks (about 1 1/2 pounds)

1. Heat coals or gas grill for direct heat.

2. In small bowl, mix all ingredients except chicken; brush over chicken.

3. Cover and grill chicken over medium heat 15 to 20 minutes; turn chicken. Cover and grill 20 to 40 minutes longer, turning 2 or 3 times, until juice of chicken is no longer pink when centers of thickest pieces are cut.

Substitute

When you're in a hurry, use 1 teaspoon of ready-to-use minced garlic that's available in jars in the produce department of your supermarket.

1 Serving: Cal. 240 (Cal. from Fat 120); Fat 14g (Sat. fat 4g); Chol. 85mg; Sodium 710mg; Carbs. 1g (Fiber 0g); Pro. 29g • **% Daily Value:** Vit. A 0%; Vit. C 0%; Calc. 2%; Iron 14% • **Exchanges:** 4 Lean Meat • **Carb. Choices:** 0

Corn-Stuffed
Turkey Burgers

Prep: 15 min
Grill: 15 min
4 sandwiches

1 1/4 pounds ground turkey
1/2 cup plain dry bread crumbs
1 tablespoon chopped chipotle chilies in adobo sauce
    (from 7-ounce can)
1/2 cup fresh corn kernels or frozen whole kernel corn
2 tablespoons thick-and-chunky salsa
1 tablespoon chopped fresh cilantro
1/2 teaspoon salt
4 slices (3/4 ounce each) Cheddar cheese
4 hamburger buns, split

1. Brush grill rack with vegetable oil. Heat coals or gas grill for direct heat.

2. In medium bowl, mix turkey, bread crumbs and chilies. Shape mixture into 8 patties, about 1/4 inch thick.

3. In small bowl, mix corn, salsa, cilantro and salt. Spoon about 2 tablespoons corn mixture onto center of 4 patties. Top with remaining patties; press edges to seal.

4. Cover and grill patties over medium heat 12 to 14 minutes, turning once, until no longer pink in center. Top patties with cheese. Cover and grill about 1 minute longer or until cheese is melted.

5. Serve burgers on buns. Serve with additional salsa and chopped cilantro if desired.

1 Sandwich: Cal. 535 (Cal. from Fat 225); Fat 25g (Sat. fat 9g); Chol. 115mg; Sodium 960mg; Carbs. 37g (Fiber 2g); Pro. 40g • **% Daily Value:** Vit. A 8%; Vit. C 2%; Calc. 22%; Iron 20% • **Exchanges:** 2 1/2 Starch, 4 1/2 Medium-Fat Meat • **Carb. Choices:** 2 1/2

1. Shape the turkey mixture into 1/4-inch thick patties. Spoon 2 tablespoons of the corn mixture onto the center of 4 patties.

2. Top with remaining patties; press edges to seal.

Blue Cheese Turkey Burgers

Prep: 10 min
Grill: 20 min
6 sandwiches

1 1/2 pounds ground turkey
1/4 cup mayonnaise or salad dressing
4 ounces crumbled blue cheese
6 onion or plain hamburger buns, split and toasted
1 large red onion sliced, if desired

1. Brush grill rack with vegetable oil. Heat coals or gas grill for direct heat.

2. In medium bowl, mix turkey, mayonnaise and blue cheese. Shape mixture into 6 patties, about 3/4 inch thick.

3. Cover and grill patties over medium heat 15 to 20 minutes, turning once, until turkey is no longer pink in center.

4. Serve burgers on buns with onion slices.

Try **This**

To toast hamburger buns, grill cut sides down about 4 minutes or until golden brown.

1 Sandwich: Cal. 400 (Cal. from Fat 200); Fat 22g (Sat. fat 7g); Chol. 95mg; Sodium 580mg; Carbs. 19g (Fiber 1g); Pro. 34g • **% Daily Value:** Vit. A 2%; Vit. C 0%; Calc. 16%; Iron 14% • **Exchanges:** 1 Starch, 4 Medium-Fat Meat, 1/2 Fat • **Carb. Choices:** 1

Honey-Dijon Brined Turkey Breast

Prep: 15 min
Marinate: 12 hr
Grill: 2 hr
Stand: 10 min
8 servings

11 cups cold water
1 cup honey
1/2 cup Dijon mustard
1/3 cup salt
5- to 6-pound bone-in whole turkey breast, thawed if frozen
3 tablespoons olive or vegetable oil
1 teaspoon dried marjoram leaves
1 teaspoon ground mustard
1 teaspoon garlic pepper

1. In 6-quart container or stockpot, stir water, honey, mustard and salt until salt and honey are dissolved. Add turkey to brine mixture. Cover and refrigerate at least 12 hours but no longer than 24 hours.

2. If using charcoal grill, place drip pan directly under grilling area, and arrange coals around edge of firebox. Heat coals or gas grill for indirect heat.

3. Remove turkey from brine mixture; rinse thoroughly under cool running water and pat dry. Discard brine. In small bowl, mix remaining ingredients; brush over turkey. Insert barbecue meat thermometer so tip is in thickest part of turkey breast and does not touch bone.

4. Cover and grill turkey over drip pan or over unheated side of gas grill over medium heat 1 hour 45 minutes to 2 hours, rotating turkey 1/2 turn after 1 hour, until thermometer reads 170°F and juice of turkey is no longer pink when center is cut. Cover with foil and let stand 5 to 10 minutes before slicing.

Shop Talk

The brine mixture adds salt and flavor to the turkey, so try to buy a turkey that hasn't been injected with saline solution. An injected turkey will work in this recipe; it will just taste a little saltier.

1 Serving: Cal. 400 (Cal. from Fat 160); Fat 18g (Sat. fat 5g); Chol. 145mg; Sodium 460mg; Carbs. 5g (Fiber 0g); Pro. 54g • **% Daily Value:** Vit. A 2%; Vit. C 0%; Calc. 2%; Iron 10% • **Exchanges:** 7 1/2 Lean Meat • **Carb. Choices:** 0

Apple-Smoked Turkey Breast

Prep: 45 min
Grill: 3 hr
Stand: 10 min
8 servings

3 cups apple wood chips
3- to 4-pound bone-in turkey breast, thawed if frozen
1 tablespoon vegetable oil
1/4 teaspoon salt
1/4 teaspoon pepper
Peppery Apple Sauce (below)

1. In large bowl, cover wood chips with water; soak 30 minutes.

2. If using charcoal grill, place drip pan directly under grilling area, and arrange coals around edge of firebox. Fill drip pan with 3 cups water. Brush grill rack with vegetable oil. Heat coals or gas grill for indirect heat.

3. Brush turkey with oil. Sprinkle with salt and pepper. Insert barbecue meat thermometer so tip is in thickest part of turkey breast and does not touch bone.

4. Drain wood chips. Add 1 cup wood chips to hot coals. For gas grill, place wood chips on piece of foil; seal tightly. Poke 6 to 8 slits in top of foil packet with sharp knife. Place on grill rack; cover grill and let packet get hot enough to start smoking, about 10 minutes. Leave packet on grill while grilling food.

5. Cover and grill turkey, skin side up, over drip pan and over low heat 2 hours 30 minutes to 3 hours, adding charcoal and drained wood chips every hour, until thermometer reads 170°F and juice of turkey is no longer pink when center is cut. (Add water to drip pan during cooking if necessary.) Meanwhile, make Peppery Apple Sauce.

6. Remove turkey from grill; brush with sauce. Cover with foil tent; let stand 10 minutes before carving. Serve with remaining sauce.

Peppery Apple Sauce

2/3 cup apple jelly
1 tablespoon cider vinegar
1/8 teaspoon ground red pepper (cayenne)
1 tablespoon chopped fresh parsley or 1 teaspoon parsley flakes

In 1-quart saucepan, mix jelly, vinegar and red pepper. Cook over low heat about 5 minutes, stirring occasionally, until jelly is melted. Stir in parsley. About 2/3 cup.

1 Serving: Cal. 285 (Cal. from Fat 90); Fat 10g (Sat. fat 3g); Chol. 90mg; Sodium 150mg; Carbs. 17g (Fiber 0g); Pro. 32g • **% Daily Value:** Vit. A 0%; Vit. C 2%; Calc. 2%; Iron 6% • **Exchanges:** 1 Other Carbs., 4 Lean Meat • **Carb. Choices:** 1

Greek Turkey Tenderloins

Prep: 15 min
Marinate: 8 hr
Grill: 30 min
Stand: 10 min
6 servings

1/2 cup plain yogurt
2 tablespoons chopped fresh parsley or 2 teaspoons parsley flakes
2 tablespoons chopped fresh or 2 teaspoons dried oregano leaves
2 tablespoons lemon juice
1/4 teaspoon pepper
1 clove garlic, finely chopped
2 turkey breast tenderloins (each about 3/4 pound)
Lemon slices, if desired
Parsley sprigs, if desired

1. In shallow glass or plastic dish or resealable plastic food-storage bag, mix all ingredients except turkey, lemon slices and parsley sprigs. Add turkey; turn to coat. Cover dish or seal bag and refrigerate at least 8 hours but no longer than 24 hours.

2. Brush grill rack with vegetable oil. Heat coals or gas grill for direct heat. Remove turkey from marinade; reserve marinade.

3. Cover and grill turkey over medium heat 25 to 30 minutes, brushing occasionally with marinade and turning after 15 minutes, until juice is no longer pink when center of thickest piece is cut. Discard any remaining marinade. Remove turkey from grill; let stand 10 minutes before cutting.

4. To serve, cut turkey diagonally into 1/2-inch slices. Garnish with lemon slices and parsley sprigs.

Serving Idea

Serve these tenderloins with a quickly tossed together salad of spinach, Kalamata olives, tomato wedges and crumbled feta cheese. Dress the salad with purchased salad dressing.

1 Serving: Cal. 125 (Cal. from Fat 10); Fat 1g (Sat. fat 0g); Chol. 75mg; Sodium 60mg; Carbs. 1g (Fiber 0g); Pro. 27g • **% Daily Value:** Vit. A 2%; Vit. C 2%; Calc. 4%; Iron 8% • **Exchanges:** 4 Very Lean Meat • **Carb. Choices:** 0

Turkey on the Grill

Prep: 30 min
Marinate: 8 hr
Grill: 4 hr
Stand: 15 min
12 to 16 servings

Lemon-Garlic Marinade (below)
12-pound whole turkey, thawed if frozen
2 tablespoons Cajun seasoning

1. Make Lemon-Garlic Marinade. Using meat injector, fill injector container to 1-ounce line with marinade. Inject marinade into turkey breasts, thighs and legs, every 1 to 2 inches, pushing plunger down slowly. Refill container and continue to inject turkey until marinade is used. (Or pour marinade over turkey in large glass dish.)

2. Sprinkle Cajun seasoning inside cavity and over outside of turkey. Fasten neck skin to back with skewer. Fold wings across back with tips touching. Tuck drumsticks under band of skin at tail. Cover and refrigerate at least 8 hours but no longer than 24 hours.

3. If using charcoal grill, place drip pan directly under grilling area, and arrange coals around edge of firebox. Heat coals or gas grill for indirect heat.

4. Insert barbecue meat thermometer in turkey so tip is in thickest part of inside thigh muscle and does not touch bone.

5. Cover and grill turkey, breast side up, over drip pan or over unheated side of gas grill over medium heat 3 to 4 hours or until thermometer reads 180°F and juice is no longer pink when center of thigh is cut. Let stand 15 minutes before carving.

Lemon-Garlic Marinade

1 cup chicken broth
1/4 cup olive or vegetable oil
2 tablespoons lemon juice
1/4 cup chopped fresh basil leaves
1/4 cup chopped fresh parsley or cilantro
1/2 teaspoon salt
1/4 teaspoon pepper
2 cloves garlic, finely chopped

In blender, cover and blend all ingredients until smooth. About 1 2/3 cups.

1 Serving: Cal. 415 (Cal. from Fat 190); Fat 21g (Sat. fat 6g); Chol. 155mg; Sodium 310mg; Carbs. 1g (Fiber 0g); Pro. 56g • **% Daily Value:** Vit. A 6%; Vit. C 2%; Calc. 4%; Iron 16% • **Exchanges:** 8 Lean Meat • **Carb. Choices:** 0

Using a meat injector, inject the marinade into the breasts, thighs and legs, making injections every 1 to 2 inches.

Sesame-Ginger Turkey Slices

Prep: 5 min
Grill: 20 min
4 servings

2 tablespoons teriyaki sauce
1 tablespoon sesame seed, toasted
1 teaspoon ground ginger
1 pound uncooked turkey breast slices, about 1/4 inch thick
4 cups hot cooked rice, if desired

1. Brush grill rack with vegetable oil. Heat coals or gas grill for direct heat.

2. In small bowl, mix teriyaki sauce, sesame seed and ginger.

3. Cover and grill turkey over medium heat 15 to 20 minutes, brushing frequently with sauce mixture and turning after 10 minutes, until no longer pink in center. Discard any remaining sauce mixture.

4. Serve turkey with rice.

Try This

To toast sesame seed, heat in an ungreased heavy skillet over medium-low heat 5 to 7 minutes, stirring frequently until browning begins, then stirring constantly until golden brown.

1 Serving: Cal. 135 (Cal. from Fat 20); Fat 2g (Sat. fat 0g); Chol. 75mg; Sodium 310mg; Carbs. 1g (Fiber 0g); Pro. 27g • **% Daily Value:** Vit. A 0%; Vit. C 0%; Calc. 2%; Iron 8% • **Exchanges:** 4 Very Lean Meat • **Carb. Choices:** 0

Turkey Breast with Plum Sauce

Prep: 10 min
Grill: 1 hr 20 min
Stand: 10 min
8 servings

4-pound boneless whole turkey breast, thawed if frozen
1/2 teaspoon lemon pepper
1/4 cup plum or raspberry jam
Plum Sauce (below)

1. Brush grill rack with vegetable oil. Heat coals or gas grill for direct heat.

2. Sprinkle turkey with lemon pepper. Insert barbecue meat thermometer in center of turkey.

3. Cover and grill turkey, skin side down, over medium heat 30 minutes; turn. Cover and grill 40 to 50 minutes longer, brushing occasionally with plum jam for last 10 minutes, until thermometer reads 170°F and juice of turkey is no longer pink when center is cut. Discard any remaining jam.

4. Meanwhile, make Plum Sauce.

5. Remove turkey from grill. Cover with foil tent and let stand 10 minutes before carving. Serve turkey with sauce.

Plum Sauce

1 cup sliced plums
1/4 cup plum or raspberry jam
1 tablespoon white vinegar

In 1-quart saucepan, mix all ingredients. Cook over medium heat about 5 minutes, stirring occasionally, until plums are tender. About 1 1/4 cups.

1 Serving: Cal. 310 (Cal. from Fat 115); Fat 13g (Sat. fat 4g); Chol. 130mg; Sodium 110mg; Carbs. 12g (Fiber 0g); Pro. 47g • **% Daily Value:** Vit. A 2%; Vit. C 2%; Calc. 2%; Iron 8% • **Exchanges:** 7 Very Lean Meat, 1 1/2 Fat • **Carb. Choices:** 1

Fish & Shellfish

Planked Salmon with Peach-Mango Salsa

Barbecued Shrimp Salad

Prep: 15 min
Grill: 5 min
4 servings

Creamy Dressing (below)
1/4 cup butter or margarine, melted
1 teaspoon blackened fish seasoning
1 1/2 pounds uncooked extra-large shrimp, peeled and deveined
1/2 cup frozen whole kernel corn (from 1-pound bag)
8 cups bite-size pieces mixed salad greens
1 medium red or orange bell pepper, cut into strips
1 avocado, pitted, peeled and sliced
1/2 cup onion-and-garlic-flavored croutons

1. Heat coals or gas grill for direct heat. Make Creamy Dressing; cover and refrigerate until serving.

2. In medium bowl, mix butter and blackened fish seasoning. Add shrimp; toss to coat.

3. Cover and grill shrimp over medium heat about 5 minutes, turning once and brushing with any remaining butter mixture, until shrimp are pink and firm.

4. Meanwhile, cook and drain corn as directed on bag. Rinse with cold water; drain. On serving platter or 4 plates, arrange salad greens. Top with bell pepper, avocado, corn and croutons. Arrange shrimp on top. Serve with dressing.

Creamy Dressing

1/4 cup mayonnaise or salad dressing
1/4 cup sour cream
2 tablespoons milk
1/2 teaspoon blackened fish seasoning
1/2 teaspoon garlic powder

In small bowl, mix all ingredients. About 1/2 cup.

Substitute

Can't find blackened fish seasoning? Use Cajun or Creole seasoning instead.

1 **Serving:** Cal. 485 (Cal. from Fat 315); Fat 35g (Sat. fat 12g); Chol. 290mg; Sodium 690mg; Carbs. 16g (Fiber 6g); Pro. 31g • **% Daily Value:** Vit. A 100%; Vit. C 100%; Calc. 14%; Iron 34% • **Exchanges:** 1/2 Starch, 2 Vegetable, 4 Lean Meat, 4 Fat • **Carb. Choices:** 1

Spicy Shrimp with Creole Sauce

Prep: 30 min
Marinate: 15 min
Grill: 6 min
4 servings

1/2 cup olive or vegetable oil
1/2 teaspoon poultry seasoning
1/2 teaspoon dried oregano leaves (do not substitute fresh)
1/2 teaspoon chili oil or crushed red pepper
1/4 teaspoon salt
1 clove garlic, finely chopped
1 pound uncooked large shrimp, peeled and deveined
Creole Sauce (below)
3 cups hot cooked rice

1. In large glass or plastic bowl, mix all ingredients except shrimp, Creole Sauce and rice. Add shrimp, stirring to coat with marinade. Cover and refrigerate at least 15 minutes but no longer than 1 hour.

2. Meanwhile, brush grill rack with vegetable oil. Heat coals or gas grill for direct heat. Make Creole Sauce; keep warm.

3. Drain shrimp; discard marinade. Cover and grill shrimp over medium heat 4 to 6 minutes, turning once, until shrimp are pink and firm. Serve shrimp and Creole Sauce over rice.

Creole Sauce

1 tablespoon butter or margarine
1 small green bell pepper, diced (1/2 cup)
2 cloves garlic, finely chopped
1 can (14.5 ounces) stewed tomatoes, undrained
1 tablespoon chopped fresh or 1 teaspoon dried thyme leaves
1/8 teaspoon pepper
1/8 teaspoon red pepper sauce
2 large dried bay leaves

In 1 1/2-quart saucepan, melt butter over medium heat. Cook bell pepper and garlic in butter, stirring occasionally, until bell pepper is crisp-tender. Stir in remaining ingredients, breaking up tomatoes. Heat to boiling; reduce heat to low. Simmer uncovered 5 to 10 minutes, stirring occasionally, until thickened. Discard bay leaves. Serve warm. About 2 cups.

1 Serving: Cal. 420 (Cal. from Fat 160); Fat 18g (Sat. fat 4g); Chol. 170mg; Sodium 560mg; Carbs. 42g (Fiber 2g); Pro. 22g • **% Daily Value:** Vit. A 12%; Vit. C 24%; Calc. 6%; Iron 24% • **Exchanges:** 2 1/2 Starch, 1 Vegetable, 2 Lean Meat, 2 Fat • **Carb. Choices:** 3

Shrimp Kabobs

Prep: 10 min
Marinate: 30 min
Grill: 8 min
4 servings

1 pound uncooked peeled deveined large shrimp, thawed if frozen
    and tails peeled
1 cup fat-free Italian dressing
1 medium red onion, cut into 8 pieces
1 medium bell pepper (any color), cut into 8 pieces
16 medium cherry tomatoes
16 small whole mushrooms

1. In shallow glass or plastic dish or heavy-duty resealable plastic food-storage bag, place shrimp and dressing. Cover dish or seal bag and refrigerate 30 minutes.

2. Heat coals or gas grill for direct heat. Remove shrimp from marinade; reserve marinade. On each of four 15-inch metal skewers, alternately thread shrimp, onion, bell pepper, tomatoes and mushrooms, leaving 1/4-inch space between each piece.

3. Cover and grill kabobs over medium heat 6 to 8 minutes, turning frequently and brushing several times with marinade, until shrimp are pink and firm. Discard any remaining marinade.

Success Tip

Leave about a 1/4-inch space between the shrimp, onion, bell pepper, tomato and mushroom pieces on the skewers to allow for even cooking.

1 Serving: Cal. 140 (Cal. from Fat 10); Fat 1g (Sat. fat 0g); Chol. 160mg; Sodium 730mg; Carbs. 13g (Fiber 2g); Pro. 20g • **% Daily Value:** Vit. A 50%; Vit. C 62%; Calc. 4%; Iron 20% • **Exchanges:** 3 Vegetable, 2 Very Lean Meat • **Carb. Choices:** 1

Pacific Rim Tuna Salad

Prep: 15 min
Grill: 10 min
4 servings

Teriyaki Pineapple Dressing (below)
12 pieces (1 1/2 inches each) fresh pineapple (2 cups)
4 tuna steaks (about 4 ounces each)
4 cups bite-size pieces mixed salad greens
1 cup grape tomatoes or cherry tomatoes, cut in half
1 small red onion, sliced and separated into rings
1/2 cup sesame oat bran sticks

1. Make Teriyaki Pineapple Dressing; reserve 2 tablespoons. Brush grill rack with vegetable oil. Heat coals or gas grill for direct heat.

2. On each of two 10-inch metal skewers, thread pineapple, leaving 1/4-inch space between each piece. Brush 1 tablespoon of the reserved dressing on pineapple; brush remaining 1 tablespoon reserved dressing on tuna steaks.

3. Cover and grill tuna over medium heat about 10 minutes, turning once and adding pineapple for last 5 minutes of grilling, until tuna flakes easily with fork.

4. On 4 plates, divide salad greens, tomatoes and onion. Top with pineapple and tuna. Sprinkle with sesame sticks. Serve with remaining dressing.

Teriyaki Pineapple Dressing

1/2 cup pineapple juice
1/4 cup teriyaki baste and glaze (from 12-ounce bottle)
1 tablespoon sesame oil
1/4 teaspoon ground ginger

In small bowl, mix all ingredients with wire whisk. About 3/4 cup.

Substitute

Stir-fry sauce can be substituted for the teriyaki baste and glaze. Choose a sauce with a syrupy, not watery, consistency. Also, if you're having a hard time finding sesame oat bran sticks, use onion-and-garlic-flavored croutons instead.

1 Serving: Cal. 345 (Cal. from Fat 110); Fat 12g (Sat. fat 3g); Chol. 45mg; Sodium 820mg; Carbs. 29g (Fiber 3g); Pro. 30g • **% Daily Value:** Vit. A 44%; Vit. C 58%; Calc. 6%; Iron 16% • **Exchanges:** 1 1/2 Fruit, 1 Vegetable, 4 Lean Meat • **Carb. Choices:** 2

Asian Tuna with Wasabi Aioli

Prep: 10 min
Marinate: 2 hr
Grill: 15 min
8 servings

2 pounds tuna steaks, 3/4 to 1 inch thick
1/2 cup vegetable oil
1/3 cup soy sauce
2 tablespoons packed brown sugar
2 teaspoons sesame oil
2 teaspoons grated gingerroot
2 cloves garlic, finely chopped
Wasabi Aioli (below)
2 teaspoons sesame seed, toasted if desired

1. If tuna steaks are large, cut into 8 serving pieces. In shallow glass or plastic dish or resealable plastic food-storage bag, mix vegetable oil, soy sauce, brown sugar, sesame oil, gingerroot and garlic. Add tuna; turn to coat with marinade. Cover dish or seal bag and refrigerate, turning once, at least 2 hours but no longer than 4 hours.

2. Meanwhile, make Wasabi Aioli.

3. Heat coals or gas grill for direct heat. Remove tuna from marinade; reserve marinade.

4. Cover and grill tuna over medium heat 10 to 15 minutes, brushing 2 to 3 times with marinade and turning once, until tuna flakes easily with fork. Discard any remaining marinade. Sprinkle tuna with sesame seed. Serve with Wasabi Aioli.

Wasabi Aioli

1/2 cup mayonnaise or salad dressing
1 teaspoon wasabi powder or prepared horseradish

In small bowl, mix ingredients. Cover and refrigerate until serving. About 1/2 cup.

1 Serving: Cal. 415 (Cal. from Fat 290); Fat 32g (Sat. fat 5g); Chol. 50mg; Sodium 730mg; Carbs. 5g (Fiber 0g); Pro. 27g • % Daily Value: Vit. A 2%; Vit. C 0%; Calc. 2%; Iron 8% • Exchanges: 4 Medium-Fat Meat, 2 1/2 Fat • Carb. Choices: 0

Tuna Sandwiches

Prep: 10 min
Marinate: 15 min
Grill: 10 min
4 sandwiches

Orange-Ginger Marinade (below)
4 tuna steaks (about 4 ounces each)
3 tablespoons mayonnaise or salad dressing
4 kaiser or hamburger buns, split
Lettuce leaves
1 large tomato, sliced
1/2 medium cucumber, thinly sliced

1. In ungreased 8-inch square glass baking dish, make Orange-Ginger Marinade; reserve 1 tablespoon. Add tuna to marinade; turn to coat. Cover and refrigerate at least 15 minutes but no longer than 2 hours.

2. Brush grill rack with vegetable oil. Heat coals or gas grill for direct heat. Remove tuna from marinade; discard marinade.

3. Cover and grill tuna over medium heat about 10 minutes, turning once, until tuna flakes easily with fork.

4. In small bowl, mix reserved 1 tablespoon marinade and the mayonnaise; spread on cut sides of buns. Layer lettuce, tuna, tomato and cucumber in buns.

Orange-Ginger Marinade

2 tablespoons soy sauce
1 tablespoon sesame or vegetable oil
1 tablespoon orange juice
1 teaspoon grated gingerroot or 1/2 teaspoon ground ginger

In small bowl, mix all ingredients. About 1/4 cup.

Success Tip

Fish generally takes about 10 minutes to grill for each inch of thickness. Add more time if the steaks are thicker, or grill the fish for slightly less time if the pieces are thinner.

1 **Sandwich:** Cal. 410 (Cal. from Fat 160); Fat 18g (Sat. fat 3g); Chol. 50mg; Sodium 650mg; Carbs. 30g (Fiber 2g); Pro. 33g • **% Daily Value:** Vit. A 14%; Vit. C 22%; Calc. 6%; Iron 18% • **Exchanges:** 2 Starch, 4 Lean Meat, 1/2 Fat • **Carb. Choices:** 2

Ginger-Lime Tuna Steaks

Prep: 15 min
Marinate: 1 hr
Grill: 20 min
6 servings

Ginger-Lime Marinade (below)
1 1/2 pounds tuna, swordfish or halibut steaks, 3/4 to 1 inch thick
Lime wedges, if desired

1. Make Ginger-Lime Marinade.

2. If fish steaks are large, cut into 6 serving pieces. In shallow glass or plastic dish or resealable plastic food-storage bag, place fish. Add marinade; turn fish to coat with marinade. Cover dish or seal bag and refrigerate at least 1 hour but no longer than 24 hours.

3. Brush grill rack with vegetable oil. Heat coals or gas grill for direct heat. Remove fish from marinade; reserve marinade.

4. Cover and grill fish over medium heat 15 to 20 minutes, brushing 2 or 3 times with marinade and turning once, until fish flakes easily with fork. Discard any remaining marinade. Serve fish with lime wedges.

Ginger-Lime Marinade

1/4 cup lime juice
2 tablespoons olive or vegetable oil
1 teaspoon finely chopped gingerroot
1/4 teaspoon salt
Dash of ground red pepper (cayenne)
1 clove garlic, crushed

In small bowl, mix all ingredients. About 1/3 cup.

Healthful Hint

Different fish have varying levels of fat. Tuna is considered moderate to high in fat; swordfish is moderate and halibut is considered a lean, low-fat fish.

1 Serving: Cal. 185 (Cal. from Fat 80); Fat 9g (Sat. fat 2g); Chol. 45mg; Sodium 110mg; Carbs. 0g (Fiber 0g); Pro. 26g • **% Daily Value:** Vit. A 0%; Vit. C 0%; Calc. 0%; Iron 6% • **Exchanges:** 3 1/2 Lean Meat • **Carb. Choices:** 0

Salmon and Asparagus Salad

**Prep: 15 min
Grill: 15 min
4 servings**

Maple-Dijon Dressing (below)
1-pound salmon fillet, 1/2 inch thick
1 pound asparagus spears
4 cups fresh baby salad greens
1 cup shredded carrots (about 1 1/2 medium)
2 hard-cooked eggs, cut into 8 wedges
Freshly ground black pepper, if desired

1. Heat coals or gas grill for direct heat. Make Maple-Dijon Dressing.

2. Cut salmon crosswise into 4 pieces. Brush salmon with 1 table-spoon of the dressing. In large bowl, toss asparagus and 1 table-spoon of the dressing. Place asparagus in grill basket (grill "wok").

3. Place salmon, skin side down, on grill. Cover and grill salmon and asparagus over medium heat, cooking asparagus 7 to 10 minutes and salmon 10 to 15 minutes, shaking grill basket or turning asparagus occasionally, until salmon flakes easily with fork and asparagus is crisp-tender.

4. Slide pancake turner between salmon and skin to remove each piece from skin. On 4 plates, divide salad greens, carrots and eggs. Top with salmon and asparagus. Sprinkle with pepper. Serve with remaining dressing.

Maple-Dijon Dressing

1/3 cup maple-flavored syrup
2 tablespoons Dijon mustard
2 tablespoons olive or vegetable oil

In small bowl, mix all ingredients with wire whisk. About 1/2 cup.

1 Serving: Cal. 385 (Cal. from Fat 155); Fat 17g (Sat. fat 4g); Chol. 180mg; Sodium 340mg; Carbs. 28g (Fiber 3g); Pro. 30g • **% Daily Value:** Vit. A 100%; Vit. C 46%; Calc. 8%; Iron 12% • **Exchanges:** 1 Starch, 3 Vegetable, 3 Lean Meat, 1 Fat • **Carb. Choices:** 2

Ginger Teriyaki Salmon with Honey-Mango Salsa

Prep: 15 min
Chill: 1 hr
Grill: 12 min
4 servings

Honey-Mango Salsa (below)
3 tablespoons teriyaki baste and glaze (from 12-ounce bottle)
1 tablespoon grated gingerroot
1-pound salmon fillet, 1/2-inch thick

1. Make Honey-Mango Salsa.

2. Meanwhile, in shallow glass or plastic dish, mix teriyaki glaze and gingerroot. Cut salmon crosswise into 4 pieces. Add salmon to dish, turning skin side up. Let stand 15 minutes.

3. Brush grill rack with vegetable oil. Heat coals or gas grill for direct heat. Remove salmon from marinade; discard marinade.

4. Place salmon, skin side up, on grill. Cover and grill over medium heat 2 minutes; turn salmon. Cover and grill 5 to 10 minutes longer or until salmon flakes easily with fork. Serve with salsa.

Honey-Mango Salsa

1 teaspoon grated lime peel
2 tablespoons lime juice
1 tablespoon honey
Dash of red pepper sauce
1 medium mango, cut lengthwise in half, seed removed and diced
    (1 cup)
2 tablespoons finely chopped red onion

In small glass or plastic bowl, mix lime peel, lime juice, honey and pepper sauce. Add mango and onion; toss. Cover and refrigerate 1 hour. About 1 1/4 cups.

Success Tip

Here's how to peel, seed and dice a mango: Score the skin lengthwise into fourths with a knife, and peel like a banana. Cut the peeled mango lengthwise close to both sides of the seed, then dice.

1 Serving: Cal. 225 (Cal. from Fat 65); Fat 7g (Sat. fat 2g); Chol. 75mg; Sodium 330mg; Carbs. 15g (Fiber 1g); Pro. 25g • **% Daily Value:** Vit. A 10%; Vit. C 14%; Calc. 2%; Iron 4% • **Exchanges:** 3 Lean Meat, 1 Fruit • **Carb. Choices:** 1

Planked Salmon with Peach-Mango Salsa

Prep: 20 min
Chill: 1 hr
Grill: 35 min
8 servings

Photo on page 132

Peach-Mango Salsa (below)
1 untreated cedar plank, 16 × 6 × 2 inches
1 large salmon fillet (about 2 pounds)
1/4 cup packed brown sugar

1. Make Peach-Mango Salsa. Meanwhile, soak cedar plank in water at least 1 hour.

2. Heat coals or gas grill for direct heat.

3. Place salmon, skin side down, on cedar plank. Make diagonal cuts in salmon every 2 inches without cutting through the skin. Rub salmon with brown sugar.

4. Place cedar plank with salmon on grill over medium heat. When cedar plank begins to smoke, cover grill. Cover and grill salmon 30 to 35 minutes or until salmon flakes easily with fork. Remove salmon from plank, using large spatula. Serve with salsa.

1. Make diagonal cuts in the salmon every 2 inches without cutting through the skin.

Peach-Mango Salsa

1/4 cup lime juice
1 tablespoon honey
1/4 teaspoon salt
1 medium mango, cut lengthwise in half, seed removed and chopped (1 cup)
2 cups chopped peeled peaches
1/4 cup chopped fresh cilantro
1 tablespoon finely chopped bell pepper

2. Place the cedar plank with the salmon on the grill.

In large glass or plastic bowl, mix lime juice, honey and salt. Add remaining ingredients; toss. Cover and refrigerate at least 1 hour. About 3 2/3 cups.

1 Serving: Cal. 210 (Cal. from Fat 55); Fat 6g (Sat. fat 2g); Chol. 65mg; Sodium 135mg; Carbs. 19g (Fiber 1g); Pro. 21g • **% Daily Value:** Vit. A 8%; Vit. C 10%; Calc. 2%; Iron 4% • **Exchanges:** 1 Fruit, 3 Very Lean Meat, 1 Fat • **Carb. Choices:** 1

Salmon with Nectarine Salsa

**Prep: 10 min
Grill: 20 min
6 servings**

2 salmon fillets, 1/2 inch thick (1 pound each)
1/2 cup lemon juice
4 medium nectarines, chopped
1/2 cup chopped fresh cilantro
2 teaspoons chopped jalapeño chili

1. Cut each salmon fillet crosswise into 3 pieces. Heat coals or gas grill for direct heat.

2. In ungreased 11 × 7-inch glass baking dish, place salmon, skin side down. Drizzle with 1/4 cup of the lemon juice.

3. Remove salmon from baking dish; place skin side down on grill. Cover and grill over medium heat 10 to 20 minutes until salmon flakes easily with fork.

4. In medium bowl, mix remaining ingredients and remaining 1/4 cup lemon juice. Serve nectarine salsa over salmon.

Substitute

Two medium peaches, cut into 1/2-inch pieces, can be used instead of the nectarines.

1 Serving: Cal. 225 (Cal. from Fat 70); Fat 8g (Sat. fat 2g); Chol. 85mg; Sodium 80mg; Carbs. 12g (Fiber 2g); Pro. 28g • **% Daily Value:** Vit. A 8%; Vit. C 18%; Calc. 2%; Iron 6% • **Exchanges:** 1 Fruit, 4 Very Lean Meat, 1/2 Fat • **Carb. Choices:** 1

Dill Salmon

Prep: 10 min
Grill: 30 min
6 servings

1 large salmon fillet (about 2 pounds)
1 tablespoon vegetable oil
1/4 teaspoon pepper
1/2 cup dill dip
2 tablespoons milk

1. Heat coals or gas grill for direct heat. Cut 24 × 18-inch piece of heavy-duty foil.

2. Place salmon fillet on foil. Brush salmon with oil; sprinkle with pepper. Wrap foil securely around salmon. Allow space on sides for circulation and expansion.

3. Cover and grill packet over medium heat 20 to 30 minutes, rotating packet 1/2 turn after 10 minutes, until salmon flakes easily with fork.

4. In small bowl, mix dill dip and milk until smooth. Serve salmon with dill sauce.

Healthful **Hint**

Perishable food should be consumed within 2 hours (1 hour if the outside temperature is over 90°F).

1 Serving: Cal. 235 (Cal. from Fat 115); Fat 13g (Sat. fat 4g); Chol. 90mg; Sodium 220mg; Carbs. 1g (Fiber 0g); Pro. 28g • **% Daily Value:** Vit. A 4%; Vit. C 0%; Calc. 4%; Iron 4% • **Exchanges:** 4 Lean Meat • **Carb. Choices:** 0

Halibut with Lime and Cilantro

Prep: 10 min
Marinate: 15 min
Grill: 20 min
2 servings

Lime-Cilantro Marinade (below)
2 halibut or salmon steaks (about 3/4 pound)
Freshly ground pepper to taste
1/2 cup salsa

1. Make Lime-Cilantro Marinade in shallow glass or plastic dish or resealable plastic food-storage bag. Add fish; turn several times to coat with marinade. Cover and refrigerate 15 minutes, turning once.

2. Brush grill rack with vegetable oil. Heat coals or gas grill for direct heat. Remove fish from marinade; discard marinade.

3. Cover and grill fish over medium heat 10 to 20 minutes, turning once, until fish flakes easily with fork. Sprinkle with pepper. Serve with salsa.

Lime-Cilantro Marinade

2 tablespoons lime juice
1 tablespoon chopped fresh cilantro
1 teaspoon olive or vegetable oil
1 clove garlic, finely chopped

In small bowl, mix all ingredients. About 3 tablespoons.

Success Tip

You may want to consider using a grill basket when grilling delicate fish that can break apart easily. Be sure to lightly brush the basket with vegetable oil before adding the fish.

1 Serving: Cal. 185 (Cal. from Fat 35); Fat 4g (Sat. fat 1g); Chol. 90mg; Sodium 420mg; Carbs. 4g (Fiber 1g); Pro. 33g • **% Daily Value:** Vit. A 10%; Vit. C 20%; Calc. 4%; Iron 6% • **Exchanges:** 5 Very Lean Meat • **Carb. Choices:** 0

Swordfish Steaks

Prep: 15 min
Marinate: 15 min
Grill: 15 min
4 servings

1/4 cup olive or vegetable oil
2 tablespoons capers
1 1/2 tablespoons lemon juice
1 tablespoon chopped fresh parsley
1/2 teaspoon pepper
2 flat anchovy fillets in oil
2 cloves garlic
4 swordfish steaks, about 1 inch thick (about 2 pounds)

1. In food processor or blender, cover and process all ingredients except swordfish until smooth.

2. In ungreased 11 × 7-inch glass baking dish, place swordfish. Pour marinade over swordfish. Cover and refrigerate at least 15 minutes but no longer than 1 hour, turning swordfish occasionally.

3. Heat coals or gas grill for direct heat. Remove swordfish from marinade; reserve marinade.

4. Cover and grill swordfish over medium-high heat 5 minutes, brushing frequently with marinade. Turn carefully; brush generously with marinade. Grill 5 to 10 minutes longer or until swordfish flakes easily with fork. Discard any remaining marinade.

Substitute

Tuna or salmon steaks could also be used in place of the swordfish. The grilling times will stay the same.

1 Serving: Cal. 325 (Cal. from Fat 180); Fat 20g (Sat. fat 4g); Chol. 110mg; Sodium 260mg; Carbs. 1g (Fiber 0g); Pro. 35g • **% Daily Value:** Vit. A 4%; Vit. C 4%; Calc. 2%; Iron 6% • **Exchanges:** 5 Lean Meat, 1 Fat • **Carb. Choices:** 0

Sea Bass with Citrus-Olive Butter

Prep: 10 min
Chill: 30 min
Grill: 13 min
4 servings

Citrus-Olive Butter (below)
1-pound sea bass fillet, about 1 inch thick
1 tablespoon olive or vegetable oil
1/4 teaspoon salt
1/8 teaspoon pepper

1. Make Citrus-Olive Butter.

2. Heat coals or gas grill for direct heat.

3. Brush all surfaces of fish fillet with oil; sprinkle with salt and pepper.

4. Cover and grill fish over medium heat 10 to 13 minutes, turning after 5 minutes, until fish flakes easily with fork. Serve with Citrus-Olive Butter.

Citrus-Olive Butter

2 tablespoons butter or margarine, softened
1 tablespoon finely chopped Kalamata olives
2 teaspoons chopped fresh parsley
1/2 teaspoon balsamic vinegar
1/4 teaspoon grated orange peel

In small bowl, mix all ingredients. Refrigerate 30 minutes or until firm. About 3 tablespoons.

1 Serving: Cal. 185 (Cal. from Fat 100); Fat 11g (Sat. fat 4g); Chol. 75mg; Sodium 300mg; Carbs. 0g (Fiber 0g); Pro. 21g • **% Daily Value:** Vit. A 6%; Vit. C 0%; Calc. 2%; Iron 2% • **Exchanges:** 3 Lean Meat, 1/2 Fat • **Carb. Choices:** 0

Monterey Fish with Lemon-Caper Sauce

Prep: 15 min
Grill: 20 min
Cook: 5 min
6 servings

1 1/2 pounds swordfish, halibut or salmon steaks,
    3/4 to 1 inch thick
1 teaspoon salt
1/4 teaspoon pepper
1/4 cup butter or margarine, melted
1 tablespoon chopped fresh or 1 teaspoon dried chervil leaves
1 tablespoon lemon juice
Lemon-Caper Sauce (below)
Lemon wedges, if desired

1. Brush grill rack with vegetable oil. Heat coals or gas grill for direct heat.

2. Sprinkle fish with salt and pepper. In small bowl, mix butter, chervil and lemon juice.

3. Cover and grill fish over medium heat 15 to 20 minutes, brushing 2 or 3 times with butter mixture and turning once, until fish flakes easily with fork.

4. Meanwhile, make Lemon-Caper Sauce. Cut fish into serving pieces. Serve with sauce and lemon wedges.

Lemon-Caper Sauce

1 lemon
1/4 cup capers, drained
1 tablespoon chopped fresh parsley
1 tablespoon butter or margarine
1/4 teaspoon salt

Peel and chop lemon, removing seeds and membrane. In 1-quart saucepan, heat lemon and remaining ingredients over medium heat, stirring occasionally, until hot. Serve warm. About 1/2 cup.

1 Serving: Cal. 215 (Cal. from Fat 135); Fat 13g (Sat. fat 7g); Chol. 85mg; Sodium 760mg; Carbs. 1g (Fiber 0g); Pro. 19g • **% Daily Value:** Vit. A 10%; Vit. C 24%; Calc. 2%; Iron 4% • **Exchanges:** 3 Medium-Fat Meat • **Carb. Choices:** 0

Tarragon Marlin Steaks with Vermouth

Prep: 10 min
Marinate: 15 min
Grill: 15 min
6 servings

1/2 cup dry vermouth or 1/4 cup lemon juice plus 1/4 cup water
1/4 teaspoon aromatic bitters
4 large sprigs fresh tarragon
1 1/2 pounds marlin, tuna or opah steaks, 1 to 1 1/2 inches thick
1 1/2 teaspoons chopped fresh or 1/2 teaspoon dried
     tarragon leaves

1. In shallow glass or plastic dish, mix vermouth and bitters. Add 2 sprigs of the tarragon. Add fish steaks; turn to coat with marinade. Top fish with remaining 2 sprigs tarragon. Cover and let stand, turning once, at least 15 minutes but no longer than 30 minutes.

2. Brush grill rack with vegetable oil. Heat coals or gas grill for direct heat. Drain fish; discard marinade but keep the tarragon sprigs.

3. Place tarragon sprigs directly on hot coals, lava rock or ceramic briquettes. Immediately cover and grill fish over medium heat 10 to 15 minutes, turning once, until fish flakes easily with fork. Remove fish to platter. Sprinkle with chopped tarragon.

Success Tip

It is generally recommended to cook fish 10 minutes for every inch of thickness. Instead of grilling the first side for half the time, try cooking the first side 1 to 2 minutes longer. Watch the fish carefully toward end of cooking time to avoid overcooking.

1 Serving: Cal. 145 (Cal. from Fat 55); Fat 6g (Sat. fat 2g); Chol. 65mg; Sodium 60mg; Carbs. 1g (Fiber 0g); Pro. 22g • **% Daily Value:** Vit. A 2%; Vit. C 0%; Calc. 2%; Iron 4% • **Exchanges:** 3 Very Lean Meat, 1 Fat • **Carb. Choices:** 0

Fish Tacos

Prep: 10 min
Grill: 7 min
8 tacos

1 pound firm white fish fillets, such as sea bass, red snapper
    or halibut
1 tablespoon olive or vegetable oil
1 teaspoon ground cumin or chili powder
1/2 teaspoon salt
1/4 teaspoon pepper
8 corn tortillas (6 inches in diameter)
1/4 cup sour cream
Toppers (shredded lettuce, chopped avocado, chopped tomato,
    chopped onion and chopped fresh cilantro), if desired
1/2 cup salsa

1. Brush grill rack with vegetable oil. Heat coals or gas grill for direct heat.

2. Brush fish with oil; sprinkle with cumin, salt and pepper.

3. Cover and grill fish over medium heat 5 to 7 minutes, turning once, until fish flakes easily with fork.

4. Heat tortillas as directed on package. Spread sour cream on tortillas. Add fish, toppers and salsa.

Try This

Fish tacos typically are made with corn tortillas instead of flour, but you can use small flour tortillas if you like. Top these flavorful fish tacos with any of your favorite condiments: shredded lettuce, chopped tomatoes, onions or avocados.

1 Taco: Cal. 125 (Cal. from Fat 35); Fat 4g (Sat. fat 1g); Chol. 30mg; Sodium 300mg; Carbs. 13g (Fiber 2g); Pro. 11g • **% Daily Value:** Vit. A 4%; Vit. C 4%; Calc. 6%; Iron 4% • **Exchanges:** 1 Starch, 1 Lean Meat • **Carb. Choices:** 0

Seafood Salad

Shallot-Thyme Vinaigrette (below)
12 uncooked large shrimp, peeled and deveined
1 pound swordfish, marlin or tuna steaks, 3/4 to 1 inch thick
1 medium fennel bulb, cut into wedges
10 cups bite-size pieces mixed salad greens
1/2 small red onion, thinly sliced
12 cherry tomatoes, cut in half
12 pitted Kalamata or ripe olives

1. Make Shallot-Thyme Vinaigrette. In shallow glass or plastic dish or heavy-duty resealable plastic food-storage bag, place shrimp and fish steaks. Add 1/4 cup of the vinaigrette; turn shrimp and fish to coat. Cover dish or seal bag and refrigerate 30 minutes. Reserve remaining vinaigrette.

2. Heat coals or gas grill for direct heat. Remove shrimp and fish from marinade; reserve marinade. Set shrimp aside.

3. Cover and grill fish and fennel over medium heat 5 minutes; brush with marinade. Add shrimp. Cover and grill 5 minutes, turning and brushing fish, fennel and shrimp with marinade 2 or 3 times, until shrimp are pink and firm, fish flakes easily with fork and fennel is tender. Discard any remaining marinade.

4. On serving platter, arrange salad greens. Cut fish into bite-size pieces. Arrange fish, fennel, shrimp and remaining ingredients on salad greens. Serve with reserved vinaigrette.

Shallot-Thyme Vinaigrette

1/3 cup olive or vegetable oil
1/4 cup balsamic vinegar
2 tablespoons white wine vinegar
1 tablespoon finely chopped shallot
1 tablespoon chopped fresh or 1 teaspoon dried thyme leaves
1 tablespoon Dijon mustard
1/4 teaspoon salt

In tightly covered container, shake all ingredients. About 3/4 cup.

1 Serving: Cal. 285 (Cal. from Fat 145); Fat 16g (Sat. fat 3g); Chol. 65mg; Sodium 340mg; Carbs. 9g (Fiber 4g); Pro. 18g • **% Daily Value:** Vit. A 66%; Vit. C 48%; Calc. 8%; Iron 16% • **Exchanges:** 2 Vegetable, 2 Lean Meat, 2 1/2 Fat • **Carb. Choices:** 1/2

1. Cut the root end and leaves off the fennel.

2. Cut the fennel into wedges.

Provençal Fish Kabobs

Prep: 20 min
Marinate: 20 min
Grill: 15 min
6 servings

1/2 cup red wine vinegar
1 tablespoon vegetable oil
2 teaspoons chopped fresh or 1/2 teaspoon dried tarragon leaves
2 teaspoons chopped fresh or 1/2 teaspoon dried thyme leaves
1 pound tuna or swordfish steaks, cut into 2-inch pieces
1 small eggplant (1 pound)
2 cups cherry tomatoes
1/2 pound medium whole mushrooms
6 large cloves garlic, peeled

1. In shallow glass or plastic dish or resealable plastic food-storage bag, mix vinegar, oil, tarragon and thyme. Add fish pieces; stir to coat with marinade. Cover dish or seal bag and refrigerate 20 minutes.

2. Brush grill rack with vegetable oil. Heat coals or gas heat for direct heat.

3. Cut eggplant into 1-inch slices; cut slices into fourths. Remove fish from marinade; reserve marinade. On each of six 15-inch metal skewers, alternately thread fish, eggplant, tomatoes and mushrooms, leaving 1/4-inch space between each piece. Thread 1 clove garlic on end of each skewer.

4. Cover and grill kabobs over medium heat 12 to 15 minutes, turning and brushing 2 to 3 times with marinade, until fish flakes easily with fork. Discard any remaining marinade.

Did You Know?

You've probably heard of Provence, a region in southern France. Recipes called "à la Provençal" simply mean "in the style of Provence." Ingredients in these dishes typically include garlic, mushrooms, tomatoes and eggplant.

1 Serving: Cal. 170 (Cal. from Fat 55); Fat 6g (Sat. fat 1g); Chol. 30mg; Sodium 40mg; Carbs. 11g (Fiber 3g); Pro. 20g • **% Daily Value:** Vit. A 12%; Vit. C 12%; Calc. 2%; Iron 10% • **Exchanges:** 2 Vegetable, 2 Very Lean Meat, 1 Fat • **Carb. Choices:** 1

Sole Fillets with Spinach

1 pound fresh spinach
1 teaspoon poultry seasoning
1/2 teaspoon chili powder
1/2 teaspoon salt
1 to 1 1/2 pounds sole, flounder or red snapper fillets,
    1/4 to 1/2 inch thick
2 tablespoons butter or margarine, melted
Lemon wedges

1. Heat coals or gas grill for direct heat. Spray 13 × 9-inch foil pan with cooking spray.

2. Rinse spinach; shake off excess water, but do not dry. Place about three-fourths of the spinach leaves in pan, covering bottom completely.

3. In small bowl, mix poultry seasoning, chili powder and salt. Lightly rub into both sides of fish. Place fish on spinach, folding thin tail ends under and, if necessary, overlapping thin edges slightly. Drizzle with butter. Cover fish completely with remaining spinach.

4. Cover and grill pan of fish and spinach over medium heat 8 to 10 minutes or until fish flakes easily with fork. Check after about 3 minutes; if top layer of spinach is charring, sprinkle with about 1/4 cup water.

5. Serve fish and spinach from pan with a slotted spoon if desired. Serve with lemon wedges.

Shop Talk

When buying spinach, look for crisp, dark green leaves. The leaves should not be discolored and should smell good. If you buy more than you need, store the leftovers in a plastic bag in your refrigerator for up to 3 days.

1 Serving: Cal.160 (Cal. from Fat 65); Fat 7g (Sat. fat 4g); Chol. 70mg; Sodium 480mg; Carbs. 3g (Fiber 2g); Pro. 21g • **% Daily Value:** Vit. A 100%; Vit. C 18%; Calc. 10%; Iron 14% • **Exchanges:** 1 Vegetable, 3 Very Lean Meat, 1/2 Fat • **Carb. Choices:** 0

Mussels with Buttery Herb Sauce

**Prep: 40 min
Grill: 5 min
4 servings**

2 pounds mussels in shells (60 to 72 mussels)
Buttery Herb Sauce (below)

1. Discard any broken-shell or open (dead) mussels. Scrub remaining mussels in cool water, removing any barnacles with a dull paring knife. Remove beards by tugging them away from shells. Place mussels in container. Cover with cool water. Agitate water with hand, then drain and discard water. Repeat several times until water runs clear; drain.

2. Make Buttery Herb Sauce.

3. Brush grill rack with vegetable oil. Heat coals or gas grill for direct heat.

4. Cover and grill mussels over medium heat 3 to 5 minutes or until mussels open, removing mussels as they open. Discard unopened mussels.

5. Place mussels on platter, or divide among shallow soup bowls. Drizzle hot sauce over mussels.

Buttery Herb Sauce

1/2 cup butter or margarine
2 teaspoons dried thyme leaves (do not substitute fresh)
2 teaspoons dried sage leaves (do not substitute fresh)
1 1/2 teaspoons celery salt
1/4 teaspoon chili oil or crushed red pepper

In 8-inch skillet, melt butter over medium heat. Stir in remaining ingredients. Reduce heat to low and cover to keep warm, or reheat just before serving. About 1/2 cup.

1 Serving: Cal. 260 (Cal. from Fat 215); Fat 24g (Sat. fat 14g); Chol. 85mg; Sodium 900mg; Carbs. 2g (Fiber 0g); Pro. 9g • **% Daily Value:** Vit. A 22%; Vit. C 6%; Calc. 4%; Iron 52% • **Exchanges:** 1 Medium-Fat Meat, 4 Fat • **Carb. Choices:** 0

Lobster Roast

Prep: 20 min
Grill: 15 min
1 to desired number of servings

Live lobsters (each 1 to 1 1/4 pounds) (see tip below)
Butter or margarine, melted
Lemon wedges, if desired
French bread, if desired

1. Allow one lobster per person. Carefully cut lobsters lengthwise in half with sharp knife or poultry shears. Remove the dark vein that runs through the center of the body and the stomach, which is just behind the head. Leave the green liver and the coral roe, which are delicacies.

2. Brush grill rack with vegetable oil. Heat coals or gas grill for direct heat.

3. Brush lobster meat generously with butter. Place lobster halves, shell sides down, on grill over medium-hot heat. Cover and grill 10 to 15 minutes, brushing frequently with butter, until meat turns white. Don't turn during grilling or you'll lose the juices that collect in the shell.

4. Serve lobsters hot with lemon wedges, additional melted butter and French bread.

Try This

If you'd prefer not to cut up a live lobster, cover it in water and parboil it for 5 to 10 minutes, then cut in half.

1 Serving: Cal. 265 (Cal. from Fat 160); Fat 18g (Sat. fat 11g); Chol. 130mg; Sodium 560mg; Carbs. 2g (Fiber 0g); Pro. 24g • **% Daily Value:** Vit. A 20%; Vit. C 0%; Calc. 8%; Iron 2% • **Exchanges:** 3 1/2 Lean Meat, 2 Fat • **Carb. Choices:** 0

Crab Legs with Lemon-Mustard Sauce

Lemon-Mustard Sauce (below)
3 pounds frozen king crab legs, thawed
1/2 cup butter or margarine, melted
Lemon wedges

1. Make Lemon-Mustard Sauce.

2. Brush grill rack with vegetable oil. Heat coals or gas grill for direct heat.

3. Carefully cut crab legs lengthwise in half through shell with sharp knife or poultry shears, leaving narrow parts of legs whole.

4. Place crab legs, shell sides down, on grill. Brush with butter. Cover and grill over medium heat 10 to 15 minutes or until shells turn red and crabmeat turns white and firm.

5. Serve crab legs with sauce and lemon wedges.

Lemon-Mustard Sauce

3/4 cup mayonnaise or salad dressing
2 tablespoons lemon juice
1 tablespoon Dijon mustard
1/8 teaspoon ground red pepper (cayenne)

In small bowl, mix all ingredients. Cover and refrigerate at least 1 hour to blend flavors. About 1 cup.

1 Serving: Cal. 675 (Cal. from Fat 530); Fat 59g (Sat. fat 20g); Chol. 250mg; Sodium 940mg; Carbs. 2g (Fiber 0g); Pro. 34g • **% Daily Value:** Vit. A 20%; Vit. C 6%; Calc. 18%; Iron 10% • **Exchanges:** 5 Lean Meat, 9 Fat • **Carb. Choices:** 0

Trout with Rosemary

Prep: 15 min
Grill: 25 min
4 servings

4 pan-dressed rainbow trout (each about 1/2 pound)
1/2 teaspoon salt
1/4 teaspoon pepper
4 sprigs rosemary (each about 3 inches long)
4 thin slices lemon
1/4 cup olive or vegetable oil
Lemon wedges, if desired

1. Heat coals or gas grill for direct heat. Brush hinged wire grill basket with vegetable oil.

2. Sprinkle cavities of trout with salt and pepper. Place 1 sprig rosemary and 1 slice lemon in each trout. Rub trout with oil. Place trout in basket.

3. Cover and grill trout over medium heat 20 to 25 minutes, brushing 2 or 3 times with oil and turning once, until trout flakes easily with fork.

4. Serve trout with lemon wedges.

Did You **Know?**

A pan-dressed fish is all ready to cook—it's been gutted and scaled, and usually the head, tail and fins have been removed.

1 Serving: Cal. 375 (Cal. from Fat 205); Fat 23g (Sat. fat 5g); Chol. 130mg; Sodium 410mg; Carbs. 0g (Fiber 0g); Pro. 42g • **% Daily Value:** Vit. A 4%; Vit. C 2%; Calc. 2%; Iron 8% • **Exchanges:** 6 Lean Meat, 1 Fat • **Carb. Choices:** 0

Paella on the Grill

Prep: 20 min
Marinate: 1 hr
Grill: 25 min
6 servings

Saffron Marinade (below)
1 pound boneless, skinless chicken breasts, cut into 1-inch pieces
1 pound uncooked medium shrimp in shells
1/2 pound chorizo sausage, cut into 1-inch pieces
8 roma (plum) tomatoes, cut into fourths
1 can (about 14 ounces) artichoke hearts, drained and cut in half
1 cup pitted Kalamata or Greek olives
Hot cooked rice, if desired

1. Make Saffron Marinade. In glass or plastic dish or resealable plastic food-storage bag, place remaining ingredients except rice. Pour marinade over mixture; stir to coat. Cover dish or seal bag and refrigerate 1 hour.

2. Heat coals or gas grill for direct heat. Remove chicken mixture from marinade; reserve marinade. Place chicken mixture in grill basket (grill "wok").

3. Cover and grill chicken mixture over medium heat 20 to 25 minutes, brushing with marinade and shaking basket or stirring occasionally, until chicken is no longer pink in center. Discard any remaining marinade. Serve chicken mixture with rice.

Saffron Marinade

1 cup chicken broth
1/2 cup sherry wine vinegar
1/2 teaspoon salt
1/4 teaspoon curry powder
1/4 teaspoon crushed saffron threads or ground turmeric
2 cloves garlic, finely chopped

In small bowl, mix all ingredients. About 1 1/2 cups.

1 Serving: Cal. 365 (Cal. from Fat 180); Fat 20g (Sat. fat 7g); Chol. 150mg; Sodium 1260mg; Carbs. 14g (Fiber 5g); Pro. 37g • **% Daily Value:** Vit. A 26%; Vit. C 16%; Calc. 8%; Iron 24% • **Exchanges:** 4 1/2 Lean Meat, 3 Vegetable, 1 Fat • **Carb. Choices:** 1

Foil Packets

Halibut Packets Vera Cruz

Cheddar Burgers and Veggies

Prep: 20 min
Grill: 20 min
6 servings

1 1/2 pounds lean (at least 80%) ground beef
1 1/2 cups shredded Cheddar cheese (6 ounces)
1 1/2 tablespoons Worcestershire sauce
3 medium green onions, chopped (3 tablespoons)
2 teaspoons peppered seasoned salt
3 medium Yukon gold potatoes, thinly sliced
2 cups baby-cut carrots
18 cherry tomatoes, cut in half, if desired
6 medium green onions, sliced (6 tablespoons)

1. Heat coals or gas grill for direct heat. Cut six 18 × 12-inch pieces of heavy-duty foil; spray half of one side of each piece with cooking spray.

2. In large bowl, mix beef, cheese, Worcestershire sauce, 3 chopped onions and 1 1/2 teaspoons of the peppered seasoned salt. Shape mixture into 6 patties, about 1 inch thick. On sprayed side of each foil piece, place potatoes. Top with beef patty, carrots, tomatoes and 6 sliced onions; sprinkle with remaining 1/2 teaspoon seasoned salt.

3. Fold foil over patties and vegetables so edges meet. Seal edges, making tight 1/2-inch fold; fold again. Allow space on sides for circulation and expansion.

4. Cover and grill packets over medium heat 17 to 20 minutes, rotating packets 1/2 turn after 10 minutes, until potatoes are tender. Place packets on plates. Cut large X across top of each packet; fold back foil.

Substitute

If you're out of peppered seasoned salt, use 1 teaspoon seasoned salt or 1/2 teaspoon salt for each teaspoon of peppered seasoned salt.

1 Serving: Cal. 440 (Cal. from Fat 235); Fat 26g (Sat. fat 12g); Chol. 95mg; Sodium 770mg; Carbs. 24g (Fiber 4g); Pro. 31g • **% Daily Value:** Vit. A 100%; Vit. C 22%; Calc. 18%; Iron 20% • **Exchanges:** 1 Starch, 2 Vegetable, 3 Medium-Fat Meat, 2 Fat • **Carb. Choices:** 1 1/2

Meat Loaf, Potato and Carrot Packets

Prep: 15 min
Grill: 30 min
6 servings

1 1/2-pound pounds lean (at least 80%) ground beef
1 envelope (1 ounce) onion recipe and soup mix
1 egg
3/4 cup milk
1/2 cup plain dry bread crumbs
1/3 cup ketchup
1 package (1 pound 4 ounces) refrigerated new potato wedges
3 cups baby-cut carrots
Fresh parsley, if desired

1. Heat coals or gas grill for direct heat. Cut six 18 × 12-inch pieces of heavy-duty foil; spray with cooking spray.

2. In large bowl, mix beef, soup mix (dry), egg, milk and bread crumbs. Shape mixture into 6 loaves, 4 × 2 1/2 × 1 inch. On one side of each foil piece, place loaf; top each with about 1 tablespoon of the ketchup. Place about 1/2 cup potatoes and 1/2 cup carrots around each loaf.

3. Fold foil over loaf and vegetables so edges meet. Seal edges, making tight 1/2-inch fold; fold again. Allow space on sides for circulation and expansion.

4. Cover and grill packets over medium heat 25 to 30 minutes, rotating packets 1/2 turn after 15 minutes, until vegetables are tender, beef is no longer pink in center and meat thermometer inserted in center of patties reads 160°F. Place packets on plates. Cut large X across top of each packet; fold back foil. Garnish with parsley.

Try This

These delicious packets can be made up to 24 hours in advance. Just pop them on the grill when you are ready to eat.

1 Serving: Cal. 425 (Cal. from Fat 160); Fat 18g (Sat. fat 7g); Chol. 100mg; Sodium 880mg; Carbs. 44g (Fiber 5g); Pro. 27g • **% Daily Value:** Vit. A 100%; Vit. C 16%; Calc. 10%; Iron 22% • **Exchanges:** 2 1/2 Starch, 1 Vegetable, 3 Medium-Fat Meat • **Carb. Choices:** 3

Pesto Chicken Packets

Prep: 15 min
Grill: 25 min
4 servings

4 boneless skinless chicken breast halves (about 1 1/4 pounds)
8 roma (plum) tomatoes, cut into 1/2-inch slices
4 small zucchini, cut into 1/2-inch slices
1/2 cup basil pesto

1. Heat coals or gas grill for direct heat. Cut four 18 × 12-inch pieces of heavy-duty foil; spray with cooking spray.

2. On one side of each foil piece, place 1 chicken breast half, one-fourth of the tomatoes and one-fourth of the zucchini. Spoon 2 tablespoons pesto over chicken mixture on each sheet.

3. Fold foil over chicken and vegetables so edges meet. Seal edges, making tight 1/2-inch fold; fold again. Allow space on sides for circulation and expansion.

4. Cover and grill packets over medium heat 20 to 25 minutes, rotating packets 1/2 turn after 10 minutes, until juice of chicken is no longer pink when centers of thickest pieces are cut. Place packets on plates. Cut large X across top of each packet; fold back foil.

Try **This**

Pesto is a sauce made of fresh basil, garlic, oil, pine nuts and grated cheese. A variety of pesto flavors is now available, and you may want to experiment with one of them in this recipe.

1 Serving: Cal. 350 (Cal. from Fat 190); Fat 21g (Sat. fat 4g); Chol. 80mg; Sodium 350mg; Carbs. 10g (Fiber 3g); Pro. 32g • **% Daily Value:** Vit. A 36%; Vit. C 26%; Calc. 16%; Iron 14% • **Exchanges:** 4 Lean Meat, 2 Vegetable, 1 Fat • **Carb. Choices:** 1

Sweet-and-Sour Chicken Packets

4 boneless, skinless chicken breast halves (about 1 1/4 pounds)
1/2 cup sweet-and-sour sauce
1 can (8 ounces) pineapple chunks, drained
1 medium bell pepper, cut into strips
1/4 small onion, cut into small wedges
1/2 cup chow mein noodles, if desired

1. Heat coals or gas grill for direct heat. Cut four 18 × 12-inch pieces of heavy-duty foil; spray with cooking spray.

2. On one side of each foil piece, place 1 chicken breast half. Top each with 1 tablespoon sweet-and-sour sauce and one-fourth of the pineapple, bell pepper and onion. Top with remaining sauce.

3. Fold foil over chicken and vegetables so edges meet. Seal edges, making tight 1/2-inch fold; fold again. Allow space on sides for circulation and expansion.

4. Cover and grill packets over medium heat 15 to 20 minutes, rotating packets 1/2 turn after 10 minutes, until juice of chicken is no longer pink when centers are cut. Place packets on plates. Cut large X across top of each packet; fold back foil. Top with chow mein noodles.

Try This

Looking for additional ways to use your bottle of sweet-and-sour sauce? Use it as a dipping sauce for pot stickers, wontons or chicken wings.

1 Serving: Cal. 230 (Cal. from Fat 45); Fat 5g (Sat. fat 1g); Chol. 75mg; Sodium 180mg; Carbs. 19g (Fiber 1g); Pro. 27g • **% Daily Value:** Vit. A 2%; Vit. C 18%; Calc. 2%; Iron 8% • **Exchanges:** 1 Fruit, 4 Very Lean Meat, 1/2 Fat • **Carb. Choices:** 1

1. Fold the foil over the chicken and vegetables so the edges meet.

2. Seal the edges, making a tight 1/2-inch fold; fold again.

Mediterranean Chicken Packets

Prep: 20 min
Grill: 25 min
4 servings

1 package (4 ounces) crumbled basil-and-tomato feta cheese
2 tablespoons grated lemon peel
1 teaspoon dried oregano leaves
4 boneless, skinless chicken breast halves
    (about 1 1/4 pounds)
4 roma (plum) tomatoes, each cut into 3 slices
1 small red onion, finely chopped (1 cup)
20 pitted Kalamata olives

1. Heat coals or gas grill for direct heat. Cut four 18 × 12-inch pieces of heavy-duty foil.

2. In small bowl, mix cheese, lemon peel and oregano. On one side of each foil piece, place 1 chicken breast half, 3 tomato slices, 1/4 cup onion and 5 olives. Spoon one-fourth of cheese mixture over chicken and vegetables on each foil piece.

3. Fold foil over chicken and vegetables so edges meet. Seal edges, making tight 1/2-inch fold; fold again. Allow space on sides for circulation and expansion.

4. Cover and grill packets over medium heat 20 to 25 minutes, rotating packets 1/2 turn after 10 minutes, until juice of chicken is no longer pink when centers of thickest pieces are cut. Place packets on plates. Cut large X across top of each packet; fold back foil.

Substitute

You can use a package of crumbled plain feta cheese instead of the flavored feta.

1 Serving: Cal. 250 (Cal. from Fat 110); Fat 12g (Sat. fat 6g); Chol. 100mg; Sodium 560mg; Carbs. 7g (Fiber 2g); Pro. 31g • **% Daily Value:** Vit. A 12%; Vit. C 10%; Calc. 18%; Iron 10% • **Exchanges:** 4 Lean Meat, 1 Vegetable • **Carb. Choices:** 1/2

180 *Betty Crocker* **GRILLING MADE EASY**

1. Fold the foil over the chicken and vegetables so the edges meet.

2. Seal the edges, making a tight 1/2-inch fold; fold again.

3. After grilling, cut a large X across the top of the packet; fold back foil.

Italian Chicken Packets

Prep: 10 min
Grill: 25 min
4 servings

4 boneless skinless chicken breast halves (about 1 1/4 pounds)
1 medium yellow bell pepper, cut into 4 wedges
4 roma (plum) tomatoes, cut in half
1 small red onion, cut into 8 wedges
1/2 cup Italian vinaigrette dressing

1. Heat coals or gas grill for direct heat. Cut four 18 × 12-inch pieces of heavy-duty foil.

2. On one side of each foil piece, place 1 chicken breast half, 1 bell pepper wedge, 2 tomato halves and 2 onion wedges. Pour 2 tablespoons dressing over chicken and vegetable mixture on each foil piece.

3. Fold foil over chicken and vegetables so edges meet. Seal edges, making tight 1/2-inch fold, fold again. Allow space on sides for circulation and expansion.

4. Cover and grill packets over medium heat 20 to 25 minutes, rotating packets 1/2 turn after 10 minutes, until juice of chicken is no longer pink when centers are cut. Place packets on plates. Cut large X across top of each packet; fold back foil.

Serving Idea

These colorful packets are a meal in themselves. Serve with French bread to soak up the flavorful juices.

1 Serving: Cal. 290 (Cal. from Fat 145); Fat 16g (Sat. fat 2g); Chol. 75mg; Sodium 340mg; Carbs. 9g (Fiber 1g); Pro. 28g • **% Daily Value:** Vit. A 10%; Vit. C 54%; Calc. 6%; Iron 8% • **Exchanges:** 2 Vegetable, 3 1/2 Lean Meat, 1 Fat • **Carb. Choices:** 1/2

Honey-Cumin BBQ Pork Packets

Prep: 20 min
Grill: 20 min
4 servings

1/2 cup barbecue sauce
1/4 cup honey
2 teaspoons ground cumin
4 pork boneless rib or loin chops, 3/4 to 1 inch thick
    (about 1 1/4 pounds)
2 large ears corn, each cut into 6 pieces
1 cup baby-cut carrots, cut lengthwise in half
2 cups refrigerated cooked new potato wedges
    (from 1-pound 4-ounce bag)
1 teaspoon salt

1. Heat coals or gas grill for direct heat. Cut four 18 × 12-inch pieces of heavy-duty foil; spray half of one side of each piece with cooking spray.

2. In small bowl, mix barbecue sauce, honey and cumin. On sprayed side of each foil piece, place 1 pork chop, 3 pieces corn, 1/4 cup carrots and 1/2 cup potato wedges. Sprinkle each with 1/4 teaspoon salt. Spoon 3 tablespoons sauce mixture over pork and vegetables on each foil piece.

3. Fold foil over pork and vegetables so edges meet. Seal edges, making tight 1/2-inch fold; fold again. Allow space on sides for circulation and expansion.

4. Cover and grill packets over medium heat 15 to 20 minutes, rotating packets 1/2 turn after 10 minutes, until pork is no longer pink in center. Place packets on plates. Cut large X across top of each packet; fold back foil.

Substitute

Look for the cooked potato wedges in the refrigerated section of the supermarket. If they are not available, cut 2 medium potatoes into wedges and place in microwavable bowl. Cover and microwave on High for about 5 minutes or until crisp-tender. Place potatoes in packet and grill as directed.

1 Serving: Cal. 385 (Cal. from Fat 70); Fat 8g (Sat. fat 3g); Chol. 55mg; Sodium 960mg; Carbs. 59g (Fiber 4g); Pro. 23g • **% Daily Value:** Vit. A 100%; Vit. C 14%; Calc. 2%; Iron 10% • **Exchanges:** 3 Starch, 2 Vegetable, 1 1/2 Very Lean Meat • **Carb. Choices:** 4

Maple Sausage, Squash and Bell Pepper Packets

Prep: 10 min
Grill: 40 min
4 servings

1 pound fully cooked kielbasa or Polish sausage, cut into
    1-inch pieces
1 small butternut squash, peeled and cut into 1-inch chunks
1 small bell pepper (any color), cut into strips
1/2 cup sliced green onions
1/4 cup maple-flavored syrup
1/4 cup orange juice
1/4 teaspoon salt

1. Heat coals or gas grill for direct heat. Cut four 18 × 12-inch pieces of heavy-duty foil.

2. On one side of each foil piece, divide sausage, squash and bell pepper. Sprinkle with onions. In small bowl, mix syrup, orange juice and salt; pour over sausage mixture on foil pieces.

3. Fold foil over sausage mixture so edges meet. Seal edges, making tight 1/2-inch fold; fold again. Allow space on sides for circulation and expansion.

4. Cover and grill packets over medium heat 35 to 40 minutes, rotating packets 1/2 turn after 15 minutes, until sausage is thoroughly heated and squash is tender. Place packets on plates. Cut large X across top of each packet; fold back foil.

Try This

Another great golden vegetable for these packets is sweet potatoes. Use 3 to 4 medium dark-orange sweet potatoes in place of the squash.

1 Serving: Cal. 480 (Cal. from Fat 280); Fat 31g (Sat. fat 12g); Chol. 65mg; Sodium 1320mg; Carbs. 28g (Fiber 2g); Pro. 15g • **% Daily Value:** Vit. A 100%; Vit. C 28%; Calc. 4%; Iron 10% • **Exchanges:** 2 Fruit, 1 Vegetable, 2 High-Fat Meat, 2 Fat • **Carb. Choices:** 2

Kielbasa and Vegetable Packets

Prep: 20 min
Grill: 40 min
8 servings

2 rings (1 pound each) fully cooked kielbasa sausage, each cut
    into 8 pieces
24 new potatoes (about 2 1/2 pounds), cut in half

Top with One or More of These Vegetables:
4 medium bell peppers, each cut lengthwise into eighths
2 medium red onions, each cut into 8 wedges
8 small zucchini, cut into 1/2-inch slices
8 ears corn, husked and each cut into fourths

Add One or More of These Seasonings:
Cajun seasoning
Garlic salt
Pepper

1. Heat coals or gas grill for direct heat. Cut eight 18 × 12-inch pieces of heavy-duty foil.

2. On one side of each foil piece, place 2 pieces kielbasa and 6 potato halves. Top each with either 4 bell pepper pieces, 2 onion wedges, 3 or 4 zucchini slices or 4 corn pieces. Sprinkle with one or more of the seasonings.

3. Fold foil over kielbasa and vegetables so edges meet. Seal edges, making tight 1/2-inch fold; fold again. Allow space on sides for circulation and expansion.

4. Cover and grill packets over medium heat 30 to 40 minutes, rotating packets 1/2 turn after 15 minutes, until potatoes are tender.* Place packets on plates. Cut large X across top of each packet; fold back foil.

Cooking time may vary depending on ingredients selected.

1 Serving: Cal. 525 (Cal. from Fat 290);
Fat 32g (Sat. fat 12g); Chol. 65mg;
Sodium 1290mg; Carbs. 47g (Fiber 5g);
Pro. 18g • **% Daily Value:** Vit. A 8%;
Vit. C 28%; Calc. 2%; Iron 18% •
Exchanges: 3 Starch, 1 Vegetable,
1 High-Fat Meat, 3 1/2 Fat •
Carb. Choices: 3

Dilled Salmon and Vegetable Packet

Prep: 20 min
Grill: 20 min
4 servings

1 1/4-pound salmon fillet, 1/2 to 3/4 inch thick
2 tablespoons olive or vegetable oil
2 teaspoons chopped fresh or 1/2 teaspoon dried dill weed
2 teaspoons chopped fresh parsley
1 teaspoon garlic salt
2 medium tomatoes, seeded and coarsely chopped (1 1/2 cups)
1 medium yellow summer squash, sliced (1 1/2 cups)
1 cup fresh snap pea pods, strings removed

1. Heat coals or gas grill for direct heat. Cut salmon fillet into 4 serving pieces.

2. In small bowl, mix oil, dill weed, parsley and garlic salt. In heavy-duty foil bag, place salmon, tomatoes, squash and pea pods. Brush oil mixture over salmon and vegetables. Double-fold open end of bag.

3. Cover and grill bag over medium heat 15 to 20 minutes, rotating bag 1/2 turn after 10 minutes, until salmon flakes easily with fork. Place bag on serving plate; unfold.

Substitute

For variety, try making this packet using halibut, tuna or swordfish instead of the salmon.

1 Serving: Cal. 285 (Cal. from Fat 135); Fat 15g (Sat. fat 2g); Chol. 95mg; Sodium 220mg; Carbs. 6g (Fiber 2g); Pro. 32g • **% Daily Value:** Vit. A 16%; Vit. C 24%; Calc. 10%; Iron 10% • **Exchanges:** 1 Vegetable, 4 1/2 Lean Meat **Carb. Choices:** 1/2

Caribbean Salmon Packets

**Prep: 20 min
Grill: 18 min
4 servings**

2 cups uncooked instant rice
1 can (14 ounces) chicken broth
1 small red bell pepper, chopped (1/2 cup)
2 medium green onions, sliced (2 tablespoons)
4 salmon fillets (6 ounces each), skin removed
1 teaspoon salt
1/2 cup chutney
1 cup pineapple chunks

1. Heat coals or gas grill for direct heat. Cut four 18 × 12-inch pieces of heavy-duty foil; spray half of one side of each piece with cooking spray.

2. In large bowl, mix rice and broth; let stand about 7 minutes or until broth is almost absorbed. Stir in bell pepper and onions. On sprayed side of each foil piece, place 3/4 cup rice mixture. Top rice with salmon. Sprinkle each salmon fillet with 1/4 teaspoon salt; top with 2 tablespoons chutney and 1/4 cup pineapple chunks.

3. Fold foil over salmon and rice mixture so edges meet. Seal edges, making tight 1/2-inch fold; fold again. Allow space on sides for circulation and expansion.

4. Cover and grill packets over medium heat 12 to 18 minutes, rotating packets 1/2 turn after 6 minutes, until salmon flakes easily with fork. Place packets on plates. Cut large X across top of each packet; fold back foil.

Success Tip

Soaking the rice in broth before grilling the packet ensures the rice will be done at the same time as the salmon.

1 Serving: Cal. 525 (Cal. from Fat 100); Fat 11g (Sat. fat 3g); Chol. 110mg; Sodium 1180mg; Carbs. 65g (Fiber 3g); Pro. 43g • **% Daily Value:** Vit. A 28%; Vit. C 40%; Calc. 4%; Iron 20% • **Exchanges:** 3 Starch, 1 Fruit, 1 Vegetable, 4 1/2 Very Lean Meat, 1 Fat • **Carb. Choices:** 4

Halibut Packets Vera Cruz

Prep: 10 min
Grill: 15 min
4 servings

Photo on page 172

4 small halibut steaks, 3/4 inch thick (about 1 1/2 pounds)
1 tablespoon vegetable oil
1/2 teaspoon salt
1/2 teaspoon ground cumin
1 cup green salsa (salsa verde)
1/2 cup fresh corn kernels or frozen whole kernel corn
1 small tomato, seeded and chopped (1/2 cup)
1 ripe avocado, pitted, peeled and chopped

1. Heat coals or gas grill for direct heat. Cut four 18 × 12-inch pieces of heavy-duty foil; spray half of one side of each piece with cooking spray.

2. Brush halibut lightly with oil. Sprinkle with salt and cumin. On sprayed side of each foil piece, place halibut. In small bowl, mix salsa, corn and tomato; spoon onto halibut.

3. Fold foil over halibut and salsa mixture so edges meet. Seal edges, making tight 1/2-inch fold; fold again. Allow space on sides for circulation and expansion.

4. Cover and grill packets over medium heat 10 to 15 minutes, rotating packets 1/2 turn after 5 minutes, until halibut flakes easily with fork. Place packets on plates. Cut large X across top of each packet; fold back foil. Sprinkle with avocado.

Shop Talk

Many different brands of green salsa are available, some spicier than others. Look for a heat level to your liking.

1 Serving: Cal. 290 (Cal. from Fat 110); Fat 12g (Sat. fat 2g); Chol. 90mg; Sodium 720mg; Carbs. 12g (Fiber 4g); Pro. 34g • **% Daily Value:** Vit. A 14%; Vit. C 14%; Calc. 4%; Iron 8% • **Exchanges:** 1 Starch, 4 Lean Meat • **Carb. Choices:** 1

Mexican Fish in Foil

Prep: 15 min
Grill: 20 min
6 servings

1 1/2 pounds halibut, cod or red snapper fillets, 1/2 to
    3/4 inch thick
1/4 cup sliced pimiento-stuffed olives
1 medium tomato, seeded and coarsely chopped (3/4 cup)
3 medium green onions, thinly sliced (3 tablespoons)
2 teaspoons capers
1 clove garlic, finely chopped
2 tablespoons lemon juice
1/4 teaspoon salt
1/8 teaspoon pepper
Lemon wedges

1. Heat coals or gas grill for direct heat. Cut six 18 × 12-inch pieces of heavy-duty foil.

2. If fish fillets are large, cut into 6 serving pieces. On one side of each foil piece, place piece of fish. In small bowl, mix olives, tomato, onions, capers and garlic; spoon over fish. Drizzle with lemon juice. Sprinkle with salt and pepper.

3. Fold foil over fish and tomato mixture so edges meet. Seal edges, making tight 1/2-inch fold; fold again. Allow space on sides for circulation and expansion.

4. Cover and grill packets over medium heat 15 to 20 minutes, rotating packets 1/2 turn after 10 minutes, until fish flakes easily with fork. Place packets on plates. Cut large X across top of each packet; fold back foil. Serve with lemon wedges.

Success Tip

To test fish for doneness, place a fork in the thickest part and gently twist. The fish will flake easily when done.

1 Serving: Cal. 115 (Cal. from Fat 20); Fat 2g (Sat. fat 0g); Chol. 60mg; Sodium 370mg; Carbs. 2g (Fiber 1g); Pro. 22g • **% Daily Value:** Vit. A 4%; Vit. C 4%; Calc. 2%; Iron 4% • **Exchanges:** 3 Very Lean Meat • **Carb. Choices:** 0

Seafaring Packets

Prep: 20 min
Grill: 20 min
8 servings

32 littleneck or cherrystone shell clams (about 2 1/2 pounds)
32 uncooked medium shrimp in shells (about 1 1/4 pounds),
    thawed if frozen
32 sea scallops (about 2 1/2 pounds)
8 ears corn, husked and each cut into fourths
32 large cherry tomatoes
Fresh chive stems or chopped fresh chives, if desired

Top with One of These Flavored Butters:
Lemon Butter (below)
Chive Butter (below)

1. Heat coals or gas grill for direct heat. Cut eight 18 × 12-inch pieces of heavy-duty foil. Make one of the Flavored Butters.

2. On one side of each foil piece, place clams, shrimp, scallops, corn and tomatoes. Drizzle 1 tablespoon of one of the Flavored Butters over seafood and vegetables on each foil piece.

3. Fold foil over seafood and vegetables so edges meet. Seal edges, making tight 1/2-inch fold; fold again. Allow space on sides for circulation and expansion.

4. Cover and grill packets over medium heat 15 to 20 minutes, rotating packets 1/2 turn after 10 minutes, until clams open, shrimp are pink and firm and vegetables are tender.* Place packets on plates. Cut large X across top of each packet; fold back foil. Top with chives.

*Cooking time may vary depending on ingredients selected.

Lemon Butter

1/2 cup butter or margarine, melted
1 tablespoon grated lemon peel

In small bowl, mix ingredients.

Chive Butter

1/2 cup butter or margarine, melted
1 tablespoon chopped fresh or 1 teaspoon freeze-dried chives

In small bowl, mix ingredients.

1 Serving: Cal. 300 (Cal. from Fat 125); Fat 14g (Sat. fat 8g); Chol. 90mg; Sodium 230mg; Carbs. 30g (Fiber 4g); Pro. 18g • % Daily Value: Vit. A 26%; Vit. C 20%; Calc. 6%; Iron 40% • Exchanges: 2 Starch, 2 Lean Meat, 1/2 Fat • Carb. Choices: 2

Herbed Seafood

**Prep: 20 min
Grill: 10 min
4 servings**

1/2 pound bay scallops
1/2 pound orange roughy fillets, cut into 1-inch pieces
1/2 pound uncooked fresh or frozen large shrimp,
      peeled and deveined
2 tablespoons chopped fresh or 2 teaspoons dried
      marjoram leaves
1/2 teaspoon grated lemon peel
1/8 teaspoon white pepper
3 tablespoons butter or margarine, melted
2 tablespoons lemon juice
4 cups hot cooked pasta or rice

1. Heat coals or gas grill for direct heat. Cut 18-inch square of heavy-duty foil; spray with cooking spray.

2. On center of foil square, arrange scallops, fish and shrimp, placing shrimp on top. Sprinkle with marjoram, lemon peel and white pepper. Drizzle with butter and lemon juice. Bring corners of foil up to center and seal loosely.

3. Cover and grill packet over medium heat 8 to 10 minutes, rotating packet 1/2 turn after 5 minutes, until scallops are white, fish flakes easily with fork and shrimp are pink and firm. Serve seafood mixture over pasta.

Substitute

Bay scallops are sweeter, more succulent and more expensive than the larger, more available (but less tender) sea scallops. If you use sea scallops, cut each in half.

1 Serving: Cal. 355 (Cal. from Fat 80); Fat 9g (Sat. fat 2g); Chol. 140mg; Sodium 270mg; Carbs. 41g (Fiber 2g); Pro. 30g • **% Daily Value:** Vit. A 12%; Vit. C 0%; Calc. 6%; Iron 24% • **Exchanges:** 3 Starch, 3 Very Lean Meat • **Carb. Choices:** 3

Lemon Pepper Halibut and Squash Packets

**Prep: 15 min
Grill: 20 min
4 servings**

1 pound halibut fillets, 1/2 to 3/4 inch thick
2 teaspoons dried basil leaves
1 teaspoon lemon pepper
1 teaspoon seasoned salt
1 medium zucchini, cut into 2 × 1-inch strips
1 medium yellow summer squash, cut into 2 × 1-inch strips
1 medium red bell pepper, cut into 1-inch pieces
2 tablespoons olive or vegetable oil

1. Heat coals or gas grill for direct heat. Cut four 18 × 12-inch pieces of heavy-duty foil; spray with cooking spray.

2. Cut halibut into 4 serving pieces if necessary. On one side of each foil piece, place piece of halibut. Sprinkle 1 teaspoon of the basil, 1/2 teaspoon of the lemon pepper and 1/2 teaspoon of the seasoned salt over halibut pieces. Top with zucchini, summer squash and bell pepper. Sprinkle with remaining basil, lemon pepper and seasoned salt. Drizzle with oil.

3. Fold foil over halibut and vegetables so edges meet. Seal edges, making tight 1/2-inch fold; fold again. Allow space on sides for circulation and expansion.

4. Cover and grill packets over medium heat 15 to 20 minutes, rotating packets 1/2 turn after 10 minutes, until halibut flakes with fork and vegetables are tender. Place packets on plates. Cut large X across top of each packet; fold back foil.

Try This

When you open the foil packet, keep the opening pointed away from you. That way, the hot steam that collected inside during grilling won't burn you.

1 Serving: Cal. 190 (Cal. from Fat 70); Fat 8g (Sat. fat 1g); Chol. 60mg; Sodium 390mg; Carbs. 6g (Fiber 2g); Pro. 23g • **% Daily Value:** Vit. A 44%; Vit. C 56%; Calc. 4%; Iron 6% • **Exchanges:** 1 Vegetable, 3 Lean Meat • **Carb. Choices:** 1/2

Veggie Burger Packets

Prep: 15 min
Grill: 25 min
4 servings

2 cups small whole mushrooms, cut in half
1 cup cut green beans
1/2 cup red bell pepper strips
1 medium red onion, cut into wedges
1/2 cup honey-mustard barbecue sauce
4 frozen vegetable burgers

1. Heat coals or gas grill for direct heat. Cut four 18 × 12-inch pieces of heavy-duty foil; spray half of one side of each piece with cooking spray.

2. In large bowl, mix mushrooms, green beans, bell pepper strips, onion and barbecue sauce. On sprayed side of each foil piece, place vegetable mixture. Top with burgers.

3. Fold foil over burgers and vegetables so edges meet. Seal edges, making tight 1/2-inch fold; fold again. Allow space on sides for circulation and expansion.

4. Cover and grill packets over medium heat 20 to 25 minutes, rotating packets 1/2 turn after 10 minutes, until vegetables are tender. Place packets on plates. Cut large X across top of each packet; fold back foil.

Try **This**

The honey-mustard barbecue sauce gives the vegetables and burgers a distinct flavor, but you can use any type of barbecue sauce you like.

1 Serving: Cal. 160 (Cal. from Fat 10); Fat 1g (Sat. fat 0g); Chol. 0mg; Sodium 590mg; Carbs. 31g (Fiber 9g); Pro. 15g • **% Daily Value:** Vit. A 18%; Vit. C 22%; Calc. 4%; Iron 18% • **Exchanges:** 1 Starch, 3 Vegetable, 1 1/2 Very Lean Meat • **Carb. Choices:** 2

Sweet Potato, Peach and Pork Packets

Prep: 10 min
Grill: 22 min
4 servings

1 large dark-orange sweet potato, peeled and thinly sliced
Dash of salt
2 tablespoons butter or margarine
4 pork boneless smoked chops
2 medium peaches or nectarines, peeled and sliced
Dash of ground cinnamon
4 medium green onions, sliced (1/4 cup)

1. Heat coals or gas grill for direct heat. Cut four 18 × 12-inch pieces of heavy-duty foil; spray with cooking spray.

2. On sprayed side of each foil piece, place one-fourth of the sweet potato slices. Sprinkle with salt. Cut butter into small pieces; sprinkle over sweet potato. Top with pork chops and peaches. Sprinkle with cinnamon.

3. Fold foil over pork mixture so edges meet. Seal edges, making tight 1/2-inch fold; fold again. Allow space on sides for circulation and expansion.

4. Cover and grill packets over medium heat 20 to 22 minutes, rotating packets 1/2 turn after 10 minutes, until sweet potatoes and peaches are tender. Place packets on plates. Cut large X across top of each packet; fold back foil. Sprinkle with onions.

Shop Talk

Smoked pork chops can be found at the fresh meat counter at the grocery store. Because you buy the chops smoked, much of the work in preparing them has already been done. Just cook them until they are thoroughly heated.

1 Serving: Cal. 245 (Cal. from Fat 110); Fat 12g (Sat. fat 6g); Chol. 55mg; Sodium 1050mg; Carbs. 17g (Fiber 3g); Pro. 17g • **% Daily Value:** Vit. A 100%; Vit. C 14%; Calc. 2%; Iron 8% • **Exchanges:** 1/2 Starch, 1/2 Fruit, 2 Lean Meat, 1 1/2 Fat • **Carb. Choices:** 1

Savory Cheese Potatoes

Prep: 5 min
Grill: 25 min
5 servings

4 cups frozen O'Brien potatoes (from 28-ounce bag)
1/2 cup ranch dressing
1 cup shredded Cheddar-American cheese blend (4 ounces)
2 tablespoons grated Parmesan cheese

1. Heat coals or gas grill for direct heat. Cut 18-inch square of heavy-duty foil; spray with cooking spray.

2. On one side of foil square, place potatoes. Drizzle with dressing; mix gently. Sprinkle with shredded cheese blend.

3. Fold foil over potatoes so edges meet. Seal edges, making tight 1/2-inch fold; fold again. Allow space on sides for circulation and expansion.

4. Cover and grill packet over medium heat 20 to 25 minutes, rotating packet 1/2 turn after 10 minutes, until potatoes are tender. Place packet on serving platter. Cut large X across top of packet; fold back foil. Sprinkle with Parmesan cheese.

Healthful Hint

Substitute reduced-fat ranch dressing for the regular. You'll save about 45 calories and 5 grams of fat per serving.

1 Serving: Cal. 350 (Cal. from Fat 190); Fat 21g (Sat. fat 7g); Chol. 35mg; Sodium 450mg; Carbs. 30g (Fiber 3g); Pro. 10g • **% Daily Value:** Vit. A 8%; Vit. C 20%; Calc. 20%; Iron 4% • **Exchanges:** 2 Starch, 1/2 High-Fat Meat, 3 Fat • **Carb. Choices:** 2

Parmesan Potatoes

Prep: 10 min
Grill: 23 min
4 servings

4 medium potatoes, thinly sliced
1/2 teaspoon salt
1/4 cup Italian-style dry bread crumbs
2 tablespoons grated Parmesan cheese
2 tablespoons butter or margarine, melted
1 tablespoon chopped fresh or 1 teaspoon dried basil leaves

1. Heat coals or gas grill for direct heat. Cut two 30 × 18-inch pieces of heavy-duty foil.

2. Divide potato slices between foil pieces. Sprinkle with salt. In small bowl, mix remaining ingredients; sprinkle over potatoes. Wrap foil securely around potatoes; pierce top of foil once or twice with fork to vent steam.

3. Cover and grill packets, seam side up, over medium heat 18 to 23 minutes, rotating packets 1/2 turn after 10 minutes, until potatoes are tender. Place packets on plates; unfold foil.

Serving **Idea**

Because of their simple, fresh flavor, these potatoes are a perfect accompaniment to grilled steak, pork chops or chicken.

1 Serving: Cal. 225 (Cal. from Fat 65); Fat 7g (Sat. fat 4g); Chol. 20mg; Sodium 460mg; Carbs. 36g (Fiber 3g); Pro. 5g • **% Daily Value:** Vit. A 6%; Vit. C 12%; Calc. 6%; Iron 12% • **Exchanges:** 2 Starch, 1/2 Other Carbs., 1 Fat • **Carb. Choices:** 2 1/2

Black Bean- and Rice-Stuffed Peppers

Prep: 10 min
Grill: 20 min
6 servings

1 can (15 ounces) black beans, rinsed and drained
3/4 cup cooked white rice
4 medium green onions, sliced (1/4 cup)
1/4 cup chopped fresh cilantro
2 tablespoons vegetable oil
2 tablespoons lime juice
1 clove garlic, finely chopped
1/4 teaspoon salt
3 large bell peppers (any color), cut lengthwise in half
    and seeds removed
1 roma (plum) tomato, diced
Additional chopped fresh cilantro, if desired

1. Heat coals or gas grill for direct heat. Cut three 18 × 12-inch pieces of heavy-duty foil; spray with cooking spray.

2. In large bowl, mix beans, rice, onions, cilantro, oil, lime juice, garlic and salt. On one side of each foil piece, place 2 bell pepper halves. Fill with bean mixture.

3. Fold foil over peppers so edges meet. Seal edges, making tight 1/2-inch fold; fold again. Allow space on sides for circulation and expansion.

4. Cover and grill packets over medium heat 15 to 20 minutes, rotating packets 1/2 turn after 10 minutes, until peppers are tender. Place packets on serving platter. Cut large X across top of each packet; fold back foil. Sprinkle with tomato and additional cilantro.

Try **This**

If you like, sprinkle the cooked peppers with shredded Cheddar or Monterey Jack cheese.

1 Serving: Cal. 180 (Cal. from Fat 45); Fat 5g (Sat. fat 1g); Chol. 0mg; Sodium 410mg; Carbs. 32g (Fiber 7g); Pro. 8g • **% Daily Value:** Vit. A 98%; Vit. C 100%; Calc. 6%; Iron 14% • **Exchanges:** 1 1/2 Starch, 1 Vegetable, 1 Fat • **Carb. Choices:** 2

Garden Vegetable Medley

Prep: 15 min
Grill: 30 min
4 servings

2 medium Yukon gold potatoes, cut into 1/8-inch slices
1 1/2 cups baby-cut carrots
4 ounces whole green beans
2 tablespoons butter or margarine, melted
1/2 teaspoon salt
1/4 teaspoon dried oregano leaves
1/4 teaspoon garlic pepper
1/4 teaspoon ground cumin

1. Heat coals or gas grill for direct heat. Cut 24 × 18-inch piece of heavy-duty foil.

2. In large bowl, toss all ingredients; spoon onto foil. Wrap foil securely around vegetable mixture. Allow space on sides for circulation and expansion.

3. Cover and grill packet over medium heat 25 to 30 minutes, rotating packet 1/2 turn after 15 minutes, until vegetables are tender. Place packet on plate; unfold foil.

Try This

This is a great packet to toss together after a trip to your local farmers' market. Feel free to substitute your favorite fresh veggies.

1 Serving: Cal. 135 (Cal. from Fat 55); Fat 6g (Sat. fat 4g); Chol. 15mg; Sodium 360mg; Carbs. 19g (Fiber 4g); Pro. 2g • **% Daily Value:** Vit. A 100%; Vit. C 10%; Calc. 4%; Iron 8% • **Exchanges:** 1 Starch, 1 Vegetable, 1 Fat • **Carb. Choices:** 1

Dilled Baby Carrots

Prep: 10 min
Grill: 1 hr
4 servings

1 bag (1-pound) baby-cut carrots
2 teaspoons dried dill weed
1 teaspoon sugar
1 teaspoon lemon juice
1 tablespoon butter or margarine

1. Heat coals or gas grill for direct heat. Cut 18 × 12-inch piece of heavy-duty foil.

2. Place carrots on foil. Sprinkle with dill weed, sugar and lemon juice. Cut butter into small pieces; sprinkle over carrots.

3. Wrap foil securely around carrots. Allow space on sides for circulation and expansion.

4. Cover and grill packet, seam side up, over medium heat about 1 hour, rotating packet 1/2 turn after 30 minutes, until carrots are tender. Place packet on plate; unfold foil.

Success Tip

Using store-bought lemon juice will work fine in this recipe, but creating your own juice by squeezing a fresh lemon will add more zing.

1 Serving: Cal. 70 (Cal. from Fat 25); Fat 3g (Sat. fat 1g); Chol. 10mg; Sodium 60mg; Carbs. 13g (Fiber 3g); Pro. 1g • **% Daily Value:** Vit. A 100%; Vit. C 8%; Calc. 2%; Iron 2% • **Exchanges:** 2 Vegetable, 1/2 Fat • **Carb. Choices:** 1

Béarnaise Corn and Potato Packets

Prep: 15 min
Grill: 35 min
4 servings

1 package (20 ounces) refrigerated diced potatoes with onions
2 ears corn, husks removed and ears cut in half
1/4 cup butter or margarine, melted
2 tablespoons Dijon mustard
1/2 teaspoon salt
1/2 teaspoon garlic pepper
1/4 teaspoon dried tarragon leaves
2 tablespoons chopped fresh chives

1. Heat coals or gas grill for direct heat. Cut four 18 × 12-inch pieces of heavy-duty foil; spray with cooking spray.

2. On one side of each foil piece, place one-fourth of the potatoes and 1 piece corn. In small bowl, mix remaining ingredients except chives; drizzle over potatoes and corn. Turn corn to coat and gently stir potatoes.

3. Fold foil over potatoes and corn so edges meet. Seal edges, making tight 1/2-inch fold; fold again. Allow space on sides for circulation and expansion.

4. Cover and grill packets over medium heat 25 to 35 minutes, rotating packets 1/2 turn after 15 minutes, until potatoes and corn are tender. Place packets on plates. Cut large X across top of each packet; unfold foil. Sprinkle with chives.

Try This

Try this recipe with dried basil, thyme or Italian seasoning instead of the tarragon. Because the flavor of tarragon is more potent, use 1/2 teaspoon of the other herbs.

1 Serving: Cal. 300 (Cal. from Fat 115); Fat 13g (Sat. fat 7g); Chol. 30mg; Sodium 570mg; Carbs. 41g (Fiber 4g); Pro. 5g • **% Daily Value:** Vit. A 12%; Vit. C 12%; Calc. 2%; Iron 4% • **Exchanges:** 2 Starch, 1 Other Carbs., 2 Fat • **Carb. Choices:** 3

Sweet Potato and Pepper Packet

Prep: 15 min
Grill: 20 min
4 servings

2 medium dark-orange sweet potatoes, peeled and cut into
1-inch pieces
1 medium yellow bell pepper, cut into 1-inch pieces
2 tablespoons butter or margarine, melted
1 tablespoon honey
1/2 teaspoon seasoned salt
1 tablespoon chopped fresh chives

1. Heat coals or gas grill for direct heat. Cut 18-inch square of heavy-duty foil; spray with cooking spray.

2. On center of foil, place sweet potatoes and bell pepper. In small bowl, mix butter, honey and seasoned salt; drizzle over potato mixture and stir to mix.

3. Fold foil over vegetables so edges meet. Seal edges, making tight 1/2-inch fold; fold again. Allow space on sides for circulation and expansion.

4. Cover and grill packet over medium heat 15 to 20 minutes, rotating packet 1/2 turn after 10 minutes, until sweet potatoes are tender. Place packet on serving platter. Cut large X across top of packet; unfold foil. Sprinkle with chives.

Healthful Hint

Sweet potatoes are an excellent source of beta-carotene, an antioxidant thought to reduce the risk of cancer.

1 Serving: Cal. 160 (Cal. from Fat 55); Fat 6g (Sat. fat 4g); Chol. 15mg; Sodium 220mg; Carbs. 25g (Fiber 3g); Pro. 2g • **% Daily Value:** Vit. A 100%; Vit. C 60%; Calc. 2%; Iron 2% • **Exchanges:** 1 Starch, 1 Vegetable, 1 Fat • **Carb. Choices:** 1 1/2

Basil, Carrot and Cauliflower Packet

3 cups cauliflowerets
1 cup baby-cut carrots, cut lengthwise in half
1 small red onion, cut into thin wedges
2 tablespoons olive or vegetable oil
1/2 teaspoon garlic pepper
1/2 teaspoon salt
1/4 cup sliced ripe olives
2 tablespoons chopped fresh basil leaves

1. Heat coals or gas grill for direct heat. Cut 18-inch square of heavy-duty foil; spray with cooking spray.

2. On center of foil, place cauliflowerets, carrots and onion. Drizzle with oil; sprinkle with garlic pepper and salt. Stir gently to mix.

3. Fold foil over vegetables so edges meet. Seal edges, making tight 1/2-inch fold; fold again. Allow space on sides for circulation and expansion.

4. Cover and grill packet over medium heat 13 to 18 minutes, rotating packet 1/2 turn after 6 minutes, until vegetables are tender. Place packet on serving platter. Cut large X across top of packet; unfold foil. Gently stir in olives and basil.

Shop Talk

Buy cauliflower that is firm and creamy white with compact flowerets. The size of the head doesn't affect the quality. Avoid heads with any sign of mold or wilted leaves. To store it, wrap cauliflower tightly and refrigerate for 3 to 5 days.

1 Serving: Cal. 115 (Cal. from Fat 70); Fat 8g (Sat. fat g); Chol. 0mg; Sodium 400mg; Carbs. 9g (Fiber 3g); Pro. 2g • **% Daily Value:** Vit. A 100%; Vit. C 32%; Calc. 4%; Iron 4% • **Exchanges:** 2 Vegetable, 1 1/2 Fat • **Carb. Choices:** 1/2

Indoor Grilling

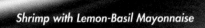

Shrimp with Lemon-Basil Mayonnaise

Jumbo Southwestern Burgers

Prep: 15 min
Grill: 12 min
4 servings

2 pounds lean (at least 80%) ground beef
2 tablespoons finely chopped onion
2 tablespoons chopped drained green chilies (from 4.5-ounce can)
1 can (4 ounces) mushroom pieces and stems, well drained and
    finely chopped
4 slices Monterey Jack cheese with jalapeño chilies, 2 × 1 × 1/4 inch
    (about 2 ounces)
4 kaiser rolls, split and toasted
1/4 cup salsa

1. Heat closed medium-size contact grill for 5 to 10 minutes. In large bowl, mix beef, onion and chilies. Shape mixture into 8 thin patties, each about 5 inches in diameter. Mound 1/4 of the mushrooms on center of 4 of the patties. Top each with 1 slice cheese. Place remaining beef patties on top; pinch edges to seal securely.

2. Place patties on grill. Close grill. Grill 10 to 12 minutes or until meat thermometer inserted in center of beef reads 160°F and patties are no longer pink in center.

3. Serve burgers in kaiser rolls with salsa.

Serving Idea

These flavor-bursting jumbo burgers beg for jumbo tortilla chips. Pick some with jumbo flavor such as taco or extra cheese.

1 Sandwich: Cal. 670 (Cal. from Fat 350); Fat 39g (Sat. fat 16g); Chol. 140mg; Sodium 710mg; Carbs. 29g (Fiber 2g); Pro. 51g • **% Daily Value:** Vit. A 8%; Vit. C 2%; Calc. 18%; Iron 32% • **Exchanges:** 2 Starch, 6 1/2 Medium-Fat Meat, 1/2 Fat • **Carb. Choices:** 2

Teriyaki Burgers

Prep: 10 min
Grill: 10 min
4 sandwiches

1 pound lean (at least 80%) ground beef
3 tablespoons teriyaki marinade
1/3 cup finely chopped water chestnuts
1/8 teaspoon pepper
2 medium green onions, finely chopped (2 tablespoons)
1 clove garlic, finely chopped
2 tablespoons teriyaki marinade
4 slices (1/2 inch thick) French bread, toasted if desired
1 small bell pepper (any color), cut into rings

1. Heat closed medium-size contact grill for 5 to 10 minutes. In medium bowl, mix beef, 3 tablespoons marinade, the water chestnuts, pepper, onions and garlic. Shape mixture into 4 patties, each about 3/4 inch thick.

2. Place patties on grill. Close grill. Grill 8 to 10 minutes, brushing with 2 tablespoons marinade, until meat thermometer inserted in center reads 160°F and patties are no longer pink in center.

3. Serve burgers on French bread, and top with bell pepper rings.

Shop Talk

Look for teriyaki marinade in the Asian-foods aisle of your grocery store. It's usually stocked with the bottles of soy sauce and hoisin sauce.

1 Sandwich: Cal. 265 (Cal. from Fat 145); Fat 16g (Sat. fat 6g); Chol. 65mg; Sodium 920mg; Carbs. 7g (Fiber 1g); Pro. 23g • **% Daily Value:** Vit. A 24%; Vit. C 30%; Calc. 2%; Iron 14% • **Exchanges:** 1 Vegetable, 3 Medium-Fat Meat, 1/2 Fat • **Carb. Choices:** 1/2

Tex-Mex Marinated Sirloin

Prep: 10 min
Marinate: 2 hr
Grill: 10 min
6 servings

1 1/2-pound beef boneless top sirloin steak, about 1 inch thick
1/4 cup soy sauce
2 tablespoons lemon juice
1 tablespoon vegetable oil
1 teaspoon ground cumin
1 teaspoon chili powder
2 cloves garlic, finely chopped

1. Pierce beef steak with fork several times on both sides. In shallow glass or plastic dish or heavy-duty plastic food-storage bag, mix remaining ingredients. Add beef; turn to coat. Cover dish or seal bag and refrigerate 2 to 3 hours, turning beef occasionally.

2. Heat closed medium-size contact grill for 5 to 10 minutes. Remove beef from marinade; discard marinade. Place beef on grill. Close grill. Grill beef 8 to 10 minutes for medium doneness.

3. To serve, cut beef across grain into 1/2-inch slices.

Shop Talk

Shave a few minutes of prep time off this Texan-inspired sirloin by using chopped garlic. Look for it in jars near the produce section of your supermarket.

1 Serving: Cal. 140 (Cal. from Fat 45); Fat 5g (Sat. fat 1g); Chol. 60mg; Sodium 500mg; Carbs. 1g (Fiber 0g); Pro. 23g • **% Daily Value:** Vit. A 0%; Vit. C 0%; Calc. 0%; Iron 12% • **Exchanges:** 3 Very Lean Meat, 1 Fat • **Carb. Choices:** 0

Béarnaise Steaks with Mushrooms

Prep: 10 min
Grill: 12 min
4 servings

1/4 cup butter or margarine, softened
1 tablespoon chopped fresh chives
1/4 teaspoon dried tarragon leaves
1 package (8 ounces) sliced fresh mushrooms
1/2 cup very thinly sliced red onion (cut in half, then sliced)
1/2 cup zesty Italian dressing
1 1/2-ounce beef boneless sirloin steak, about 1 inch thick

1. Heat closed medium-size contact grill for 5 to 10 minutes. In small bowl, mix butter, chives and tarragon. Refrigerate until serving.

2. In medium bowl, mix mushrooms, onion and dressing. With slotted spoon, place mushrooms and onion on grill; reserve dressing in bowl. Close grill. Grill 3 to 5 minutes or until vegetables are crisp-tender. Remove from grill; cover to keep warm.

3. Brush both sides of beef steak with dressing from bowl. Place beef on grill. Close grill. Grill 5 to 7 minutes for medium-rare, brushing with dressing once or twice, or grill until desired doneness.

4. To serve, cut beef into serving pieces. Serve with vegetables and butter mixture.

Success **Tip**

It's important to let the steak rest a couple of minutes after you take it off the grill. That way, you won't lose all the flavorful juices when you cut into it.

1 Serving: Cal. 555 (Cal. from Fat 385); Fat 43g (Sat. fat 15g); Chol. 135mg; Sodium 420mg; Carbs. 7g (Fiber 1g); Pro. 36g • **% Daily Value:** Vit. A 12%; Vit. C 2%; Calc. 4%; Iron 24% • **Exchanges:** 1 Vegetable, 4 Medium-Fat Meat, 3 1/2 Fat • **Carb. Choices:** 1/2

Spicy Pork Chops

Prep: 5 min
Marinate: 30 min
Grill: 10 min
6 servings

1 tablespoon chili powder
1 tablespoon vegetable oil
1 teaspoon ground cumin
1/4 teaspoon ground red pepper (cayenne)
1/4 teaspoon salt
1 large clove garlic, finely chopped
6 pork loin or rib chops, about 1/2 inch thick (about 2 pounds)

1. In small bowl, mix all ingredients except pork. Cut outer edge of fat on pork chops diagonally at 1-inch intervals to prevent curling (do not cut into meat). Spread chili powder mixture evenly on both sides of pork. Cover and refrigerate at least 30 minutes.

2. Heat closed medium-size contact grill for 5 to 10 minutes. Place pork on grill. Close grill. Grill 8 to 10 minutes or until no longer pink when cut near bone.

Shop Talk

Look for individually packed pork chops in the freezer section of your grocery store. They're a handy way to buy pork chops because you only buy only as many as you need.

1 Serving: Cal. 195 (Cal. from Fat 100); Fat 11g (Sat. fat 3g); Chol. 65mg; Sodium 150mg; Carbs. 1g (Fiber 0g); Pro. 23g • **% Daily Value:** Vit. A 8%; Vit. C 0%; Calc. 0%; Iron 6% • **Exchanges:** 3 Lean Meat, 1/2 Fat • **Carb. Choices:** 0

Pesto-Stuffed
Pork Chops

Prep: 15 min
Grill: 6 min
4 servings

4 pork boneless loin chops, 3/4 to 1 inch thick
1/4 cup basil pesto
1/2 teaspoon seasoned salt
1/2 teaspoon coarsely ground black pepper

1. Heat closed medium-size contact grill for 5 to 10 minutes. With sharp knife, make 1 1/2-inch slit in side of each pork chop, then cut into chop to make pocket (do not enlarge slit). Place 1 tablespoon pesto in each pocket. Sprinkle pork with seasoned salt and pepper.

2. Place pork on grill with pockets toward back of grill to help keep pesto in pockets.) Close grill. Grill 4 to 6 minutes or until pork is no longer pink in center.

Substitute

All sorts of flavored pestos are on the market, from cilantro to mint. You may even want to try whipping up a batch of your own. You'll find several recipes for pesto on page 299.

1 Serving: Cal. 295 (Cal. from Fat 190); Fat 21g (Sat. fat 6g); Chol. 70mg; Sodium 470mg; Carbs. 1g (Fiber 0g); Pro. 25g • **% Daily Value:** Vit. A 2%; Vit. C 0%; Calc. 6%; Iron 6% • **Exchanges:** 3 1/2 Medium-Fat Meat, 1/2 Fat • **Carb. Choices:** 0

Pork Ribs with Barbecue Sauce

Prep: 15 min
Bake: 2 hr
Grill: 24 min
4 servings

3 tablespoons packed brown sugar
1 tablespoon vegetable oil
4 teaspoons chopped fresh or 1 1/2 teaspoons dried thyme leaves
1/2 teaspoon salt
1/4 teaspoon pepper
3 pounds pork loin back ribs
1 cup barbecue sauce

1. Heat oven to 300°F. In small bowl, mix all ingredients except ribs and barbecue sauce. Rub mixture on ribs.

2. In 13 × 9-inch pan, place ribs. Cover and bake 2 hours or until no longer pink when cut near bone; drain ribs.

3. Heat closed medium-size contact grill for 5 to 10 minutes. Place ribs on grill. Close grill. Grill 20 to 24 minutes, brushing ribs with barbecue sauce 2 or 3 times during last 10 minutes of grilling.

Try This

The spice level of these pork chops is determined by the type of barbecue sauce you buy. Go mild or wild—it's up to you.

1 Serving: Cal. 795 (Cal. from Fat 475); Fat 53g (Sat. fat 19g); Chol. 200mg; Sodium 1070mg; Carbs. 32g (Fiber 0g); Pro. 48g • **% Daily Value:** Vit. A 2%; Vit. C 2%; Calc. 10%; Iron 20% • **Exchanges:** 2 Other Carbs., 7 High-Fat Meat • **Carb. Choices:** 2

Bratwurst Patties with Apple-Mustard Glaze

Prep: 5 min
Grill: 14 min
4 servings

1/4 cup frozen (thawed) apple juice concentrate
1/2 teaspoon ground mustard
1/4 teaspoon ground ginger
1 medium unpeeled apple, cut into 1/4-inch slices
4 bratwurst patties (3 to 4 ounces each), thawed if frozen

1. Heat closed medium-size contact grill for 5 to 10 minutes. In small bowl, mix apple juice concentrate, mustard and ginger. Add apple slices; toss to coat. Reserve juice mixture. With slotted spoon or tongs, place apple slices on grill; reserve juice mixture. Close grill. Grill 3 to 4 minutes or until apples are crisp-tender. Remove from grill; cover to keep warm.

2. Place bratwurst patties on grill. Close grill. Grill 3 minutes. Brush both sides of bratwurst with reserved juice mixture. Close grill. Grill 5 to 7 minutes longer, brushing once or twice with juice mixture, until bratwurst are no longer pink in center. Serve with apples. Discard any remaining apple juice mixture.

Serving Idea

These fruity bratwurst patties make a nice breakfast or brunch main dish. Serve them with scrambled eggs and toasted English muffins.

1 Serving: Cal. 360 (Cal. from Fat 250); Fat 28g (Sat. fat 10g); Chol. 60mg; Sodium 930mg; Carbs. 16g (Fiber 1g); Pro. 11g • **% Daily Value:** Vit. A 2%; Vit. C 2%; Calc. 2%; Iron 4% • **Exchanges:** 1 Fruit, 1 1/2 High-Fat Meat, 3 1/2 Fat • **Carb. Choices:** 1

Cajun Sausage Kabobs

Prep: 15 min
Grill: 14 min
4 servings

1 pound fully cooked smoked Polish or kielbasa sausage, cut into
    3/4- to 1-inch pieces
1 medium red or green bell pepper, cut into 1- to 1 1/2-inch pieces
16 refrigerated potato wedges (from 20-ounce bag)
1/2 cup chili sauce
2 tablespoons Worcestershire sauce
1 to 2 teaspoons red pepper sauce
1/2 teaspoon dried thyme leaves

1. Heat closed medium-size contact grill for 5 to 10 minutes. On each of eight 6- to 8-inch metal skewers, alternately thread sausage, bell pepper and potatoes, leaving 1/4-inch space between each piece. In small bowl, mix chili sauce, Worcestershire sauce, pepper sauce and thyme.

2. Place 4 kabobs on grill. Close grill. Grill 3 minutes. Brush both sides of kabobs with chili sauce mixture. Grill 3 to 4 minutes longer, brushing with sauce mixture 2 or 3 times, until peppers and potatoes are tender. Repeat with remaining kabobs.

Success Tip

Why leave a 1/4-inch space between each piece? It helps the kabob pieces cook evenly.

1 Serving: Cal. 460 (Cal. from Fat 290); Fat 32g (Sat. fat 12g); Chol. 70mg; Sodium 1570mg; Carbs. 28g (Fiber 2g); Pro. 14g • **% Daily Value:** Vit. A 44%; Vit. C 56%; Calc. 4%; Iron 10% • **Exchanges:** 2 Starch, 1 High-Fat Meat, 4 1/2 Fat • **Carb. Choices:** 2

Italian Sausages with Tomato Salsa

1 medium tomato, seeded and chopped (3/4 cup)
2 medium green onions, sliced (2 tablespoons)
1 jalapeño chili, seeded and finely chopped
2 tablespoons Italian dressing
4 uncooked hot or mild Italian sausage links (about 1 pound)
4 hot dog buns, split

1. In small glass or plastic bowl, mix tomato, onions and chili; toss with dressing. Cover and refrigerate at least 30 minutes.

2. Heat closed medium-size contact grill for 5 to 10 minutes. Place sausages on grill. Close grill. Grill 15 to 17 minutes or until no longer pink in center. Serve on buns with tomato salsa.

Try This

You can easily "class up" these Italian sausages by using a different type of bread. Try dark whole-grain or herb-flavored buns instead of the hot dog buns.

1 Serving: Cal. 385 (Cal. from Fat 205); Fat 23g (Sat. fat 7g); Chol. 55mg; Sodium 940mg; Carbs. 26g (Fiber 2g); Pro. 18g • **% Daily Value:** Vit. A 6%; Vit. C 16%; Calc. 8%; Iron 14% • **Exchanges:** 2 Starch, 2 High-Fat Meat, 1/2 Fat • **Carb. Choices:** 2

Double-Cheese and Bacon Sandwiches

Prep: 10 min
Grill: 20 min
4 sandwiches

8 slices bacon
4 slices red onion, 1/4 inch thick
4 slices (3/4 ounces each) Cheddar cheese
4 slices (3/4 ounces each) mozzarella cheese
8 slices sourdough or Vienna bread, 1/2 inch thick

1. Heat closed medium-size contact grill for 5 to 10 minutes. Place bacon on grill. (If necessary, cook 4 slices at a time.) Close grill. Grill 3 to 4 minutes or until browned. Remove bacon from grill; drain on paper towels. Cut bacon slices crosswise in half.

2. Carefully scrape most of drippings from grill into drip tray, using rubber scraper. Place onion on grill. Close grill. Grill 4 to 6 minutes or until tender.

3. To make sandwiches, layer Cheddar cheese, bacon, onion and mozzarella cheese between bread slices. Place 2 sandwiches on grill. Close grill. Grill 3 to 5 minutes or until bread is toasted and cheese is melted. Repeat with remaining sandwiches.

Try This

This tasty version of a classic comfort food can be tailor-made to please everyone at the table. Experiment with different types of cheeses and breads to find your family's favorite.

1 Sandwich: Cal. 330 (Cal. from Fat 160); Fat 18g (Sat. fat 9g); Chol. 45mg; Sodium 660mg; Carbs. 23g (Fiber 1g); Pro. 19g • **% Daily Value:** Vit. A 2%; Vit. C 0%; Calc. 8%; Iron 20% • **Exchanges:** 1 1/2 Starch, 2 High-Fat Meat, 1/2 Fat • **Carb. Choices:** 1 1/2

Cilantro- and Jalapeño-Topped Chicken Breasts

Prep: 10 min
Grill: 8 min
4 servings

4 boneless, skinless chicken breast halves (about 1 1/4 pounds)
1 teaspoon chili powder
1/2 teaspoon ground cumin
1/2 teaspoon garlic pepper
1/2 teaspoon salt
1/4 cup green or red hot pepper (jalapeño) jelly
2 tablespoons lime juice
2 tablespoons chopped fresh cilantro

1. Heat closed medium-size contact grill for 5 to 10 minutes. Sprinkle chicken with chili powder, cumin, garlic pepper and salt. Place chicken on grill. Close grill. Grill 6 to 8 minutes or until juice of chicken is no longer pink when centers of thickest pieces are cut.

2. Meanwhile, in small microwavable bowl, mix jelly and lime juice. Microwave uncovered on High 40 to 60 seconds, stirring every 20 seconds, until melted and smooth. Stir in cilantro.

3. To serve, spoon warm jelly mixture over chicken.

Shop Talk

As you might guess from its name, jalapeño jelly adds a jalapeño flavor to foods and can be made from green or red chilies. It varies in spiciness, but unlike salsa, it is smooth in texture. Look for bottles or jars of jalapeño jelly in the same aisle as the salsas at your supermarket.

1 Serving: Cal. 200 (Cal. from Fat 35); Fat 4g (Sat. fat 1g); Chol. 75mg; Sodium 670mg; Carbs. 14g (Fiber 1g); Pro. 27g • **% Daily Value:** Vit. A 4%; Vit. C 2%; Calc. 2%; Iron 8% • **Exchanges:** 1 Other Carbs., 4 Very Lean Meat • **Carb. Choices:** 1

Chicken Fajita Quesadillas

Prep: 5 min
Grill: 27 min
4 servings

2 tablespoons taco seasoning mix (from 1.25-ounce envelope)
2 tablespoons lime juice
1 teaspoon honey
1 pound chicken breast tenders (not breaded)
2 cups frozen stir-fry bell peppers and onions (from 1-pound bag),
    thawed and drained
8 flour tortillas (8 inches in diameter)
1 cup shredded Colby-Monterey Jack cheese (4 ounces)
1 medium avocado, pitted, peeled and thinly sliced

1. Heat closed medium-size contact grill for 5 to 10 minutes. In medium bowl, mix taco seasoning mix, lime juice and honey. Add chicken; toss to coat. Set aside.

2. Place stir-fry vegetables on grill. Close grill. Grill 2 to 3 minutes or until crisp-tender. Remove from grill; cover to keep warm.

3. Place chicken on grill. Close grill. Grill 3 to 4 minutes or until chicken is no longer pink in center.

4. On 4 tortillas, layer stir-fry vegetables, chicken, cheese and avocado. (Cut chicken pieces lengthwise in half if very large.) Top with remaining tortillas. Place 1 quesadilla at a time on grill. Close grill. Grill 3 to 5 minutes or until golden brown and cheese is melted. Cut each quesadilla into 4 wedges.

Serving Idea

Serve these zesty quesadillas with toppings such as sour cream, salsa and ripe olives.

1 Serving: Cal. 640 (Cal. from Fat 250); Fat 28g (Sat. fat 10g); Chol. 95mg; Sodium 1070mg; Carbs. 62g (Fiber 6g); Pro. 41g • **% Daily Value:** Vit. A 22%; Vit. C 48%; Calc. 34%; Iron 26% • **Exchanges:** 3 1/2 Starch, 1 Vegetable, 4 Lean Meat, 2 1/2 Fat • **Carb. Choices:** 4

Peppered Sage Turkey Mignons

Prep: 10 min
Grill: 12 min
4 servings

4 slices bacon
1 turkey breast tenderloin (3/4 to 1 pound)
1 tablespoon olive or vegetable oil
1 teaspoon dried sage leaves
1/2 teaspoon garlic pepper
1/4 teaspoon salt

1. Heat closed medium-size contact grill for 5 to 10 minutes. Place bacon in grill. Close grill. Grill 2 to 3 minutes or until brown but not crisp. Drain on paper towels just until cool enough to handle.

2. Cut turkey tenderloin crosswise into 4 pieces. Brush both sides of each piece with oil; sprinkle with sage, garlic pepper and salt. Wrap 1 bacon slice around each turkey piece; secure with toothpick. (Fold or press together the end piece to resemble round piece.)

3. Place turkey on grill. Close grill. Grill 7 to 9 minutes or until turkey is no longer pink in center.

Healthful Hint

Turkey and other poultry should be stored in the coldest part of your refrigerator as soon as you get it home from the grocery store. Be sure to use it by the "sell-by" date, as poultry tends to lose its freshness fast.

1 Serving: Cal. 135 (Cal. from Fat 65); Fat 7g (Sat. fat 2g); Chol. 50mg; Sodium 280mg; Carbs. 0g (Fiber 0g); Pro. 18g • **% Daily Value:** Vit. A 0%; Vit. C 0%; Calc. 0%; Iron 6% • **Exchanges:** 2 1/2 Lean Meat • **Carb. Choices:** 0

Turkey Patty Melts

Prep: 10 min
Grill: 12 min
4 sandwiches

2 medium onions, thinly sliced
1 pound ground turkey
1 tablespoon Dijon mustard
2 teaspoons chopped fresh or 1/2 teaspoon dried thyme leaves
2 teaspoons chopped fresh or 1/2 teaspoon dried oregano leaves
1/2 teaspoon salt
1/8 teaspoon pepper
1 clove garlic, finely chopped
4 slices (3/4 ounces each) Swiss cheese
4 hamburger buns, split

1. Brush medium-size contact grill with vegetable oil. Heat closed contact grill for 5 to 10 minutes. Place onions on grill. Close grill. Grill 5 to 7 minutes or until golden brown. Remove from grill; cover to keep warm.

2. Meanwhile, in medium bowl, mix remaining ingredients except cheese and buns. Shape mixture into 4 patties, each about 3/4 inch thick.

3. Place patties on grill. Close grill. Grill 8 to 10 minutes or until no longer pink in center. Top patties with cheese. Grill uncovered about 1 minute longer or until cheese is melted.

4. Serve burgers in buns with onions.

Try This

Weep no more! If your grocery store has a salad bar, pick up some sliced onions there instead of chopping them yourself.

1 Sandwich: Cal. 385 (Cal. from Fat 135); Fat 15g (Sat. fat 6g); Chol. 95mg; Sodium 760mg; Carbs. 28g (Fiber 2g); Pro. 35g • **% Daily Value:** Vit. A 6%; Vit. C 2%; Calc. 28%; Iron 14% • **Exchanges:** 2 Starch, 4 Lean Meat • **Carb. Choices:** 2

Shrimp with Lemon-Basil Mayonnaise

Prep: 10 min
Grill: 6 min
4 servings

Photo on page 212

2 tablespoons butter or margarine, melted
1 tablespoon lemon juice
1/4 teaspoon garlic powder
3/4 teaspoon lemon pepper
1 1/2 pounds uncooked peeled deveined large shrimp,
    thawed if frozen and tails peeled
1/2 cup mayonnaise or salad dressing
2 tablespoons chopped drained roasted red bell peppers
    (from 7-ounce jar)
2 tablespoons chopped fresh basil leaves
1/2 teaspoon grated lemon peel

1. Heat closed medium-size contact grill for 5 to 10 minutes. In large bowl, mix butter, lemon juice, garlic powder and 1/2 teaspoon of the lemon pepper. Add shrimp; toss to coat.

2. Place shrimp on grill. Close grill. Grill 4 to 6 minutes or until shrimp are pink and firm.

3. Meanwhile, in small bowl, mix mayonnaise, bell peppers, basil, lemon peel and remaining 1/4 teaspoon lemon pepper. Serve with shrimp.

Success Tip

To devein shrimp, use a small, pointed knife or a shrimp deveiner to make a shallow cut along the center back of each shrimp, then wash out the vein.

1 Serving: Cal. 340 (Cal. from Fat 260); Fat 29g (Sat. fat 7g); Chol. 190mg; Sodium 440mg; Carbs. 2g (Fiber 0g); Pro. 18g • **% Daily Value:** Vit. A 18%; Vit. C 10%; Calc. 4%; Iron 16% • **Exchanges:** 2 1/2 Lean Meat, 4 1/2 Fat • **Carb. Choices:** 0

Spicy Balsamic Salmon

Prep: 5 min
Grill: 6 min
4 servings

1-pound salmon fillet, 3/4 to1 inch thick
1/2 teaspoon black and red pepper blend
1/4 teaspoon salt
1/4 teaspoon ground ginger
3 tablespoons balsamic vinegar
3 tablespoons orange marmalade

1. Heat closed medium-size contact grill for 5 to 10 minutes. Cut salmon into 4 serving pieces. Sprinkle salmon with pepper blend, salt and ginger. In 1-quart saucepan, mix vinegar and marmalade.

2. Place salmon, skin side down, on grill. Close grill. Grill 3 minutes. Brush with vinegar mixture. Grill 2 to 3 minutes longer, brushing with vinegar mixture once or twice, until salmon flakes easily with fork.

3. Heat remaining vinegar mixture to boiling; boil and stir 1 minute. Serve with salmon.

Try This

Use salmon steaks in place of the fillets in this recipe. You may also want to experiment with the many flavors of marmalade that are available.

1 Serving: Cal. 180 (Cal. from Fat 55); Fat 6g (Sat. fat 2g); Chol. 65mg; Sodium 500mg; Carbs. 11g (Fiber 0g); Pro. 21g • **% Daily Value:** Vit. A 2%; Vit. C 2%; Calc. 2%; Iron 4% • **Exchanges:** 1 Other Carbs., 3 Very Lean Meat, 1/2 Fat • **Carb. Choices:** 1

Smokers

Turkey with Chili–Corn Bread Dressing

Four-Pepper Beef Brisket

Prep: 10 min
Smoke: 5 hr
12 servings

2 cups hickory wood chips
Four-Pepper Rub (below)
5-pound well-trimmed fresh beef brisket (not corned beef)
1/2 cup barbecue sauce

1. In medium bowl, cover wood chips with water; soak 30 minutes.

2. Drain wood chips. Prepare and heat smoker using wood chips and adding water to water pan following manufacturer's directions.

3. Make Four-Pepper Rub. Rub pepper mixture into all sides of beef.

4. Brush smoker rack with vegetable oil. Cover and smoke beef about 4 hours. Brush beef with barbecue sauce; continue smoking about 1 hour longer or until meat thermometer reads 160°F. If smoking stops, add additional wood chips through side door of smoker.

Four-Pepper Rub

1 tablespoon cracked black pepper
1 tablespoon cracked white pepper
1 tablespoon cracked red pepper
1 tablespoon lemon pepper

In small bowl, mix all ingredients. About 1/4 cup.

Try This

Add even more zip to this peppery brisket with your favorite barbecue sauce, or make your own sauce with a recipe chosen from the Sauces, Marinades & Rubs chapter.

1 Serving: Cal. 300 (Cal. from Fat 125); Fat 14g (Sat. fat 5g); Chol. 110mg; Sodium 290mg; Carbs. 4g (Fiber 0g); Pro. 41g • **% Daily Value:** Vit. A 2%; Vit. C 0%; Calc. 2%; Iron 20% • **Exchanges:** 5 1/2 Lean Meat • **Carb. Choices:** 0

Apple-Smoked Pork with Salsa

Prep: 20 min
Chill: 1 hr
Smoke: 3 hr
8 servings

Pear Salsa (below)
4 cups apple wood chips
2 pork tenderloins (about 1 pound each)
1 teaspoon garlic salt
1 small onion, cut into 1/4-inch slices

1. Make Pear Salsa.

2. In large bowl, cover wood chips with water; soak 30 minutes.

3. Drain wood chips. Prepare and heat smoker using wood chips and adding water to water pan following manufacturer's directions.

4. Sprinkle pork with garlic salt. Make diagonal cuts across pork at 1-inch intervals to within 1/2 inch of bottom of pork. Insert onion pieces in cuts in pork.

5. Place pork on rack in smoker. Cover and smoke about 3 hours or until meat thermometer inserted in center of pork reads 160°F. If smoking stops, add additional wood chips through side door of smoker. Top pork with salsa.

Pear Salsa

1 1/2 cups chopped unpeeled pear (about 1 large)
2 tablespoons chopped green onions
2 tablespoons chopped fresh cilantro
2 tablespoons chopped hot yellow chili
2 teaspoons grated lemon peel
2 tablespoons lemon juice
1/2 teaspoon salt

In small glass or plastic bowl, mix all ingredients. Cover and refrigerate 1 hour. About 1 3/4 cups.

1 Serving: Cal. 170 (Cal. from Fat 45); Fat 5g (Sat. fat 2g); Chol. 70mg; Sodium 320mg; Carbs. 5g (Fiber 1g); Pro. 26g • **% Daily Value:** Vit. A 2%; Vit. C 12%; Calc. 0%; Iron 8% • **Exchanges:** 4 Very Lean Meat, 1/2 Fat • **Carb. Choices:** 0

Ginger-Soy Pork Loin Roast

Prep: 25 min
Marinate: 4 hr
Smoke: 4 hr
6 servings

1/4 cup plus 2 tablespoons soy sauce
1 tablespoon chopped gingerroot
3 tablespoons dry white wine
3 tablespoons lemon juice
1 tablespoon vegetable oil
1/4 teaspoon pepper
1/8 teaspoon seasoned salt
1 clove garlic, finely chopped
2- to 2 1/2-pound pork boneless loin roast
6 to 8 hickory wood chunks*
Apricot Sauce (page 284)

1. In small bowl, mix soy sauce, gingerroot, wine, lemon juice, oil, pepper, seasoned salt and garlic.

2. In shallow glass or plastic dish or heavy-duty resealable plastic food-storage bag, place pork roast. Pour soy sauce mixture over pork; turn pork to coat. Cover dish or seal bag and refrigerate, turning pork occasionally, at least 4 hours but no longer than 24 hours.

3. In large bowl, cover wood chunks with water; soak 30 minutes.

4. Drain wood chunks. Prepare and heat smoker using wood chunks and adding water to water pan following manufacturer's directions.

5. Brush smoker rack with vegetable oil. Remove pork from marinade and drain; discard marinade.

6. Place pork, fat side up, on rack in smoker. Cover and smoke 3 hours 30 minutes to 4 hours or until meat thermometer inserted in center of pork reads 160°F (pork will remain pink when done). If smoking stops, add additional wood chunks through side door of smoker.

7. Make Apricot Sauce. Serve pork with warm sauce.

*Three cups hickory wood chips can be substituted.

1 Serving: Cal. 610 (Cal. from Fat 380); Fat 42g (Sat. fat 9g); Chol. 120mg; Sodium 880mg; Carbs. 23g (Fiber 0g); Pro. 35g • **% Daily Value:** Vit. A 0%; Vit. C 2%; Calc. 2%; Iron 10% • **Exchanges:** 1/2 Starch, 1 Other Carbs., 5 1/2 Lean Meat, 4 1/2 Fat • **Carb. Choices:** 1 1/2

Hot and Spicy Ribs

Prep: 10 min
Smoke: 5 hr
6 servings

4 cups hickory wood chips
Spicy Rib Rub (below)
5 pounds pork spareribs (not cut into serving pieces)
Barbecue sauce, if desired

1. In large bowl, cover wood chips with water; soak 30 minutes.

2. Drain wood chips. Prepare and heat smoker using wood chips and adding water to water pan following manufacturer's directions.

3. Make Spicy Rib Rub. Cut rack of pork in half to fit on smoker rack if necessary. Rub spice mixture into pork.

4. Place pork on rack in smoker. Cover and smoke 4 hours 30 minutes to 5 hours or until tender. If smoking stops, add additional wood chips through side door of smoker. Serve pork with barbecue sauce.

Spicy Rib Rub

1 tablespoon garlic powder
1 tablespoon paprika
2 teaspoons ground red pepper (cayenne)
2 teaspoons dried thyme leaves, crumbled
1 teaspoon salt
1 teaspoon pepper

In small bowl, mix all ingredients. About 3 tablespoons.

Serving Idea

These spicy-hot ribs are great served with your favorite coleslaw, potato salad and iced tea—or any other drink that suits your mood.

1 Serving: Cal. 585 (Cal. from Fat 405); Fat 45g (Sat. fat 16g); Chol. 180mg; Sodium 530mg; Carbs. 2g (Fiber 0g); Pro. 43g • **% Daily Value:** Vit. A 14%; Vit. C 0%; Calc. 6%; Iron 16% • **Exchanges:** 6 Medium-Fat Meat, 3 Fat • **Carb. Choices:** 0

Smoked Brown Sugar-Brined Pork Chops

Prep: 10 min
Marinate: 3 hr
Smoke: 1 hr 30 min
6 servings

1/2 cup packed brown sugar
1/4 cup salt
2 dried bay leaves
1 clove garlic, crushed
1 teaspoon whole black peppercorns
4 cups water
6 bone-in center-cut pork loin chops, about 1 inch thick
    (4 to 5 pounds)
4 to 6 wood chunks for smoking (hickory, mesquite or apple)*
2 tablespoons packed brown sugar
1/2 teaspoon garlic powder
1/2 teaspoon black pepper
1/4 teaspoon ground red pepper (cayenne)

1. In 2-gallon-size heavy-duty resealable plastic food-storage bag, mix 1/2 cup brown sugar, the salt, bay leaves, garlic, peppercorns and 4 cups water. Seal bag and squeeze to mix until sugar and salt have dissolved. Place pork chops in bag of brine; seal bag. Refrigerate at least 3 hours but no longer than 8 hours.

2. In medium bowl, cover wood chunks with water; soak at least 30 minutes.

3. Drain wood chunks. Prepare and heat smoker using wood chunks and adding water to water pan following manufacturer's directions.

4. Meanwhile, remove pork chops from brine; discard brine. Blot pork chops dry with paper towels. In small bowl, mix 2 tablespoons brown sugar, garlic powder, black pepper and red pepper. Rub each side of pork chops with slightly less than 1 teaspoon brown sugar mixture.

5. Arrange pork chops 1 inch apart on top and bottom smoker racks. Cover and smoke about 1 hour 30 minutes or until meat thermometer inserted in center of pork reads 160°F (pork will remain pink when done). If smoking stops, add additional wood chunks through side door of smoker.

Three cups hickory, mesquite or apple wood chips can be substituted.

1 Serving: Cal. 180 (Cal. from Fat 70); Fat 8g (Sat. fat 3g); Chol. 60mg; Sodium 430mg; Carbs. 6g (Fiber 0g; Pro. 21g • **% Daily Value:** Vit. A 0%; Vit. C 0%; Calc. 0%; Iron 4% • **Exchanges:** 1/2 Other Carbs., 3 Lean Meat • **Carb. Choices:** 1/2

Southwestern Smoked Chicken

Prep: 15 min
Marinate: 4 hr
Smoke: 4 hr
4 servings

1/4 cup red wine vinegar
1/2 cup vegetable oil
2 tablespoons chopped fresh cilantro
2 tablespoons packed brown sugar
2 teaspoons chili powder
1/4 teaspoon salt
1/8 teaspoon ground cumin
2 cloves garlic, finely chopped
3- to 4-pound whole broiler-fryer chicken
6 to 8 wood chunks for smoking (hickory, mesquite or apple)*

1. In small bowl, beat vinegar, oil, cilantro, brown sugar, chili powder, salt, cumin and garlic with wire whisk until well blended.

2. In shallow glass or plastic dish or heavy-duty gallon-size resealable plastic food-storage bag, place whole chicken. Pour vinegar mixture over chicken; turn chicken to coat. Cover dish or seal bag and refrigerate, turning chicken occasionally, at least 4 hours but no longer than 24 hours.

3. In large bowl, cover wood chunks with water; soak 30 minutes.

4. Drain wood chunks. Prepare and heat smoker using wood chunks and adding water to water pan following manufacturer's directions.

5. Remove chicken from marinade and drain; discard remaining marinade.

6. Place chicken on rack in smoker. Cover and smoke 3 hours 30 minutes to 4 hours or until meat thermometer inserted in thickest part of inside thigh muscle (not touching bone) reads 180°F and juice is no longer pink when center of thigh is cut. If smoking stops, add additional wood chunks through side door of smoker.

*Three cups hickory, mesquite or apple wood chips can be substituted.

1 Serving: Cal. 470 (Cal. from Fat 295); Fat 33g (Sat. fat 7g); Chol. 130mg; Sodium 200mg; Carbs. 4g (Fiber 0g); Pro. 40g • **% Daily Value:** Vit. A 2%; Vit. C 0%; Calc. 2%; Iron 10% • **Exchanges:** 6 Medium-Fat Meat, 1/2 Fat • **Carb. Choices:** 0

Citrus-Marinated Turkey Breast

Prep: 25 min
Marinate: 8 hr
Smoke: 4 hr
10 servings

3/4 cup frozen (thawed) orange juice concentrate
(from 12-ounce can)
3/4 cup frozen (thawed) limeade concentrate (from 12-ounce can)
1/2 cup honey
1/2 teaspoon paprika
1/2 teaspoon ground ginger
6- to 7-pound whole bone-in turkey breast, thawed if frozen
10 to 15 wood chunks for smoking (hickory, mesquite or apple)*
1 tablespoon cornstarch

1. In small bowl, mix orange juice concentrate, limeade concentrate, honey, paprika and ginger. Reserve 1 cup of the juice mixture to make the sauce in step 7.

2. In shallow glass or plastic dish or heavy-duty 2-gallon resealable plastic food-storage bag, place turkey breast. Pour remaining juice mixture over turkey; turn turkey to coat. Cover dish or seal bag and refrigerate, turning turkey occasionally, at least 8 hours but no longer than 24 hours.

3. In large bowl, cover wood chunks with water; soak 30 minutes.

4. Drain wood chunks. Prepare and heat smoker using wood chunks and adding water to water pan following manufacturer's directions.

5. Brush smoker rack with vegetable oil. Remove turkey from marinade and drain; discard remaining marinade.

6. Place turkey on rack in smoker. Cover and smoke 3 to 4 hours or until meat thermometer inserted in thickest part of turkey (not touching bone) reads 170°F and juice is no longer pink when center is cut. If smoking stops, add additional wood chunks through side door of smoker.

7. In small bowl, mix cornstarch and 3 tablespoons of the reserved marinade. In 1-quart saucepan, heat remaining reserved marinade to boiling over medium heat. Stir in cornstarch mixture. Cook about 2 minutes, stirring constantly, until thickened. Drizzle sauce over sliced turkey.

*Five cups hickory, mesquite or apple wood chips can be substituted.

1 Serving: Cal. 420 (Cal. from Fat 125); Fat 14g (Sat. fat 4g); Chol. 140mg; Sodium 115mg; Carbs. 23g (Fiber 0g); Pro. 52g • **% Daily Value:** Vit. A 2%; Vit. C 18%; Calc. 2%; Iron 10% • **Exchanges:** 1/2 Fruit, 1 Other Carbs., 7 1/2 Very Lean Meat, 1 1/2 Fat • **Carb. Choices:** 1 1/2

Turkey with Chili-Corn Bread Dressing

Prep: 30 min
Smoke: 6 hr 30 min
10 servings

Photo on page 236

4 cups hickory wood chips
10- to 12-pound whole turkey
Chili–Corn Bread Dressing (below)

1. In large bowl, cover wood chips with water; soak 30 minutes.

2. Drain wood chips. Prepare and heat smoker using wood chips and adding water to water pan following manufacturer's directions.

3. Fasten neck skin of turkey to back with skewer. Fold wings across back with tips touching. Tuck drumsticks under band of skin at tail, or tie or skewer to tail.

4. Brush smoker rack with vegetable oil. Place turkey, breast side up, on rack in smoker. Cover and smoke turkey 6 hours to 6 hours 30 minutes or until meat thermometer inserted in thickest part of inside thigh muscle (not touching bone) reads 180°F and juice is no longer pink when center of thigh is cut. If smoking stops, add additional wood chips through side door of smoker.

5. Meanwhile, make Chili–Corn Bread Dressing. Cover dressing with foil and refrigerate. Add dressing, covered, for last 2 hours of smoking or until hot.

Chili–Corn Bread Dressing

1 cup water
1 cup butter or margarine, melted
1 medium green bell pepper, chopped (1 cup)
1/2 chopped red onion
2 cans (4.5 ounces each) chopped green chiles, drained
1 package (16 ounces) corn bread stuffing mix

In 13 × 9-inch foil pan, mix water, butter, bell pepper, onion and chiles. Add stuffing mix; toss.

1 Serving: Cal. 680 (Cal. from Fat 360); Fat 40g (Sat. fat 18g); Chol. 240mg; Sodium 910mg; Carbs. 12g (Fiber 1g); Pro. 69g • **% Daily Value:** Vit. A 22%; Vit. C 10%; Calc. 6%; Iron 24% • **Exchanges:** 1 Starch, 9 Lean Meat, 2 1/2 Fat • **Carb. Choices:** 1

Herbed Salmon Fillet with Cucumber Sauce

Prep: 20 min
Smoke: 1 hr 30 min
8 servings

2 cups apple wood chips
4 sprigs dill weed
4 sprigs tarragon
1 small bunch thyme
1 large salmon fillet (about 2 pounds)
Cucumber Sauce (below)

1. In medium bowl, cover wood chips with water; soak 30 minutes.

2. Drain wood chips. Prepare and heat smoker using wood chips and adding water to water pan following manufacturer's directions.

3. Place dill weed, tarragon and thyme lengthwise on top of salmon fillet; secure with string.

4. Brush smoker rack with vegetable oil. Place salmon, skin side down, on rack in smoker. Cover and smoke about 1 hour 30 minutes or until salmon flakes easily with a fork. If smoking stops, add additional wood chips through side door of smoker.

5. Meanwhile, make Cucumber Sauce. Serve salmon with sauce.

Cucumber Sauce

1 large cucumber, seeded and chopped (1 cup)
1 cup sour cream or plain yogurt
2 tablespoons chopped fresh parsley or 1 teaspoon parsley flakes
2 tablespoons chopped fresh or 1 teaspoon freeze-dried chives
1/4 teaspoon salt
1 clove garlic, finely chopped

In small bowl, mix all ingredients. Cover and refrigerate at least 1 hour. About 2 cups.

1 Serving: Cal. 195 (Cal. from Fat 110); Fat 12g (Sat. fat 4g); Chol. 70mg; Sodium 130mg; Carbs. 2g (Fiber 0g); Pro. 20g • **% Daily Value:** Vit. A 8%; Vit. C 2%; Calc. 4%; Iron 4% • **Exchanges:** 3 Lean Meat, 1/2 Fat • **Carb. Choices:** 0

Smoked Brined Salmon

Prep: 10 min
Marinate: 3 hr
Smoke: 1 hr
6 servings

1/2 cup sugar
1/4 cup salt
1 tablespoon grated orange peel (from 1 small orange)
1 medium onion, sliced
1 teaspoon whole black peppercorns
4 cups water
2 1/2- to 3-pound skin-on salmon fillet
4 to 6 wood chunks for smoking (hickory, mesquite or apple)*
2 tablespoons vegetable oil
1/2 teaspoon paprika
1/4 teaspoon pepper

1. In large heavy-duty resealable plastic food-storage bag, mix sugar, salt, orange peel, onion, peppercorns and 4 cups water. Seal bag and squeeze to mix until sugar and salt have dissolved. Place salmon in bag of brine; seal bag. Refrigerate at least 3 hours but no longer than 4 hours.

2. In medium bowl, cover wood chunks with water; soak at least 30 minutes.

3. Drain wood chunks. Prepare and heat smoker using wood chunks and adding water to water pan following manufacturer's directions.

4. Meanwhile, remove salmon from brine; discard brine. Blot salmon dry with paper towels. Brush both sides of salmon with oil. Place salmon, skin side down. Sprinkle with paprika and pepper.

5. Place salmon, skin side down, on top grill rack in smoker. Cover and smoke about 1 hour or until salmon flakes easily with fork. If smoking stops, add additional wood chunks through side door of smoker.

6. Place salmon, skin side up, on foil. Peel skin from fish and discard. Use foil to turn fish onto serving platter.

*Two cups hickory, mesquite or apple wood chips can be substituted.

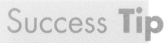

Success Tip

Take care not to brine longer than the recipe indicates or the salmon will taste salty.

1 Serving: Cal. 270 (Cal. from Fat 115); Fat 13g (Sat. fat 3g); Chol. 105mg; Sodium 490mg; Carbs. 4g (Fiber 0g); Pro. 34g • **% Daily Value:** Vit. A 2%; Vit. C 2%; Calc. 2%; Iron 6% • **Exchanges:** 5 Lean Meat • **Carb. Choices:** 0

Trout with Hazelnut Stuffing

Prep: 25 min
Smoke: 1 hr 30 min
4 servings

2 cups apple or other fruitwood chips
Hazelnut Stuffing (below)
4 pan-dressed rainbow trout (about 1/2 pound each)

1. In medium bowl, cover wood chips with water; soak 30 minutes.

2. Drain wood chips. Prepare and heat smoker using wood chips and adding water to water pan following manufacturer's directions.

3. Make Hazelnut Stuffing. Spoon about 1/4 cup stuffing mixture into cavity of each trout; secure with string.

4. Brush smoker rack with vegetable oil. Place trout on rack in smoker. Cover and smoke trout about 1 hour 30 minutes or until trout flakes easily with a fork. If smoking stops, add additional wood chips through side door of smoker.

Hazelnut Stuffing

1 cup seasoned stuffing crumbs
1/4 cup chopped hazelnuts (filberts) or pecans, toasted if desired
2 tablespoons butter or margarine, melted
2 tablespoons apple juice
1/2 teaspoon dried sage leaves, crumbled

In small bowl, mix all ingredients. About 1 cup.

Try This

This Hazelnut Stuffing also pairs well with pork chops and chicken breasts.

1 Serving: Cal. 425 (Cal. from Fat 200); Fat 22g (Sat. fat 7g); Chol. 145mg; Sodium 370mg; Carbs. 11g (Fiber 1g); Pro. 45g • **% Daily Value:** Vit. A 8%; Vit. C 2%; Calc. 6%; Iron 12% • **Exchanges:** 1 Starch, 6 Lean Meat • **Carb. Choices:** 1

Mediterranean Potato Salad

Sides

Baked Potatoes on the Grill

Prep: 5 min
Grill: 1 hr 15 min
4 servings

4 medium baking potatoes
Rock or kosher salt

1. Heat coals or gas grill for direct heat.

2. Gently scrub potatoes. Pierce potatoes several times with fork to allow steam to escape while potatoes bake.

3. In 2 disposable 8 × 4-inch foil loaf pans, pour 1-inch layer of salt. Place 2 potatoes in salt in each pan; pour salt over potatoes until completely covered.

4. Cover and grill potatoes over medium heat 1 hour to 1 hour 15 minutes or until potatoes are tender when pierced in center with fork. Carefully remove potatoes from salt.

Serving Idea

Here's a delicious, fun new way to make "baked" potatoes without heating up the oven. They're perfect to throw on the grill with Beer Can Chicken (page 110) or other foods that grill a long time.

1 Serving: Cal. 905 (Cal. from Fat 0); Fat 0g (Sat. fat 0g); Chol. 0mg; Sodium 600mg; Carbs. 21g (Fiber 1g); Pro. 2g • **% Daily Value:** Vit. A 0%; Vit. C 10%; Calc. 0%; Iron 2% • **Exchanges:** 1 Starch • **Carb. Choices:** 1

Three-Potato Medley

Prep: 15 min
Microwave: 10 min
Grill: 15 min
8 servings

4 small unpeeled red potatoes, cut into 3/4-inch pieces
4 small unpeeled Yukon gold potatoes, cut into 3/4-inch pieces
1 medium dark-orange sweet potato, peeled and cut into
    3/4-inch pieces
3 tablespoons honey mustard barbecue sauce
1 tablespoon fresh lemon juice
1 tablespoon vegetable oil
1 teaspoon chopped fresh sage, if desired
1/2 teaspoon salt
1 small green bell pepper, cut into 1-inch pieces
1 large onion, cut into thin wedges

1. Heat coals or gas grill for direct heat.

2. In shallow microwavable dish, place red, Yukon gold and sweet potato pieces. Cover with microwavable plastic wrap, folding back one edge or corner 1/4 inch to vent steam. Microwave on High 8 to 10 minutes, stirring once after 4 minutes, until tender. Cool slightly.

3. Meanwhile, in medium bowl, mix barbecue sauce, lemon juice, oil, sage and salt. Stir in potatoes, bell pepper and onion. Place in grill basket (grill "wok").

4. Cover and grill vegetables over medium heat 10 to 15 minutes, shaking basket or stirring vegetables 2 or 3 times, until potatoes are tender and lightly browned.

Did You Know?

Sage has long been used for medicinal purposes as well as for cooking. This pungent herb with its musty aroma is a nice complement to the homey, earthy potatoes.

1 Serving: Cal. 140 (Cal. from Fat 20); Fat 2g (Sat. fat 0g); Chol. 0mg; Sodium 210mg; Carbs. 28g (Fiber 4g); Pro. 2g • **% Daily Value:** Vit. A 44%; Vit. C 22%; Calc. 2%; Iron 10% • **Exchanges:** 1 Starch, 1 Other Carbs. • **Carb. Choices:** 2

Garlic and Cumin New Potatoes

Prep: 10 min
Grill: 15 min
4 servings

12 unpeeled small red potatoes, cut into fourths
2 tablespoons butter or margarine, melted
1/2 teaspoon garlic powder
1/2 teaspoon ground cumin
1/2 teaspoon paprika
1/2 teaspoon peppered seasoned salt
1/4 cup chopped fresh cilantro

1. Heat coals or gas grill for direct heat.

2. In large bowl, place potatoes. Add remaining ingredients except cilantro; toss to coat. Place in grill basket (grill "wok").

3. Cover and grill potatoes over medium heat 10 to 15 minutes, shaking basket or stirring potatoes frequently, until tender.

4. Sprinkle potatoes with cilantro; toss to coat.

Success Tip

Shake the grill basket often to "stir" the potatoes so they cook evenly and don't burn.

1 Serving: Cal. 185 (Cal. from Fat 55); Fat 6g (Sat. fat 4g); Chol. 15mg; Sodium 220mg; Carbs. 30g (Fiber 3g); Pro. 3g • **% Daily Value:** Vit. A 6%; Vit. C 12%; Calc. 2%; Iron 8% • **Exchanges:** 1 Starch, 1 Other Carbs., 1 Fat • **Carb. Choices:** 2

Mediterranean Potato Salad

Prep: 10 min
Cook: 20 min
Grill: 10 min
6 to 8 servings

Photo on page 252

1 1/2 pounds unpeeled small red potatoes
1/2 teaspoon salt
2 tablespoons olive or vegetable oil
Basil Vinaigrette (below)
1 small red bell pepper, chopped (1/2 cup)
1/2 cup pitted ripe olives

1. In 2-quart saucepan, place potatoes; add enough water just to cover potatoes. Add salt. Cover and heat to boiling; reduce heat to low. Cook covered about 15 minutes or just until potatoes are tender; drain. Cool slightly; cut potatoes in half. Toss with oil.

2. Heat coals or gas grill for direct heat.

3. Cover and grill potatoes over medium heat 5 to 10 minutes, turning occasionally, until golden brown and tender.

4. Meanwhile, make Basil Vinaigrette. In large bowl, toss potatoes, bell pepper, olives and vinaigrette.

Basil Vinaigrette

1/3 cup olive or vegetable oil
2 tablespoons chopped fresh basil leaves
3 tablespoons white wine vinegar
1 teaspoon Dijon mustard
1 teaspoon salt

In tightly covered container, shake all ingredients. About 1/2 cup.

1 Serving: Cal. 255 (Cal. from Fat 160); Fat 18g (Sat. fat 2g); Chol. 0mg; Sodium 760mg; Carbs. 22g (Fiber 3g); Pro. 2g • **% Daily Value:** Vit. A 16%; Vit. C 30%; Calc. 4%; Iron 14% • **Exchanges:** 1 Starch, 1/2 Other Carbs., 3 Fat • **Carb. Choices:** 1 1/2

Potato Salad with Chile Vinaigrette

Prep: 20 min
Grill: 30 min
4 servings

1 can (4.5 ounces) chopped green chiles
Chile Vinaigrette (below)
4 unpeeled small red potatoes, cut into 1/2-inch pieces (1 1/2 cups)
2 unpeeled Yukon gold potatoes, cut into 1/2-inch pieces
     (2 1/2 cups)
2 tablespoons olive or vegetable oil
1/2 teaspoon salt
1 medium yellow bell pepper, cut into 1/2-inch pieces
3 medium roma (plum) tomatoes, coarsely chopped (1 cup)

1. Heat coals or gas grill for direct heat.

2. Reserve 2 tablespoons of the chiles for Chile Vinaigrette; reserve remaining chiles for salad. Make Chile Vinaigrette.

3. Place red and Yukon gold potatoes in grill basket (grill "wok"). Drizzle with oil; sprinkle with salt. Shake basket to mix and turn potatoes.

4. Cover and grill potatoes over medium heat 25 to 30 minutes, shaking basket or stirring potatoes occasionally, until tender. Add bell pepper to basket for last 5 minutes of grilling.

5. In large bowl, place Chile Vinaigrette; stir in tomatoes and remaining green chiles. Add potatoes and bell pepper; toss to mix.

Chile Vinaigrette

1/4 cup white balsamic vinegar
Reserved 2 tablespoons chopped green chiles
2 tablespoons olive or vegetable oil
1/4 teaspoon black and red pepper blend
1/4 teaspoon salt

In blender, cover and blend all ingredients about 10 seconds or until smooth. About 1/2 cup.

1 Serving: Cal. 290 (Cal. from Fat 125); Fat 14g (Sat. fat 2g); Chol. 0mg; Sodium 990mg; Carbs. 42g (Fiber 5g); Pro. 4g • **% Daily Value:** Vit. A 14%; Vit. C 70%; Calc. 2%; Iron 16% • **Exchanges:** 1 Starch, 1 1/2 Other Carbs., 1 Vegetable, 2 Fat • **Carb. Choices:** 3

Sweet Potatoes with Chipotle-Honey Sauce

Prep: 10 min
Grill: 10 min
6 servings

Chipotle-Honey Sauce (below)
6 medium dark-orange sweet potatoes
1/3 cup olive or vegetable oil
2 teaspoons coarse salt

1. Brush grill rack with vegetable oil. Heat coals or gas grill for direct heat.

2. Make Chipotle-Honey Sauce; set aside.

3. Cut each sweet potato lengthwise into 4 or 5 slices; brush both sides with oil.

4. Place potatoes on grill rack over medium heat; sprinkle with 1 teaspoon of the salt. Cover and grill 8 to 10 minutes, turning once and sprinkling with remaining salt, until potatoes are tender. Serve with sauce.

Chipotle-Honey Sauce

1 cup honey
4 chipotle chilies in adobo sauce, finely chopped
2 tablespoons adobo sauce (from can of chilies)

In small bowl, mix all ingredients. About 1 1/4 cups.

1 Serving: Cal. 410 (Cal. from Fat 110); Fat 12g (Sat. fat 2g); Chol. 0mg; Sodium 510mg; Carbs. 77g (Fiber 4g); Pro. 2g • **% Daily Value:** Vit. A 100%; Vit. C 24%; Calc. 4%; Iron 4% • **Exchanges:** 1 Starch, 4 Other Carbs., 2 Fat • **Carb. Choices:** 5

Nutty Veggie Combo

Prep: 12 min
Grill: 15 min
6 servings

2 tablespoons butter or margarine, melted
2 tablespoons chopped fresh parsley
1/4 teaspoon salt
1 cup small cauliflowerets
8 Brussels sprouts, cut in half
8 baby yellow pattypan squash
1/2 cup walnut halves

1. Heat coals or gas grill for direct heat.

2. In small bowl, mix butter, parsley and salt. Place vegetables and walnuts in grill basket (grill "wok").

3. Cover and grill vegetables over medium heat 10 to 15 minutes, turning and brushing with butter mixture 2 or 3 times, until crisp-tender.

Shop Talk

Farmers' markets and local gardens may offer unusual varieties of cauliflower and squash in a rainbow of colors, such as green squash and orange or purple cauliflower.

1 Serving: Cal. 145 (Cal. from Fat 100); Fat 11g (Sat. fat 3g); Chol. 10mg; Sodium 135mg; Carbs. 8g (Fiber 3g); Pro. 4g • **% Daily Value:** Vit. A 12%; Vit. C 28%; Calc. 4%; Iron 4% • **Exchanges:** 2 Vegetable, 2 Fat • **Carb. Choices:** 1/2

Cajun Corn

Prep: 20 min
Grill: 26 min
6 servings

1/4 cup butter or margarine, melted
1 tablespoon Cajun seasoning
2 or 3 drops red pepper sauce
6 ears corn with husks

1. Heat coals or gas grill for direct heat.

2. In small bowl, mix butter, Cajun seasoning and pepper sauce. Reserve 1 tablespoon butter mixture.

3. Carefully pull back husks of each ear of corn; remove silk. Generously brush butter mixture over corn. Pull husks back over ears; tie husks securely with thin piece of husk or string.

4. Cover and grill corn over medium heat 20 to 26 minutes, turning frequently, until tender. Remove husks. Brush corn with reserved 1 tablespoon butter.

Shop Talk

Use corn at its very freshest for maximum sweetness and juiciness. Fresh-picked corn with plump kernels will give you the best-tasting Cajun corn.

1 Serving: Cal. 195 (Cal. from Fat 80); Fat 9g (Sat. fat 5g); Chol. 20mg; Sodium 75mg; Carbs. 25g (Fiber 3g); Pro. 3g • **% Daily Value:** Vit. A 14%; Vit. C 4%; Calc. 0%; Iron 4% • **Exchanges:** 1 Starch, 1/2 Other Carbs., 2 Fat • **Carb. Choices:** 1 1/2

Easy Italian Veggies

Prep: 15 min
Grill: 20 min
4 servings

1/4 cup butter or margarine, softened
2 tablespoons lemon pepper
1 unpeeled large potato, cut lengthwise into fourths
1 medium zucchini, cut lengthwise in half
1 medium yellow summer squash, cut lengthwise in half
2 large bell peppers (any color), cut lengthwise into fourths
    and seeded
1 medium onion, cut into 1/2-inch slices
1/4 cup Italian dressing

1. Heat coals or gas grill for direct heat.

2. In small bowl, mix butter and lemon pepper. Brush on potato, zucchini, summer squash, bell peppers and onion.

3. Cover and grill vegetables over medium heat 10 to 20 minutes, turning frequently, until tender. As vegetables become done, remove from grill to platter. Sprinkle with dressing. Serve warm.

Healthful Hint

For 0 grams of fat and only 105 calories per serving, omit the butter, spray vegetables with butter-flavored cooking spray before grilling and use fat-free Italian dressing.

1 Serving: Cal. 265 (Cal. from Fat 160); Fat 18g (Sat. fat 7g); Chol. 35mg; Sodium 220mg; Carbs. 22g (Fiber 4g); Pro. 4g • **% Daily Value:** Vit. A 24%; Vit. C 70%; Calc. 6%; Iron 8% • **Exchanges:** 1/2 Starch, 3 Vegetable, 3 Fat • **Carb. Choices:** 1 1/2

Asian Summer Squash Medley

Prep: 10 min
Grill: 10 min
4 servings

2 medium zucchini, cut into 1/2-inch slices
1 medium yellow summer squash, cut into 1/2-inch slices
1 cup baby pattypan squash
1/3 cup Asian dressing and marinade (from 16-ounce bottle)
1 tablespoon creamy peanut butter
2 medium green onions, sliced (2 tablespoons)
2 tablespoons chopped peanuts

1. Heat coals or gas grill for direct heat.

2. In large bowl, place zucchini, summer squash and pattypan squash. Add dressing; toss to coat. Place squash mixture in grill basket (grill "wok"), using slotted spoon; reserve dressing in bowl.

3. Cover and grill squash over medium heat 8 to 10 minutes, shaking basket or stirring squash occasionally, until crisp-tender.

4. Stir peanut butter into dressing in bowl until well mixed. Add grilled squash and onions to dressing mixture in bowl; toss to coat. Sprinkle with peanuts.

Shop Talk

Grill baskets, sometimes called grill "woks," can be found where grill equipment and cookware are sold. They usually have a punched-hole design or crisscross pattern. Choose a basket with small openings so food doesn't fall through. For a super-simple "grill basket," poke holes in a large piece of foil and turn up the edges slightly.

1 Serving: Cal. 180 (Cal. from Fat 125); Fat 14g (Sat. fat 2g); Chol. 0mg; Sodium 260mg; Carbs. 10g (Fiber 3g); Pro. 4g • **% Daily Value:** Vit. A 18%; Vit. C 18%; Calc. 4%; Iron 6% • **Exchanges:** 2 Vegetable, 3 Fat • **Carb. Choices:** 1/2

Tomato-Artichoke Kabobs

Prep: 10 min
Grill: 8 min
4 servings

1 jar (6 to 7 ounces) marinated artichoke hearts
12 cherry tomatoes

1. Brush grill rack with vegetable oil. Heat coals or gas grill for direct heat.

2. Drain artichoke hearts; reserve liquid. On each of four 10- to 12-inch metal skewers, alternately thread artichoke hearts and tomatoes, leaving 1/4-inch space between each piece. Brush with artichoke liquid.

3. Cover and grill kabobs over medium heat 6 to 8 minutes, brushing with artichoke liquid and turning 2 or 3 times, until hot.

Substitute

If you're not a fan of artichokes, simply use large fresh white mushrooms instead.

1 Serving: Cal. 40 (Cal. from Fat 10); Fat 1g (Sat. fat 0g); Chol. 0mg; Sodium 130mg; Carbs. 7g (Fiber 3g); Pro. 2g • **% Daily Value:** Vit. A 8%; Vit. C 10%; Calc. 2%; Iron 4% • **Exchanges:** 1 1/2 Vegetable • **Carb. Choices:** 1/2

Skewered Ratatouille

Prep: 10 min
Stand: 30 min
Grill: 20 min
6 servings

1 small eggplant (about 3/4 pound)
3/4 teaspoon salt
2 small zucchini
1 medium green bell pepper
1 small onion
1/3 cup Italian dressing
1 cup tomato pasta sauce or Italian-style tomato sauce, heated

1. Cut eggplant into 1-inch chunks. Place eggplant in colander over bowl or sink. Sprinkle with salt. Let drain 30 minutes. Rinse and pat dry.

2. Brush grill rack with vegetable oil. Heat coals or gas grill for direct heat.

3. Cut zucchini, bell pepper and onion into 1-inch chunks. On each of six 10-inch metal skewers, alternately thread eggplant, zucchini, bell pepper and onion, leaving 1/4-inch space between each piece. Brush with dressing.

4. Cover and grill kabobs over medium heat 15 to 20 minutes, turning and brushing twice with dressing, until vegetables are crisp-tender. In small pan or can with label removed, heat pasta sauce during last 10 minutes of grilling, stirring occasionally. Serve kabobs with sauce.

Success Tip

If you sprinkle the eggplant with a little salt and let it stand 30 minutes, the bitter taste often found in eggplant will be eliminated.

1 Serving: Cal. 140 (Cal. from Fat 65); Fat 7g (Sat. fat 1g); Chol. 0mg; Sodium 620mg; Carbs. 17g (Fiber 3g); Pro. 2g • **% Daily Value:** Vit. A 14%; Vit. C 24%; Calc. 4%; Iron 4% • **Exchanges:** 2 Vegetable, 1/2 Other Carbs., 1 1/2 Fat • **Carb. Choices:** 2

Mushrooms with Herbs

Prep: 10 min
Marinate: 1 hr
Grill: 20 min
4 servings

1/2 cup olive or vegetable oil
3 tablespoons lemon juice
1 teaspoon chopped fresh or 1/4 teaspoon dried oregano leaves
1 teaspoon chopped fresh or 1/4 teaspoon dried thyme leaves
1 clove garlic, crushed
1 pound large white mushrooms (about 2 1/2 inches in diameter)
1/4 teaspoon salt
1/8 teaspoon pepper

1. In large glass or plastic bowl or resealable plastic food-storage bag, mix oil, lemon juice, oregano, thyme and garlic. Add mushrooms; stir to coat. Cover and refrigerate at least 1 hour but no longer than 8 hours.

2. Heat coals or gas grill for direct heat. Remove mushrooms from marinade (mushrooms will absorb most of the marinade).

3. Cover and grill mushrooms over medium heat 15 to 20 minutes, turning 2 or 3 times, until tender and golden brown. Sprinkle with salt and pepper.

Try This

You can use smaller mushrooms, if you like—just be sure to use a grilling screen or foil pan, and check for doneness after half the grilling time.

1 Serving: Cal. 245 (Cal. from Fat 215); Fat 24g (Sat. fat 3g); Chol. 0mg; Sodium 150mg; Carbs. 5g (Fiber 1g); Pro. 3g • **% Daily Value:** Vit. A 0%; Vit. C 4%; Calc. 0%; Iron 6% • **Exchanges:** 1 Vegetable, 5 Fat • **Carb. Choices:** 0

Vegetables and Ravioli

Prep: 10 min
Grill: 12 min
4 servings

1/4 cup olive or vegetable oil
1 teaspoon garlic pepper
1/2 teaspoon salt
2 small zucchini, cut lengthwise in half
2 medium red, yellow or green bell peppers, cut lengthwise in half and seeded
1 small red onion, cut into fourths
1 package (9 ounces) refrigerated cheese-filled ravioli
1 tablespoon chopped fresh or 1 teaspoon dried basil leaves
1 teaspoon chopped fresh or 1/4 teaspoon dried thyme leaves
1/4 cup shredded Parmesan cheese

1. Brush grill rack with vegetable oil. Heat coals or gas grill for direct heat.

2. In small bowl, mix 2 tablespoons of the oil, the garlic pepper and salt. Brush on cut sides of vegetables.

3. Cover and grill zucchini, bell peppers and onion, cut sides down, over medium heat 10 to 12 minutes, brushing occasionally with oil mixture, until crisp-tender.

4. Meanwhile, cook and drain ravioli as directed on package. Return to saucepan.

5. Cut zucchini crosswise into 1/4-inch slices. Cut bell peppers into slices. Separate onion into pieces. Toss ravioli, vegetables, remaining 2 tablespoons oil, and the basil and thyme; heat through. Sprinkle with cheese.

Serving Idea

Fresh doesn't get much better than this! Full of garden goodies, this pasta is perfect served with a light salad, warm breadsticks and an icy sorbet for dessert.

1 Serving: Cal. 295 (Cal. from Fat 180); Fat 20g (Sat. fat 6g); Chol. 70mg; Sodium 940mg; Carbs. 18g (Fiber 3g); Pro. 11g • **% Daily Value:** Vit. A 84%; Vit. C 100%; Calc. 22%; Iron 8% • **Exchanges:** 1 Starch, 1 Medium-Fat Meat, 3 Fat • **Carb. Choices:** 1

Caesar Vegetable Salad

Prep: 25 min
Grill: 7 min
4 servings

1/3 cup Caesar dressing
1/4 cup chopped fresh parsley
4 large fresh portabella mushrooms, cut into fourths
4 medium yellow summer squash, cut into 1/2-inch slices
2 medium bell peppers (any color), cut into 1/2-inch strips
3 tablespoons olive or vegetable oil
1 cup cherry tomatoes, cut into fourths
1/3 cup shredded Parmesan cheese

1. Heat coals or gas grill for direct heat.

2. In small bowl, mix dressing and parsley; set aside. Brush mushrooms, summer squash and bell peppers with oil.

3. Place mushrooms, summer squash and bell peppers in grill basket (grill "wok") or directly on grill rack. Cover and grill over medium heat 5 to 7 minutes, shaking basket or stirring or turning vegetables occasionally, until vegetables are crisp-tender.

4. To serve, arrange mushrooms around edge of serving platter and remaining grilled vegetables in center; sprinkle with tomatoes. Drizzle dressing over vegetables. Sprinkle with cheese. Serve at room temperature.

Healthful Hint

To reduce the fat in this recipe to 4 grams per serving, use fat-free Caesar dressing and spray the vegetables with cooking spray instead of brushing with olive oil.

1 Serving: Cal. 270 (Cal. from Fat 190); Fat 21g (Sat. fat 4g); Chol. 15mg; Sodium 360mg; Carbs. 17g (Fiber 5g); Pro. 8g • **% Daily Value:** Vit. A 92%; Vit. C 100%; Calc. 20%; Iron 10% • **Exchanges:** 3 Vegetable, 4 1/2 Fat • **Carb. Choices:** 1

Pepper Salad

Prep: 15 min
Stand: 1 hr 15 min
Grill: 20 min
6 servings

6 medium bell peppers (any color)
1/4 cup olive or vegetable oil
1/2 teaspoon salt
1/4 teaspoon pepper

1. Brush grill rack with vegetable oil. Heat coals or gas grill for direct heat.

2. Cover and grill bell peppers over medium heat 15 to 20 minutes, turning frequently, until skin is blistered on all sides. Wrap peppers in clean towel or place in brown paper bag; cool 15 minutes.

3. Remove skin from peppers with knife. Cut peppers lengthwise in half; remove stems and seeds. Cut peppers into 1/4- to 1/2-inch-wide strips; place in glass or plastic bowl. Drizzle with oil. Sprinkle with salt and pepper. Cover and refrigerate at least 1 hour but no longer than 3 days.

Try This

This simple salad is also excellent served at room temperature. If you'd like more flavor, stir in 1 tablespoon chopped fresh herbs or 1 teaspoon dried herbs such as oregano or basil or 1 clove finely chopped garlic.

1 Serving: Cal. 115 (Cal. from Fat 80); Fat 9g (Sat. fat 1g); Chol. 0mg; Sodium 200mg; Carbs. 8g (Fiber 2g); Pro. 1g • **% Daily Value:** Vit. A 100%; Vit. C 100%; Calc. 0%; Iron 2% • **Exchanges:** 1/2 Other Carbs., 2 Fat • **Carb. Choices:** 1/2

Vegetable Pasta Salad

Prep: 25 min
Grill: 25 min
4 servings

2 cups uncooked gemelli or rotini pasta (8 ounces)
1 small red onion, cut into thin wedges
1 1/2 cups baby-cut carrots
1/2 cup balsamic vinaigrette
1/2 teaspoon seasoned salt
8 ounces fresh asparagus spears, cut into 2-inch pieces
1 jar (6 to 7 ounces) marinated artichoke hearts, drained
    and liquid reserved
2 slices bacon, crisply cooked and crumbled

1. Heat coals or gas grill for direct heat.

2. Cook and drain pasta as directed on package.

3. Meanwhile, in large bowl, place onion and carrots; drizzle with about 1/4 cup of the vinaigrette. Sprinkle with seasoned salt; toss to coat. Place onion and carrots in grill basket (grill "wok"), using slotted spoon; reserve vinaigrette in bowl.

4. Cover and grill onion and carrots over medium heat 15 minutes, shaking basket or stirring vegetables occasionally. Add asparagus to vinaigrette in bowl; toss to coat. Add asparagus to onion and carrots in grill basket. Cover and grill 8 to 10 minutes longer or until vegetables are crisp-tender.

5. Add cooked pasta, grilled vegetables and artichoke liquid to vinaigrette in bowl. Drizzle with remaining 1/4 cup vinaigrette; toss. Stir in artichokes. Sprinkle with bacon.

Success Tip

Before cutting the asparagus into pieces, wash it under cool running water to remove any sand. Then snap off the end of each stalk where it breaks naturally.

1 Serving: Cal. 405 (Cal. from Fat 145); Fat 16g (Sat. fat 2g); Chol. 5mg; Sodium 640mg; Carbs. 59g (Fiber 6g); Pro. 12g • **% Daily Value:** Vit. A 100%; Vit. C 12%; Calc. 8%; Iron 18% • **Exchanges:** 3 1/2 Starch, 1 Vegetable, 2 Fat • **Carb. Choices:** 4

Double-Cheese and Herb Bread

Prep: 10 min
Grill: 3 min
4 servings

4 slices Italian bread, 1/2 inch thick
Cooking spray
1 tablespoon chopped fresh or 1/2 teaspoon dried basil leaves
1 tablespoon chopped fresh or 1/2 teaspoon dried oregano leaves
1/4 teaspoon garlic powder
1/2 cup shredded Colby or mild Cheddar cheese (2 ounces)
1/2 cup shredded Havarti cheese (2 ounces)

1. Heat coals or gas grill for direct heat.

2. Spray both sides of each bread slice with cooking spray. Sprinkle one side with basil, oregano and garlic powder. Top with cheeses.

3. Cover and grill bread over medium heat 2 to 3 minutes or until bread is toasted and cheese is melted.

Substitute

Sourdough bread can be used instead of the Italian bread.

1 Serving: Cal. 170 (Cal. from Fat 100); Fat 11g (Sat. fat 6g); Chol. 30mg; Sodium 310mg; Carbs. 10g (Fiber 1g); Pro. 8g • **% Daily Value:** Vit. A 8%; Vit. C 0%; Calc. 20%; Iron 4% • **Exchanges:** 1 Starch, 1/2 High-Fat Meat, 1 Fat • **Carb. Choices:** 1/2

Southwestern Rub

Sauces, Rubs & Marinades

Zesty Barbecue Sauce

Prep: 10 min
Cook: 5 min
About 1 1/2 cups sauce

1/2 cup ketchup
2 tablespoons red wine vinegar
1 tablespoon prepared horseradish
1 small onion, finely chopped (1/4 cup)
1 can (8 ounces) jellied cranberry sauce

1. In 1-quart saucepan, mix all ingredients. Heat to boiling; reduce heat to low. Simmer uncovered about 5 minutes, stirring frequently, until cranberry sauce is melted.

2. Cool sauce slightly. Serve sauce with grilled beef, pork or turkey. Cover and refrigerate up to 2 weeks.

For a sauce with an added bite, increase the horseradish to 2 tablespoons.

1/4 Cup: Cal. 85 (Cal. from Fat 0); Fat 0g (Sat. fat 0g); Chol. 0mg; Sodium 250mg; Carbs. 22g (Fiber 1g); Pro. 0g • **% Daily Value:** Vit. A 4%; Vit. C 8%; Calc. 0%; Iron 2% • **Exchanges:** 1 1/2 Carbs. • **Carb. Choices:** 1 1/2

Spicy Texas Barbecue Sauce

Prep: 15 min
Cook: 1 hr
About 5 cups sauce

1 cup ketchup
1/2 cup packed brown sugar
1/4 cup lime juice
2 to 3 tablespoons ground red chilies or chili powder
1 tablespoon vegetable oil
1 tablespoon Worcestershire sauce
3 medium onions, chopped (1 1/2 cups)
2 jalapeño chilies, seeded and finely chopped
2 cloves garlic, finely chopped
1 can (12 ounces) tomato paste
1 can or bottle (12 ounces) regular or nonalcoholic beer

1. In 2-quart saucepan, heat all ingredients to boiling; reduce heat to low. Cover and simmer 1 hour, stirring occasionally.

2. Serve warm sauce with grilled ribs, steak, chicken or brisket.

Success Tip

Capsaicin is the substance in chilies that makes them hot, hot, hot. You may want to wear plastic gloves when chopping chilies, as capsaicin can be irritating to your skin.

1 Serving (1 tablespoon): Cal. 20 (Cal. from Fat 0); Fat 0g (Sat. fat 0g); Chol. 0mg; Sodium 75mg; Carbs. 4g (Fiber 0g); Pro. 0g • **% Daily Value:** Vit. A 4%; Vit. C 2%; Calc. 0%; Iron 0% • **Exchanges:** Free • **Carb. Choices:** 0

Honey-Pecan Sauce

Prep: 5 min
About 1/2 cup
sauce

3 tablespoons honey
2 tablespoons butter or margarine, melted
2 tablespoons chopped pecans, toasted
2 teaspoons lemon juice
1 teaspoon ground mustard

1. In small bowl, mix all ingredients.

2. Serve sauce with grilled pork or chicken.

Success Tip

Toasting the pecans adds a flavor boost to the nuts and gives them a nice crunch. To toast, cook in a small skillet over medium-low heat 5 to 7 minutes, stirring frequently until they begin to brown, then stirring constantly until they are golden brown.

1 Serving (2 Tablespoons): Cal. 130 (Cal. from Fat 70); Fat 8g (Sat. fat 4g); Chol. 15mg; Sodium 55mg; Carbs. 14g (Fiber 0g); Pro. 0g • **% Daily Value:** Vit. A 4%; Vit. C 2%; Calc. 0%; Iron 0% • **Exchanges:** 1 Carbs., 1 1/2 Fat • **Carb. Choices:** 1

Apricot Sauce

1 cup mayonnaise (not salad dressing)
1/4 cup honey
1/4 cup apricot preserves
2 tablespoons Dijon mustard

1. In 1-quart saucepan, stir all ingredients until well mixed. Heat over low heat, stirring occasionally, until warm (do not boil).

2. Serve warm sauce with grilled pork, poultry or fish.

Try This

This flavorful sauce is a great match for the Ginger-Soy Pork Loin Roast, page 242. Or, try it as a spread for your favorite sandwich. You may also want to try replacing the apricot preserve with peach preserve.

1 Serving (2 tablespoons): Cal. 360 (Cal. from Fat 260); Fat 29g (Sat. Fat 4.5g); Chol. 20mg; Sodium 340mg; Carbs. 22g (Fiber 0g); Pro. 0g • **% Daily Value:** Vit. A 2%; Vit. C 0%; Calc. 0%; Iron 2% • **Exchanges:** 1 1/2 Other Carbs., 6 Fat • **Carb. Choices:** 1 1/2

Green Herb Sauce

Prep: 10 min
About 1/2 cup
sauce

1 cup lightly packed fresh cilantro
1/4 cup lightly packed fresh parsley
2 tablespoons lightly packed fresh basil leaves
2 tablespoons coarsely chopped fresh chives
1/4 cup chicken broth
2 tablespoons olive or vegetable oil
1 clove garlic, chopped
1/2 to 1 jalapeño chili, seeded and chopped
1/4 cup grated Parmesan cheese
1/4 teaspoon salt

1. In food processor or blender, cover and process all ingredients, stopping to scrape sides if necessary, until smooth.

2. Serve sauce with grilled pork, poultry or fish.

Shop Talk

You'll find cilantro in bunches in the produce area next to the parsley. Cilantro can be refrigerated for several days wrapped tightly in a plastic bag or with the stems in a container of water. If you store it in water, be sure to change the water every 2 or 3 days.

1 Serving (2 Tablespoons): Cal. 50 (Cal. from Fat 35); Fat 4g (Sat. fat 1g); Chol. 0mg; Sodium 170mg; Carbs. 1g (Fiber 0g); Pro. 2g • **% Daily Value:** Vit. A 8%; Vit. C 18%; Calc. 4%; Iron 2% • **Exchanges:** 1 Fat • **Carb. Choices:** 0

Herbed Garlic Pepper Rub

Prep: 5 min
About 2
tablespoons rub

1 1/2 teaspoons dried oregano leaves
1 teaspoon garlic pepper
1/2 teaspoon salt
1/2 teaspoon onion powder
1/2 teaspoon chili powder
1/8 teaspoon ground red pepper (cayenne)

1. In small bowl, mix all ingredients.

2. Spread rub evenly on 1 pound boneless meat (pork or beef). Grill meat as desired.

Healthful Hint

Because this dry rub uses no oil, it adds no extra fat to your food. It's a great low-fat way to cook lean meat!

1 Serving (2 teaspoons): Cal. 5 (Cal. from Fat 0); Fat 0g (Sat. fat 0g); Chol. 0mg; Sodium 200mg; Carbs. 1g (Fiber 0g); Pro. 0g • **% Daily Value:** Vit. A 2%; Vit. C 0%; Calc. 0%; Iron 0% • **Exchanges:** Free • **Carb. Choices:** 0

Cajun Spice Rub

Prep: 5 min
About 1 tablespoon rub

1 teaspoon black pepper
1/2 teaspoon white pepper
1/2 teaspoon ground red pepper (cayenne)
1/2 teaspoon salt
1/2 teaspoon ground cumin
1/2 teaspoon ground nutmeg
1 tablespoon vegetable oil

1. In small bowl, mix all ingredients except oil.

2. Brush oil on both sides of 1 pound meat (chicken, pork, beef). Spread rub evenly on meat. Grill meat as desired.

Substitute

If you don't have white pepper, increase the amount of black pepper to 1 1/2 teaspoons.

1 Serving (1 teaspoon): Cal. 5 (Cal. from Fat 0); Fat 0g (Sat. fat 0g); Chol. 0mg; Sodium 390mg; Carbs. 1g (Fiber 0g); Pro. 0g • **% Daily Value:** Vit. A 0%; Vit. C 0%; Calc. 0%; Iron 0% • **Exchanges:** Free • **Carb. Choices:** 0

Southwestern Rub

Photo on page 278

Prep: 10 min
About 3
tablespoons rub

1 tablespoon chili powder
1 tablespoon vegetable oil
1 teaspoon ground cumin
1/4 teaspoon salt
1/4 teaspoon ground red pepper (cayenne)
1 large clove garlic, finely chopped

1. In small bowl, mix all ingredients.

2. Spread rub evenly on 1 pound boneless meat (chicken, pork, beef) or 2 1/2 pounds 1/2-inch-thick pork chops. Grill meat as desired.

Did You Know?

Because this rub has oil in it, it's known as a "wet rub" rather than the more typical "dry rub."

1 Serving (1 teaspoon): Cal. 20 (Cal. from Fat 20); Fat 2g (Sat. fat 0g); Chol. 0mg; Sodium 75mg; Carbs. 1g (Fiber 0g); Pro. 0g • **% Daily Value:** Vit. A 2%; Vit. C 0%; Calc. 0%; Iron 2% • **Exchanges:** Free • **Carb. Choices:** 0

Fajita Marinade

Prep: 5 min
Marinate: 8 hr
About 1/2 cup
marinade

1/4 cup vegetable oil
1/4 cup red wine vinegar
1 teaspoon sugar
1 teaspoon dried oregano leaves
1 teaspoon chili powder
1/2 teaspoon garlic powder
1/2 teaspoon salt
1/4 teaspoon pepper

1. In shallow glass or plastic dish or resealable plastic food storage bag, mix all ingredients. Add about 1 or 1 1/2 pounds beef, pork or boneless chicken; turn to coat. Cover dish or seal bag and refrigerate, turning meat occasionally, at least 8 hours but no longer than 24 hours.

2. Remove meat from marinade; reserve marinade. Grill meat as desired, brushing occasionally with marinade. Discard any remaining marinade.

Try This

Don't limit yourself to using this tasty marinade for only fajitas (see Sizzling Fajitas, page 58). Meats marinated in this mixture and then cooked also make great salads or sandwiches.

1 Serving (4 teaspoons): Cal. 45 (Cal. from Fat 40); Fat 4.5g (Sat. Fat 0.5g); Chol. 0mg; Sodium 100mg; Carbs. 0g (Fiber 0g); Pro. 0g • **% Daily Value:** Vit. A 0%; Vit. C 0%; Calc. 0%; Iron 0% • **Exchanges:** 1 Fat • **Carb. Choices:** 0

Lemon-Herb Marinade

Prep: 5 min
Marinate: 30 min
About 2/3 cup
marinade

1/3 cup olive or vegetable oil
1/4 cup lemon juice
1 tablespoon chopped fresh or 1 teaspoon dried basil leaves
2 teaspoons chopped fresh or 1/2 teaspoon dried thyme leaves
1/4 teaspoon salt
1/4 teaspoon pepper
2 cloves garlic, finely chopped

1. In shallow glass or plastic dish or resealable plastic food-storage bag, mix all ingredients. Add about 1 pound fish, 1 pound seafood, 1 pound boneless chicken or 3 1/2 pounds bone-in chicken; turn to coat. Cover dish or seal bag and refrigerate at least 30 minutes but no longer than 24 hours.

2. Remove meat from marinade; reserve marinade. Grill meat as desired, brushing occasionally with marinade. Heat remaining marinade to boiling to serve as sauce with grilled meat.

Success Tip

As a general rule, marinate fish fillets, seafood and vegetables about 30 minutes, pork chops and chicken at least 1 hour and larger meat cuts up to 24 hours. Turn the food once or twice during the marinating time, so the marinade can reach all surfaces.

1 Serving (1 Tablespoon): Cal. 65 (Cal. from Fat 65); Fat 7g (Sat. fat 1g); Chol. 0mg; Sodium 55mg; Carbs. 1g (Fiber 0g); Pro. 0g • **% Daily Value:** Vit. A 0%; Vit. C 2%; Calc. 0%; Iron 0% • **Exchanges:** 1 1/2 Fat • **Carb. Choices:** 0

Peppery Teriyaki Marinade

1/4 cup soy sauce
2 tablespoons water
1 tablespoon lemon juice
1 tablespoon vegetable oil
1 teaspoon packed brown sugar
1/4 teaspoon coarsely ground pepper
1 clove garlic, finely chopped

1. In shallow glass or plastic dish or resealable plastic food-storage bag, mix all ingredients. Add about 1 1/2 pounds meat (pork, chicken, beef); turn to coat. Cover dish or seal bag and refrigerate at least 8 hours but no longer than 24 hours.

2. Remove meat from marinade; reserve marinade. Grill meat as desired, brushing occasionally with marinade. Discard any remaining marinade.

Healthful Hint

If you're trying to lower the sodium in your diet, check your supermarket shelf for low- or reduced-sodium soy sauce.

1 Serving (1 Tablespoon): Cal. 30 (Cal. from Fat 20); Fat 2g (Sat. fat 0g); Chol. 0mg; Sodium 460mg; Carbs. 3g (Fiber 0g); Pro. 0g • **% Daily Value:** Vit. A 0%; Vit. C 0%; Calc. 0%; Iron 0% • **Exchanges:** 1/2 Fat • **Carb. Choices:** 0

Fresh Tomato Salsa

Prep: 20 min
About 3 1/2 cups
salsa

3 large tomatoes, seeded and chopped (3 cups)
8 medium green onions, sliced (1/2 cup)
1 small green bell pepper, chopped (1/2 cup)
3 cloves garlic, finely chopped
2 jalapeño chilies, finely chopped (1 tablespoon)
2 tablespoons chopped fresh cilantro
2 to 3 tablespoons lime juice
1/2 teaspoon salt

1. In large glass or plastic bowl, mix all ingredients.

2. Serve salsa with grilled fish, chicken, chops, steak or tortilla chips.

Success Tip

Make this fresh salsa when tomatoes are at their peak, June through September. You can find just about all the ingredients you need at your local farmers' market.

1 Serving (1/4 cup): Cal. 10 (Cal. from Fat 0); Fat 0g (Sat. fat 0g); Chol. 0mg; Sodium 90mg; Carbs. 3g (Fiber 0g); Pro. 0g • **% Daily Value:** Vit. A 8%; Vit. C 26%; Calc. 0%; Iron 2% • **Exchanges:** Free • **Carb. Choices:** 0

Roasted-Corn Salsa

Prep: 15 min
Grill: 20 min
Cool: 20 min
**About 2 1/2 cups
salsa**

3 ears corn, husks removed
4 medium green onions
2 teaspoons vegetable oil
1 medium red bell pepper, chopped (1 cup)
2 tablespoons finely chopped Anaheim or serrano chili
3 tablespoons lemon juice
1/4 teaspoon salt

1. Brush grill rack with vegetable oil. Heat coals or gas grill for direct heat.

2. Brush corn and onions with oil.

3. Cover and grill corn and onions over medium-hot heat 5 minutes. Remove onions from grill; set aside. Turn corn. Cover and grill about 15 minutes longer, turning twice, until tender. Remove corn from grill; cool 20 minutes.

4. Cut corn from ears. Cut onions into slices. In medium glass or plastic bowl, mix corn, onions and remaining ingredients.

5. Serve salsa with grilled chicken or fish.

Success Tip

Roasting adds a special flavor to this easy salsa. It's particularly good with smoked meats such as chicken, turkey or pork.

1 Serving (1/4 Cup): Cal. 50 (Cal. from Fat 10); Fat 1g (Sat. fat 0g); Chol. 0mg; Sodium 65mg; Carbs. 9g (Fiber 1g); Pro. 1g • **% Daily Value:** Vit. A 16%; Vit. C 26%; Calc. 0%; Iron 2% • **Exchanges:** 1/2 Starch • **Carb. Choices:** 1/2

Tropical Fruit Salsa

Prep: 15 min
Chill: 1 hr
**About 2 cups
salsa**

2 kiwifruit, peeled and chopped
1 medium mango, cut lengthwise in half, seed removed and
    chopped (1 cup)
1 medium papaya, peeled, seeded and chopped (1 1/2 cups)
1 jalapeño chili, seeded and finely chopped
1 cup pineapple chunks
1 tablespoon finely chopped red onion
1 tablespoon chopped fresh cilantro
2 tablespoons lime juice

1. In medium glass or plastic bowl, mix all ingredients. Cover and
refrigerate 1 to 2 hours to blend flavors.

2. Serve with grilled poultry, pork and seafood.

Substitute

If mangoes and papayas aren't readily available, try substituting a
combination of peaches, nectarines, plums and apricots.

1 Serving (1/4 Cup): Cal. 60 (Cal. from
Fat 0); Fat 0g (Sat. fat 0g); Chol. 0mg;
Sodium 5mg; Carbs. 14g (Fiber 2g);
Pro. 1g • **% Daily Value:** Vit. A 12%;
Vit. C 90%; Calc. 2%; Iron 0% •
Exchanges: 1 Fruit • **Carb. Choices:** 1

Two-Tomato Relish

Prep: 5 min
2 cups relish

2 medium tomatoes, finely chopped (1 1/2 cups)
2 medium yellow pear tomatoes, finely chopped (1/2 cup)
1 tablespoon red wine vinegar
1 teaspoon chopped fresh or 1/4 teaspoon dried oregano leaves

1. In medium glass or plastic bowl, mix all ingredients. Cover and refrigerate until serving.

2. Serve with grilled bratwurst, Polish sausage or chicken.

Substitute

You can choose whatever tomatoes you have on hand in this simple yet flavorful relish recipe. It's nice to have a mix of color, but 4 red tomatoes will also taste great.

1 Serving (2 Tablespoons): Cal. 10 (Cal. from Fat 0); Fat 0g (Sat. fat 0g); Chol. 0mg; Sodium 5mg; Carbs. 2g (Fiber 0g); Pro. 0g • **% Daily Value:** Vit. A 6%; Vit. C 12%; Calc. 0%; Iron 0% • **Exchanges:** Free • **Carb. Choices:** 0

Pesto

Prep: 10 min
About 1 1/3 cups
sauce

2 cups firmly packed fresh basil leaves
3/4 cup grated Parmesan cheese
3/4 cup olive or vegetable oil
1/4 cup pine nuts
3 cloves garlic

1. In blender or food processor, cover and blend all ingredients on medium speed about 3 minutes, stopping blender occasionally to scrape sides, until smooth.

2. Serve with grilled chicken, fish, pork or beef or tossed with hot cooked pasta.

   Cilantro Pesto: Substitute 1 1/2 cups firmly packed fresh cilantro and 1/2 cup firmly packed fresh parsley for the 2 cups fresh basil.

   Spinach Winter Pesto: Substitute 2 cups firmly packed fresh spinach leaves and 1/2 cup firmly packed fresh or 1/4 cup dried basil leaves for the 2 cups fresh basil.

   Sun-Dried Tomato Pesto: Omit basil. Decrease oil to 1/3 cup. Add 1/2 cup oil-packed sun-dried tomatoes, undrained. Use food processor.

Try This

In addition to tasting great with grilled meats, poultry and fish, these pestos taste delicious spread on toasted baguette slices.

1 Tablespoon: Cal. 100 (Cal. from Fat 90); Fat 10g (Sat. fat 2g); Chol. 5mg; Sodium 65mg; Carbs. 1g (Fiber 0g); Pro. 2g • **% Daily Value:** Vit. A 6%; Vit. C 0%; Calc. 6%; Iron 2% • **Exchanges:** 2 Fat • **Carb. Choices:** 0

Beginnings & Endings

Grilled Italian Pesto Pizza

Roasted Garlic with French Bread

Prep: 5 min
Grill: 35 min
6 servings

2 large bulbs garlic
2 tablespoons olive or vegetable oil
Salt and pepper, if desired
12 thin slices French bread

1. Heat coals or gas grill for direct heat.

2. Peel loose paperlike layers from garlic bulbs, but do not separate cloves. Cut two 18 × 12-inch pieces of heavy-duty foil. On each foil piece, place garlic bulb. Brush bulbs generously with oil. Sprinkle with salt and pepper. Wrap foil securely around bulbs.

3. Cover and grill garlic over medium heat 25 to 35 minutes or until cloves are very soft. Add bread for last 5 minutes of grilling, turning once, until golden brown.

4. To serve, squeeze garlic pulp from papery skin onto bread and spread.

Try This

If you like the taste of roasted garlic, double the amount and use the extra to make garlic butter or add to mashed potatoes.

1 Serving: Cal.140 (Cal. from Fat 55); Fat 6g (Sat. fat 1g); Chol. 0mg; Sodium 190mg; Carbs. 19g (Fiber 1g); Pro. 3g • **% Daily Value:** Vit. A 0%; Vit. C 2%; Calc. 4%; Iron 6% • **Exchanges:** 1 Starch, 1 Fat • **Carb. Choices:** 1

Grilled Italian Pesto Pizza

Prep: 15 min
Grill: 8 min
4 servings

Photo on page 300

1/2 cup basil pesto
1 package (14 ounces) ready-to-serve original Italian pizza crust
    or other 12-inch ready-to-serve pizza crust
2 cups shredded mozzarella cheese (8 ounces)
3 large roma (plum) tomatoes, cut into 1/4-inch slices
1/2 cup whole basil leaves
1/4 cup shredded Parmesan cheese

1. Heat coals or gas grill for direct heat.

2. Spread pesto over pizza crust. Sprinkle 1 cup of the mozzarella cheese over pesto. Arrange tomato slices and basil leaves on cheese. Sprinkle with remaining 1 cup mozzarella cheese and the Parmesan cheese.

3. Cover and grill pizza over medium heat 6 to 8 minutes or until crust is crisp and cheese is melted. (If crust browns too quickly, place a piece of foil between crust and grill.)

Substitute

Instead of purchasing basil pesto, try making one of the homemade pestos on page 299 to see which you like best.

1 Serving: Cal. 665 (Cal. from Fat 295); Fat 33g (Sat. fat 11g); Chol. 40mg; Sodium 1190mg; Carbs. 66g (Fiber 4g); Pro. 30g • **% Daily Value:** Vit. A 28%; Vit. C 8%; Calc. 64%; Iron 28% • **Exchanges:** 4 Starch, 1 Vegetable, 2 High-Fat Meat, 2 1/2 Fat • **Carb. Choices:** 4 1/2

Mexican Quesadillas

Prep: 15 min
Grill: 15 min
4 servings

8 whole wheat flour tortillas (8 inches in diameter)
1 large tomato, chopped (1 cup)
1 can (4.5 ounces) chopped green chiles, drained
1 1/2 cups shredded Monterey Jack cheese (6 ounces)
1/2 cup sour cream

1. Heat coals or gas grill for direct heat. Cut four 30 × 18-inch pieces of heavy-duty foil.

2. On each foil piece, place 1 tortilla. Top each with one-fourth of the tomato and chiles. Sprinkle each with one-fourth of the cheese. Top with remaining tortillas. Wrap foil securely around quesadillas; pierce top of foil packets once or twice with fork to vent steam.

3. Cover and grill quesadillas, seam side up, over medium heat about 15 minutes or until cheese is melted. Cut each quesadilla into 6 wedges. Top with sour cream.

Healthful Hint

For just 305 calories and 5 grams of fat per serving, prepare these quesadillas with fat-free Monterey Jack cheese and fat-free sour cream.

1 Serving: Cal. 385 (Cal. from Fat 190); Fat 21g (Sat. fat 12g); Chol. 55mg; Sodium 720mg; Carbs. 38g (Fiber 7g); Pro. 18g • **% Daily Value:** Vit. A 22%; Vit. C 32%; Calc. 36%; Iron 14% • **Exchanges:** 2 Starch, 1 Vegetable, 1 1/2 High-Fat Meat, 1 Fat • **Carb. Choices:** 2 1/2

Picnic Taco Nachos

Prep: 5 min
Grill: 10 min
4 servings

5 cups tortilla chips
1 can (15 ounces) black beans, rinsed, drained and mashed
1 can (4.5 ounces) chopped green chiles, drained
2 teaspoons taco seasoning mix (from 1.25-ounce envelope)
2 roma (plum) tomatoes, chopped
2 medium green onions, sliced (2 tablespoons)
2 cups finely shredded Colby-Monterey Jack cheese (8 ounces)

1. Heat coals or gas grill for direct heat. Cut one 30 × 18-inch piece of heavy-duty foil; spray with cooking spray.

2. Spread tortilla chips on foil. In medium bowl, mix beans, chiles and taco seasoning mix; spoon evenly over tortilla chips. Top with tomatoes and onions. Sprinkle with cheese. Wrap foil securely around nachos.

3. Cover and grill nachos, seam side up, over medium heat 8 to 10 minutes or until cheese is melted.

Healthful **Hint**

For merely 360 calories and 11 grams of fat per serving, prepare these nachos with baked tortilla chips and reduced-fat Monterey Jack cheese.

1 Serving: Cal. 465 (Cal. from Fat 225); Fat 25g (Sat. fat 13g); Chol. 55mg; Sodium 1010mg; Carbs. 44g (Fiber 10g); Pro. 23g • **% Daily Value:** Vit. A 20%; Vit. C 16%; Calc. 42%; Iron 20% • **Exchanges:** 3 Starch, 2 Medium-Fat Meat, 2 Fat • **Carb. Choices:** 3

Bruschetta

Prep: 10 min
Grill: 6 min
16 servings

1/2 cup olive or vegetable oil
2 tablespoons chopped fresh or 2 teaspoons dried basil leaves
2 cloves garlic, finely chopped
1 loaf unsliced French bread (about 12 inches), cut horizontally
   in half

1. Brush grill rack with vegetable oil. Heat coals or gas grill for direct heat.

2. In small bowl, mix oil, basil and garlic. Brush or drizzle on cut sides of bread.

3. Cover and grill bread, cut sides up, over medium heat about 6 minutes, rotating once, until toasted. To serve, cut into sixteen 1 1/2-inch slices.

Did You Know?

The name of this traditional Italian garlic bread means "to roast over coals." Olive oil is used generously, and for the best flavor, try extra-virgin olive oil. If you like, sprinkle the bruschetta with salt and pepper before grilling.

1 Serving: Cal. 390 (Cal. from Fat 260); Fat 29g (Sat. fat 4g); Chol. 0mg; Sodium 310mg; Carbs. 27g (Fiber 2g); Pro. 5g • **% Daily Value:** Vit. A 2%; Vit. C 0%; Calc. 4%; Iron 10% • **Exchanges:** 2 Starch, 5 Fat • **Carb. Choices:** 2

Crispy Honey Wings

Prep: 15 min
Grill: 25 min
32 servings

16 chicken wings (about 3 pounds)
3/4 cup honey
1/4 cup white Worcestershire sauce
1/2 teaspoon ground ginger

1. Brush grill rack with vegetable oil. Heat coals or gas grill for direct heat.

2. Cut each chicken wing at joints to make 3 pieces; discard tip. In small bowl, mix remaining ingredients.

3. Cover and grill chicken over medium heat 20 to 25 minutes, brushing frequently with honey mixture and turning after 10 minutes, until juice of chicken is no longer pink when centers of thickest pieces are cut. Discard any remaining honey mixture.

Try This

For an added twist, you may want to try using a flavored honey in these finger-licking wings. Raspberry, peach, lemon and apricot are just a few choices available. Look for flavored honey at gourmet stores.

1 Serving: Cal. 70 (Cal. from Fat 25); Fat 3g (Sat. fat 1g); Chol. 15mg; Sodium 30mg; Carbs. 7g (Fiber 0g); Pro. 4g • **% Daily Value:** Vit. A 0%; Vit. C 0%; Calc. 0%; Iron 2% • **Exchanges:** 1/2 Other Carbs., 1/2 Fat • **Carb. Choices:** 1/2

Firecracker Chicken Wings

Prep: 10 min
Marinate: 1 hr
Grill: 25 min
12 servings

12 chicken wings (about 2 1/2 pounds)
2 tablespoons chili powder
1 1/2 teaspoons dried oregano leaves
1 1/4 teaspoons ground red pepper (cayenne)
1 teaspoon garlic salt
1 teaspoon ground cumin
1 teaspoon pepper
Sour cream, if desired
Paprika, if desired

1. Fold chicken wing tips under opposite ends to form triangles.

2. In resealable plastic food-storage bag, place remaining ingredients except sour cream and paprika. Seal bag and shake to blend seasonings. Add chicken. Seal bag and shake until chicken is coated with seasonings. Refrigerate at least 1 hour but no longer than 24 hours.

3. Brush grill rack with vegetable oil. Heat coals or gas grill for direct heat.

4. Cover and grill chicken over medium heat 20 to 25 minutes, turning after 10 minutes, until juice of chicken is no longer pink when centers of thickest pieces are cut.

5. Serve chicken with sour cream sprinkled with paprika.

Serving Idea

Serve these fiery-hot chicken wings with purchased blue cheese salad dressing for dipping.

1 Appetizer: Calories 105 (Calories from Fat 65); Fat 7g (Saturated 2g); Cholesterol 30mg; Sodium 125mg; Carbohydrate 1g (Dietary Fiber 0g); Protein 10g • **% Daily Value:** Vitamin A 12%; Vitamin C 0%; Calcium 0%; Iron 4% • **Exchanges:** 1 1/2 Med-Fat Meat • **Carb. Choices:** 0

Tangy Onion Flowers

**Prep: 20 min
Grill: 1 hr
4 servings**

4 medium onions (4 to 5 ounces each)
Vegetable oil
1/4 cup balsamic or cider vinegar
1 tablespoon chopped fresh or 1 teaspoon dried oregano leaves
1 tablespoon packed brown sugar
1/4 teaspoon salt
1/4 teaspoon pepper
1/3 cup seasoned croutons, crushed

1. Heat coals or gas grill for direct heat. Cut four 18 × 12-inch pieces of heavy-duty foil.

2. Peel onions; cut 1/2-inch slice from top of each onion and leave root end. Cut each onion from top into 8 wedges to within 1/2 inch of root end. Gently pull wedges apart, leaving root end attached.

3. Brush oil over foil pieces. Place 1 onion on each foil piece; loosely shape foil around onion. Sprinkle onions with vinegar, oregano, brown sugar, salt and pepper. Wrap foil securely around onions.

4. Cover and grill onions over medium heat 50 to 60 minutes or until very tender. To serve, sprinkle croutons over onions.

Serving Idea

Here's a delicious and low-fat alternative to the deep-fried onion blossom featured at many restaurants; serve with ketchup for dipping, if desired.

1 Serving: Cal. 90 (Cal. from Fat 20); Fat 2g (Sat. fat 0g); Chol. 0mg; Sodium 190mg; Carbs. 16g (Fiber 2g); Pro. 2g • **% Daily Value:** Vit. A 2%; Vit. C 6%; Calc. 2%; Iron 2% • **Exchanges:** 1/2 Other Carbs., 1 Vegetable, 1/2 Fat • **Carb. Choices:** 1

1. Cut 1/2-inch slice from the top of each onion.

2. Cut each onion into 8 wedges.

3. Place the onion on the foil square, and sprinkle with topping.

4. Wrap the foil securely around the onion.

Summer Cobbler

Prep: 15 min
Grill: 30 min
8 servings

1/4 cup butter or margarine, melted
1 1/4 cups Original Bisquick® mix
1/2 cup sugar
1/2 cup milk
1 medium nectarine or peach, sliced (1 cup)
1 cup blueberries or blackberries
1/4 cup sugar
1/2 teaspoon ground cinnamon

1. Heat coals or gas grill for direct heat.

2. In 9-inch round foil pan, melt butter on grill. Meanwhile, in small bowl, mix baking mix, 1/2 cup sugar and the milk with spoon; beat 30 seconds. Pour over butter in pan. Top batter with nectarine and blueberries. Sprinkle with 1/4 cup sugar and the cinnamon.

3. Cover and grill cobbler over medium heat about 30 minutes or until toothpick inserted in center comes out clean.

Success Tip

After this fruity cobbler is baked, move it to the side of the grill to keep warm until you're ready to serve it.

1 Serving: Cal. 230 (Cal. from Fat 80); Fat 9g (Sat. fat 4g); Chol. 15mg; Sodium 320mg; Carbs. 36g (Fiber 1g); Pro. 2g • **% Daily Value:** Vit. A 6%; Vit. C 2%; Calc. 6%; Iron 4% • **Exchanges:** 1 Starch, 1/2 Fruit, 1 Other Carbs., 1 1/2 Fat • **Carb. Choices:** 2 1/2

Fresh Cherries Jubilee

Prep: 15 min
Stand: 1 hr
Grill: 12 min
4 servings

2 cups dark sweet cherries, pitted
1 tablespoon packed brown sugar
1 tablespoon brandy, cherry liqueur or apple juice
1 pint (2 cups) vanilla frozen yogurt or ice cream

1. In 8-inch square foil pan, mix cherries, brown sugar and brandy. Cover and let stand 1 hour.

2. Heat coals or gas grill for direct heat.

3. Stir cherry mixture. Cover with foil, sealing edges securely.

4. Cover and grill pan over medium heat 10 to 12 minutes, shaking pan occasionally, until cherries are hot and tender. Cool slightly. Spoon cherry mixture over frozen yogurt.

Try This

You can make this recipe in a snap if you use canned dark sweet cherries.

1 Serving: Cal. 175 (Cal. from Fat 20); Fat 2g (Sat. fat 1g); Chol. 5mg; Sodium 60mg; Carbs. 34g (Fiber 1g); Pro. 5g • **% Daily Value:** Vit. A 2%; Vit. C 4%; Calc. 16%; Iron 2% • **Exchanges:** 1 Starch, 1 Fruit, 1/2 Fat • **Carb. Choices:** 2

Gingered Fruit Kabobs

Prep: 25 min
Grill: 8 min
24 servings

1 large pineapple (about 4 pounds)
4- to 5-pound watermelon wedge
8 firm medium bananas
6 kiwifruit
3/4 cup butter or margarine
2 tablespoons honey
2 tablespoon lime juice
2 teaspoons grated gingerroot

1. Heat coals or gas grill for direct heat.

2. Cut 1/2-inch slice off top and bottom of pineapple; carefully cut off rind. Cut pineapple and watermelon each into 48 chunks. Cut each banana into 6 pieces. Cut each kiwifruit into 8 pieces. On twenty-four 12-inch metal skewers, alternately thread fruits, leaving 1/4-inch space between each piece.

3. In 1-quart saucepan, heat remaining ingredients over medium heat, stirring occasionally, until butter is melted.

4. Cover and grill kabobs over medium heat 6 to 8 minutes, brushing occasionally with butter mixture and turning 2 or 3 times, until hot.

Try This

You can knock several minutes off the prep time in this recipe by purchasing precut pineapple pieces and watermelon chunks.

1 Serving : Cal. 140 (Cal. from Fat 55); Fat 6g (Sat. fat 4g); Chol. 15mg; Sodium 40mg; Carbs. 21g (Fiber 2g); Pro. 1g • **% Daily Value:** Vit. A 10%; Vit. C 50%; Calc. 0%; Iron 2% • **Exchanges:** 1 1/2 Fruit, 1 Fat • **Carb. Choices:** 1

Grilled Pineapple with Coconut

Prep: 15 min
Stand: 1 hr
Grill: 15 min
6 servings

1 medium pineapple (about 3 pounds)
1 tablespoon rum or apple juice
1 teaspoon granulated sugar
1/2 cup plain yogurt
1 tablespoon packed brown sugar
1/4 cup flaked or shredded coconut, toasted if desired

1. Cut 1/2-inch slice off top and bottom of pineapple; carefully cut off rind. Cut pineapple crosswise into 6 slices. Drizzle rum over pineapple. Sprinkle with granulated sugar. Let stand 1 hour.

2. Meanwhile, in small bowl, mix yogurt and brown sugar; cover and refrigerate until serving.

3. Heat coals or gas grill for direct heat.

4. Cover and grill pineapple over medium heat 10 to 15 minutes, turning once, until hot. Top with yogurt mixture and coconut.

Success Tip

To toast coconut, cook in an ungreased heavy skillet over medium-low heat 6 to 14 minutes, stirring frequently until coconut starts to brown, then stirring constantly until golden brown. If you'd rather use your microwave, spread coconut in a microwavable pie plate and microwave uncovered on High 1 minute 30 seconds to 2 minutes, stirring every 30 seconds, until golden brown.

1 Serving: Cal. 70 (Cal. from Fat 10); Fat 1g (Sat. fat 0g); Chol. 0mg; Sodium 15mg; Carbs. 14g (Fiber 2g); Pro. 1g • **% Daily Value:** Vit. A 0%; Vit. C 10%; Calc. 4%; Iron 2% • **Exchanges:** 1 Fruit • **Carb. Choices:** 1

Toasted Butter-Rum Pound Cake

Prep: 15 min
Grill: 5 min
8 servings

1/2 cup sour cream
2 tablespoons packed brown sugar
1 package (10.75 ounces) frozen pound cake loaf
1/4 cup rum, if desired
1/4 cup butter or margarine, softened
1/2 cup sliced almonds

1. Brush grill rack with vegetable oil. Heat coals or gas grill for direct heat.

2. In small bowl, mix sour cream and brown sugar; set aside.

3. Cut frozen pound cake into 8 slices. On each side, sprinkle with rum, spread with butter, then press almonds onto butter. Place cake slices on grilling screen.

4. Cover and grill cake over medium heat about 5 minutes, turning once, until golden brown. To serve, top with sour cream mixture.

Substitute

If you'd like to keep the rum flavor but prefer not to use alcohol, mix 1 tablespoon rum extract and 3 tablespoons water and substitute for the 1/4 cup rum in this recipe.

1 Serving: Cal. 345 (Cal. from Fat 215); Fat 24g (Sat. fat 12g); Chol. 75mg; Sodium 85mg; Carbs. 27g (Fiber 1g); Pro. 5g • **% Daily Value:** Vit. A 8%; Vit. C 0%; Calc. 6%; Iron 6% • **Exchanges:** 1 Starch, 1 Other Carbs., 4 1/2 Fat • **Carb. Choices:** 2

Striped S'mores

Prep: 5 min
Grill: 5 min
6 servings

12 large marshmallows
24 fudge-striped shortbread cookies

1. Heat coals or gas grill for direct heat.

2. On each of 6 metal skewers, thread 2 marshmallows.

3. Hold marshmallows over medium heat 3 to 5 minutes, turning frequently, until golden brown.

4. Place 1 marshmallow between bottoms of 2 cookies; press tightly.

For "s'more" fun, spread peanut butter on bottoms of the cookies before sandwiching the marshmallows.

1 Serving (: Cal. 285 (Cal. from Fat 100); Fat 11g (Sat. fat 3g); Chol. 0mg; Sodium 170mg; Carbs. 44g (Fiber 1g); Pro. 4g • **% Daily Value:** Vit. A 0%; Vit. C 0%; Calc. 0%; Iron 10% • **Exchanges:** 1 Starch, 2 Other Carbs., 2 Fat • **Carb. Choices:** 3

Cherry Pie in the Sky

Prep: 5 min
Grill: 18 min
4 servings

2 tablespoons butter or margarine, softened
8 slices white sandwich bread
1/3 cup cherry pie filling
1 package (3 ounces) cream cheese, sliced
2 teaspoons sugar, if desired

1. Heat coals or gas grill for direct heat.

2. Spread butter on 1 side of 2 slices of bread. On sandwich press, place 1 slice, butter side out. Spoon one-fourth of the pie filling onto center of bread. Top with one-fourth of the cream cheese. Top with other slice of bread, butter side out. Close press; trim excess bread.

3. Grill uncovered over medium heat 15 to 18 minutes, turning once, until bread is golden brown and cream cheese is melted. Sprinkle with 1/2 teaspoon of the sugar. Repeat with remaining ingredients. Serve warm.

Substitute

Instead of cherry pie filling, use strawberry jam or grape jelly instead.

1 Serving: Cal. 280 (Cal. from Fat 135); Fat 15g (Sat. fat 9g); Chol. 40mg; Sodium 370mg; Carbs. 31g (Fiber 1g); Pro. 6g • **% Daily Value:** Vit. A 10%; Vit. C 0%; Calc. 6%; Iron 10% • **Exchanges:** 2 Starch, 3 Fat • **Carb. Choices:** 2

Grilled Doughnut Desserts

Prep: 5 min
Grill: 3 min
6 servings

3 plain cake doughnuts
3 large marshmallows
6 milk chocolate candy drops or pieces, unwrapped

1. Heat coals or gas grill for direct heat.

2. Cut doughnuts and marshmallows horizontally in half.

3. Place doughnuts, cut side down, on grill rack over medium heat. Place marshmallow halves, cut side down, over holes in doughnuts.

4. Cover and grill 2 to 3 minutes or until cut sides of doughnuts are golden brown and marshmallows are soft. Immediately push chocolate candy, point side down, into each marshmallow.

Try This

Cut marshmallows in half with kitchen scissors dipped in water.

1 Serving: Cal. 140 (Cal. from Fat 65); Fat 7g (Sat. fat 2g); Chol. 10mg; Sodium 65mg; Carbs. 17g (Fiber 0g); Pro. 2g • **% Daily Value:** Vit. A 2%; Vit. C 0%; Calc. 2%; Iron 2% • **Exchanges:** 1 Starch, 1 1/2 Fat • **Carb. Choices:** 1

Turtle Brownies with Grilled Tropical Fruit

Prep: 25 min
Grill: 15 min
12 servings

1 medium pineapple (about 3 pounds)
3 medium mangoes
4 medium firm bananas
1/4 cup butter or margarine, melted
3 tablespoons orange juice
2 tablespoons packed brown sugar
12 brownies (3 inch square)
1 cup caramel topping

1. Heat coals or gas grill for direct heat.

2. Cut 1/2-inch slice off top and bottom of pineapple; carefully cut off rind. Cut pineapple into 1-inch chunks (3 cups). Cut mangoes lengthwise in half, remove seed and cut into 1-inch chunks (3 cups). Cut bananas into 1-inch slices (3 cups). In small bowl, mix butter, orange juice and brown sugar.

3. On each of twenty-four 10-inch metal skewers, alternately thread pineapple, mango and banana pieces, leaving 1/4-inch space between each piece. Brush butter mixture over fruit.

4. Cover and grill fruit over medium-low heat 10 to 15 minutes, turning frequently and brushing with butter mixture, until fruit is lightly browned.

5. Cut brownies diagonally in half. On each plate, arrange 2 brownie triangles. Remove fruit from skewers, and arrange around and over brownies. Drizzle with caramel topping.

Shop Talk

Buy "green tip" bananas, which are ripe but still firm enough to withstand grilling.

1 Serving: Cal. 650 (Cal. from Fat 250); Fat 28g (Sat. fat 11g); Chol. 75mg; Sodium 145mg; Carbs. 93g (Fiber 5g); Pro. 6g • **% Daily Value:** Vit. A 14%; Vit. C 20%; Calc. 4%; Iron 12% • **Exchanges:** 2 Starch, 2 Fruit, 2 Other Carbs., 5 1/2 Fat • **Carb. Choices:** 6

Helpful Nutrition & Cooking Information

Nutrition Guidelines

We provide nutrition information for each recipe that includes calories, fat, cholesterol, sodium, carbohydrate, fiber and protein. Individual food choices can be based on this information.

Recommended intake for a daily diet of 2,000 calories as set by the Food and Drug Administration

Total Fat	Less than 65g
Saturated Fat	Less than 20g
Cholesterol	Less than 300mg
Sodium	Less than 2,400mg
Total Carbohydrate	300g
Dietary Fiber	25g

Criteria Used for Calculating Nutrition Information

▶ The first ingredient was used wherever a choice is given (such as 1/3 cup sour cream or plain yogurt).

▶ The first ingredient amount was used wherever a range is given (such as 3- to 3-1/2–pound cut-up broiler-fryer chicken).

▶ The first serving number was used wherever a range is given (such as 4 to 6 servings).

▶ "If desired" ingredients and recipe variations were not included (such as sprinkle with brown sugar, if desired).

▶ Only the amount of a marinade or frying oil that is estimated to be absorbed by the food during preparation or cooking was calculated.

Ingredients Used in Recipe Testing and Nutrition Calculations

▶ Ingredients used for testing represent those that the majority of consumers use in their homes: large eggs, 2% milk, 80%-lean ground beef, canned ready-to-use chicken broth and vegetable oil spread containing not less than 65% fat.

▶ Fat-free, low-fat or low-sodium products were not used, unless otherwise indicated.

▶ Solid vegetable shortening (not butter, margarine, nonstick cooking sprays or vegetable oil spread as they can cause sticking problems) was used to grease pans, unless otherwise indicated.

Equipment Used in Recipe Testing

We use equipment for testing that the majority of consumers use in their homes. If a specific piece of equipment (such as a wire whisk) is necessary for recipe success, it is listed in the recipe.

▶ Cookware and bakeware without nonstick coatings were used, unless otherwise indicated.
▶ No dark-colored, black or insulated bakeware was used.
▶ When a pan is specified in a recipe, a metal pan was used; a baking dish or pie plate means ovenproof glass was used.
▶ An electric hand mixer was used for mixing only when mixer speeds are specified in the recipe directions. When a mixer speed is not given, a spoon or fork was used.

Cooking Terms Glossary

Beat: Mix ingredients vigorously with spoon, fork, wire whisk, hand beater or electric mixer until smooth and uniform.

Boil: Heat liquid until bubbles rise continuously and break on the surface and steam is given off. For rolling boil, the bubbles form rapidly.

Chop: Cut into coarse or fine irregular pieces with a knife, food chopper, blender or food processor.

Cube: Cut into squares 1/2 inch or larger.

Dice: Cut into squares smaller than 1/2 inch.

Grate: Cut into tiny particles using small rough holes of grater (citrus peel or chocolate).

Grease: Rub the inside surface of a pan with shortening, using pastry brush, piece of waxed paper or paper towel, to prevent food from sticking during baking (as for some casseroles).

Julienne: Cut into thin, matchlike strips, using knife or food processor (vegetables, fruits, meats).

Mix: Combine ingredients in any way that distributes them evenly.

Sauté: Cook foods in hot oil or margarine over medium-high heat with frequent tossing and turning motion.

Shred: Cut into long thin pieces by rubbing food across the holes of a shredder, as for cheese, or by using a knife to slice very thinly, as for cabbage.

Simmer: Cook in liquid just below the boiling point on top of the stove; usually after reducing heat from a boil. Bubbles will rise slowly and break just below the surface.

Stir: Mix ingredients until uniform consistency. Stir once in a while for stirring occasionally, often for stirring frequently and continuously for stirring constantly.

Toss: Tumble ingredients (such as green salad) lightly with a lifting motion, usually to coat evenly or mix with another food.

Metric Conversion Guide

Volume

U.S. Units	Canadian Metric	Australian Metric
1/4 teaspoon	1 mL	1 ml
1/2 teaspoon	2 mL	2 ml
1 teaspoon	5 mL	5 ml
1 tablespoon	15 mL	20 ml
1/4 cup	50 mL	60 ml
1/3 cup	75 mL	80 ml
1/2 cup	125 mL	125 ml
2/3 cup	150 mL	170 ml
3/4 cup	175 mL	190 ml
1 cup	250 mL	250 ml
1 quart	1 liter	1 liter
1 1/2 quarts	1.5 liters	1.5 liters
2 quarts	2 liters	2 liters
2 1/2 quarts	2.5 liters	2.5 liters
3 quarts	3 liters	3 liters
4 quarts	4 liters	4 liters

Weight

U.S. Units	Canadian Metric	Australian Metric
1 ounce	30 grams	30 grams
2 ounces	55 grams	60 grams
3 ounces	85 grams	90 grams
4 ounces (1/4 pound)	115 grams	125 grams
8 ounces (1/2 pound)	225 grams	225 grams
16 ounces (1 pound)	455 grams	500 grams
1 pound	455 grams	1/2 kilogram

Measurements

Inches	Centimeters
1	2.5
2	5.0
3	7.5
4	10.0
5	12.5
6	15.0
7	17.5
8	20.5
9	23.0
10	25.5
11	28.0
12	30.5
13	33.0

Temperatures

Fahrenheit	Celsius
32°	0°
212°	100°
250°	120°
275°	140°
300°	150°
325°	160°
350°	180°
375°	190°
400°	200°
425°	220°
450°	230°
475°	240°
500°	260°

Note: The recipes in this cookbook have not been developed or tested using metric measures. When converting recipes to metric, some variations in quality may be noted.

Index

Note: Page numbers in *italics* indicate illustrations.

W–Z

Complete your cookbook library with these *Betty Crocker* titles

Betty Crocker Baking for Today

Betty Crocker's Best Bread Machine Cookbook

Betty Crocker's Best Chicken Cookbook

Betty Crocker's Best Christmas Cookbook

Betty Crocker's Best of Baking

Betty Crocker's Best of Healthy and Hearty Cooking

Betty Crocker's Best-Loved Recipes

Betty Crocker's Bisquick® Cookbook

Betty Crocker Bisquick® II Cookbook

Betty Crocker Bisquick® Impossibly Easy Pies

Betty Crocker Celebrate!

Betty Crocker's Complete Thanksgiving Cookbook

Betty Crocker's Cook Book for Boys and Girls

Betty Crocker's Cook It Quick

Betty Crocker's Cookbook, 9th Edition—*The* **BIG RED** *Cookbook*®

Betty Crocker's Cookbook, Bridal Edition

Betty Crocker's Cookie Book

Betty Crocker's Cooking Basics

Betty Crocker's Cooking for Two

Betty Crocker's Cooky Book, Facsimile Edition

Betty Crocker's Diabetes Cookbook

Betty Crocker Dinner Made Easy with Rotisserie Chicken

Betty Crocker Easy Family Dinners

Betty Crocker's Easy Slow Cooker Dinners

Betty Crocker's Eat and Lose Weight

Betty Crocker's Entertaining Basics

Betty Crocker's Flavors of Home

Betty Crocker 4-Ingredient Dinners

Betty Crocker Healthy Heart Cookbook

Betty Crocker's Healthy New Choices

Betty Crocker's Indian Home Cooking

Betty Crocker's Italian Cooking

Betty Crocker's Kids Cook!

Betty Crocker's Kitchen Library

Betty Crocker's Living with Cancer Cookbook

Betty Crocker's Low-Fat, Low-Cholesterol Cooking Today

Betty Crocker More Slow Cooker Recipes

Betty Crocker's New Cake Decorating

Betty Crocker's New Chinese Cookbook

Betty Crocker One-Dish Meals

Betty Crocker's A Passion for Pasta

Betty Crocker's Pasta Favorites

Betty Crocker's Picture Cook Book, Facsimile Edition

Betty Crocker's Quick & Easy Cookbook

Betty Crocker's Slow Cooker Cookbook

Betty Crocker's Ultimate Cake Mix Cookbook

Betty Crocker's Vegetarian Cooking